AN
EASTERN
SAGA

MARVIN FARKAS

Make-Do Publishing

An Eastern Saga
Mavin Farkas
ISBN 978-988-18419-5-7

First published in 2010

Make-Do Publishing
Hong Kong

Typesetting: Lamma Studio Design
Cover design: Timothy McEvenue

Dedicated to Dick Farkas who was my twin brother.

AN EASTERN SAGA

1

SLOW BOAT TO HONG KONG

April 16, 1954. Osaka Dockyards. Pier Six. I got my first look at the ship that would be home for the next five days, the *Eastern Saga*. It wasn't very large and had two black and orange smokestacks belching puffs of dirty black smoke as the engineer cleared the engines ahead of start-up. It was a gray, drizzly day, not the best weather to begin an ocean voyage over restive seas, but I had my visa at last and was finally on my way to Hong Kong.

The crew was loading cargo. Bills of lading read: general household goods, Jardine Matheson and Company; rubber dinghies and outboard engines consigned to American Motorboats, Inc.; Nikon cameras, lenses and ancillary equipment going to Shriro, China Limited.

At the top, a crewman pointed me toward of a big hand-painted sign tacked onto the hatch that read 'Customs and Immigration Inspection. Enter by this port and descend ladder to the mess deck.' In the mess hall I found two uniformed Japanese officials checking papers and bags.

Cargo vessels usually have enough cabins for eight passengers, but on this trip there were to be only four. The first two were a portly British man attired in a safari jacket and his wife, as slim as he was substantial, dressed primly in a plain black dress and tightly pinned bun. She spoke English with a thick British accent though she was actually a Portuguese Eurasian. The third passenger was a Dutchman, stylishly arrayed in a crisp light blue suit and neatly trimmed goatee. And then there was me.

When they finally got around to me, the customs man opened my bag, gave it a cursory inspection and then handed me over to the immigration official who thumbed through my passport, found a blank space, and stamped me out of Japan.

My cabin consisted of a bunk bed with a neatly folded towel on the pillow and a small clothes closet with a mirror. I dumped my knapsack onto the bed and went up on deck just in time to see the seamen cast off the mooring lines that tied the *M.V. Eastern Saga* to the wharf. With all engines ahead, the ship moved away from the pier, heading for the open sea and Hong Kong.

That night, I took a stroll on deck. The night was clear and a full moon reflected on the black water. The gentle rolling of the sea, the familiar odor of the engine room and the steady chug, chug of the motors took me back to when I had come to Hong Kong with the U.S. Navy just as the Second World War was ending. I was on a destroyer again, taking the midnight till 4 a.m. watch, looking out for mines and enemy submarines.

Our ship had carried U.N. officials in charge of digging up the graves of Americans killed during the war in China. We carried the remains back to Hong Kong for transshipment to the States. When I was in the Navy, I didn't have a rank, I had a rating. I was a Seaman Second Class; you can't get any lower than that. I had got a sideline glimpse of China but I had wanted to come back and get a good look at it as a civilian, and now I had got the chance.

Not that I would ever have wanted to return to those days. We went all over the Pacific from Qingdao to Hainan. But I was a chronic seasick. When I read on the ship's 'plan of the day' that we were to get 'underway' I began to feel woozy and I remained seasick for the next three or four days. It was horrible.

Fortunately the weather later in our voyage was sunny and bright. The sky was clear blue and so was the ocean. The first officer strolled by in his officer's cap and black jacket with three stripes on the epaulets that told his rank. Under his jacket he wore a turtleneck sweater and dungaree trousers—the official uniform of the merchant sailor. 'Beautiful day,' he said.

'Without a doubt. Everything going alright with the ship?' I asked.

'No complaints. The ship is ten years old, but very sturdy. It'll probably be running for quite a few years more.'

'Can an old ship take very rough seas?' I asked, curious what exactly 'sturdy' meant.

'Of course it can. The Pacific is supposed to be the calmest of the five oceans but I've seen it get very wild. You'll have a sample of just how rough it can be tomorrow night. The weather report shows a storm brewing in the Formosa Straits. If you're on deck you'll see thirty-foot swells breaking fore and aft, but I don't recommend you stand outside to watch.

The Formosa Straits separates the province of Fujian in southeastern China from the island of Taiwan. 'Formosa' translates to beautiful, named by Portuguese explorers who first arrived back in the 16th century. But the straits are more than 100 miles wide and the roughest stretch of water between Japan and Hong Kong. It seems there is always a storm brewing in the Formosa Straits.

'Are you ever afraid when you get those really violent storms hitting the ship?'

'Well, not afraid but I might say 'uncomfortable'. In my twenty-five years at sea I've seen lots of bad storms. They're inevitable so what can you do about them? You just set your instruments, slow the engines, hold onto the wheel and ride 'em out. Don't worry though, it has been a lot of years since we lost a ship to a storm.

Enjoy the good weather while it lasts,' he said, saluting and walking away.

The following night we had just finished dinner and were starting drinks when the storm struck. The wind had been picking up most of the afternoon and the sea was rough. Earlier, I had taken a walk on deck to watch the clouds forming and followed it with an Adabrin pill. So by dinner, aside from a bit of drowsiness, I wasn't feeling any pain. I was talking to the Dutchman about the big poker game he was heading to in Macau when a wave suddenly crashed against the side and the ship shuddered, rolling violently to the left and then to the right. Wave after wave slammed against the deck and the bulkheads, spraying the windows with heavy streams of water. I looked at the thin portholes. If they didn't hold we could be flooded in less than a minute.

From a left-right rolling action the ship began to pitch, up and down like a roller coaster. Into the trough it went and then up onto the crest of the waves, down again and up again over and over. The ship began to swing wildly, pitching and rolling at the same time. The roar as the waves struck was terrifying. I slid all over the mess hall along with everything that wasn't nailed down, holding onto the words of the first mate like a prayer, 'Just set the instruments, hold onto the wheel and ride her out.'

My fellow passengers were tossing back scotches in between the rolling and the pitching, but I declined any drinks. The Adabrin held my nausea somewhat at bay although I was really scared.

The storm held its grip through the night, not abating until morning when it gradually tapered out. I saw members of the crew led by the first mate carrying lanterns and assessing the damage. Surprisingly to me, there was very little. Ships are constructed to withstand the constant battering and unless they encounter the worst possible storm scenario, they do exactly as the first mate said — 'ride it out.'

On the fifth day, the Eastern Saga sailed through Lei Yue Mun Gap into Hong Kong Harbor in one piece and right on schedule. It was as I remembered it. In the harbor, Chinese junks, sampans and little craft scurried in all directions. Some had torn sails with huge holes patched with flour bags. Many of the larger junks had engines and flat bottoms and were used as lighters for loading and unloading cargos from ocean-going freighters.

The harbor pilot's small boat flying its red and white 'H' flag came alongside the *Eastern Saga* and the pilot climbed aboard, took over the helm and guided the ship safely to berth 7A located in the middle of the harbor with Hong Kong on one side and Kowloon on the other.

2

GO WEST

On a sudden urge, I had decided to leave behind the life I knew and begin a new one in a far-away place. As foolish as it may have seemed, the die was cast and I was not about to turn back.

I was from a Jewish family in a gritty neighborhood of the Bronx in New York City. My old man was a nice enough guy but I don't think he thought much of my abilities. He had immigrated from Hungary in 1920 and started in New York as a darkroom assistant, working his way up to become one of the city's most important commercial photographers. At one time he was the official photographer for the Bloomingdale's department store on Lexington Avenue. Although firmly of the conviction that I didn't live up to his standards, apparently he figured he owed me a living. So at the age of 26 I had the humiliating job of being the delivery boy at his studio.

As I'd do my routes, my thoughts would often drift back to my days in the Navy when we were stationed in Hong Kong. It was my first experience away from home and my first taste of the mysterious East. I missed the excitement of that life.

Then one morning as I drove to work I made a spur of the

moment decision — I'd sell my one-year old Chrysler sedan, buy an air ticket and go back to Hong Kong.

I was due at the office, but instead I headed straight for the used car showrooms on Broadway. At the first one the salesman offered me $1,500 but I wasn't ready to bite. I worked my way through the showrooms only to discover that $1,500 really was the best deal I was going to get. It was my first experience selling a car,and it was enough for me to classify used car salesmen among the lowest forms of humanity. When I went back to the first salesman he said he'd talked it over with his boss and they could really only manage $1,350. Take it or leave it.

Three hours late, I arrived at the studio with the money in my pocket and before my father could say anything I announced I was going to Hong Kong. I told him how I'd reached my decision and how I was in possession of $1,350, more money than I'd ever had before. I wasn't deluded into thinking that I would really be missed. My twin brother Dick was repping the studio and was bringing in some very big business. As for my contribution to the company, they could always find a kid with a bike to cover for me.

My father took the whole thing with stoicism. He went to a closet, handed me a beat up old Rolleiflex camera and advised me to get experience as a photographer. Then in a sudden burst of generosity (which was definitely not his style) wrote me a check for $500. I was on my way.

My inspired plan hit its first snag though when I tried to get a visa for Hong Kong from the British Embassy in Washington, D.C. I wanted to leave right away and they said getting a visa would take months. At that point I figured the closer I got to Hong Kong the less complicated the process would be so I decided to head west to San Francisco. But I found the same hang up there. The British Consulate in San Francisco told me that my application would be processed in London and it would take two months. There had to be a better way.

'Why not try Hawaii,' I thought. A small back-alley travel agent was touting cheap tickets to Hawaii on an obscure airline called Trans-Oceanic. They had a flight to Honolulu leaving the next day, so I bought a ticket.

Trans-Oceanic Airline had only one airplane, a huge clipper, and due to the extraordinarily cheap price, every seat was taken. Not only were the regular seats taken, but those in the lounge as well, and 10 passengers just sat on the floor. After a few chilling seconds when the pilot struggled to lift this huge load off the runway, we settled down to six-and-a-half hours of one of the most extraordinary plane rides I have ever experienced.

The stewardesses did a brisk business selling drinks and got into the spirit of things by sitting on passengers' laps and posing for photographs. At one point the purser took over the microphone and regaled us with exciting tales of the Hawaiian Islands, King Kamehameha and the benefits of eating pineapples. The man sitting next to me had a ukulele and started strumming a few favorites. Some passengers danced in the aisles, others joined in the sing along, and everybody seemed to be enjoying themselves.

With no seatbelts for many of the passengers I don't know what would have happened if we had met some real turbulence, but there was hardly a ripple the whole trip. Every minute of the flight was full of fun, and as we approached

Honolulu the pilot took a few extra turns around Diamond Head, giving us courtside view of the iconic (and gratefully extinct) volcano at the eastern end of Waikiki Beach.

As we came around for final approach, the purser's voice became serious. 'In a few minutes we will be touching down in beautiful Honolulu. We know you've enjoyed the trip and so please, please refrain from mentioning the few passengers we couldn't find seats for to members of the ground staff. They are a bit straitlaced.'

And then he said, 'Now as a tribute to you wonderful people, the crew joins me in wishing you, in the tradition of the islands, *Aloha 'Oe.*'

It seemed a pity that within a week Trans-Oceanic Airlines had closed down forever.

Honolulu was the most beautiful city I had ever seen. The houses were made of lath and plaster and some had green-tiled Oriental roofs, offering the visitor a hint of its ethnic mix. The streets were broad, the air balmy, the breezes gentle and palms swayed everywhere I looked. The temperature was 72 degrees but I figured there must be rain sometime; how else could you account for such lush greenery? Hawaii was truly a Garden of Eden.

I arrived in the early afternoon and decided the British Consulate could wait until the next morning. First, I had to answer the call of the beautiful beach. I can swim okay but I never cared for it very much, especially in the saltwater. For the moment I was only interested in lying in the sand and looking at the beauties in their scant bathing costumes. I put on my swimming trunks, took a towel from the bathroom and headed for legendary Waikiki Beach.

The sand was deep and hot on the bottoms of my feet so I steered toward a palm tree that promised a cool respite. I spread my towel under it and sat down among the sand dunes to watch the passing parade.

My vigil paid off. Later, a pretty farm girl from Kansas called Ruth joined me under the palm. She was wearing a one-piece cotton bathing suit and I talked her into going for a night walk on the beach. We took off our shoes and headed toward the water, soft moonlight illuminating the sand and docile waves as they unfurled on the shore. We held hands and as we walked along the water's edge I was deep in reflection.

Now that I was actually in Hawaii I had sort of painted myself into a corner. The only thing that lay between me and Hong Kong was about 6,000 miles of ocean, and if I couldn't get a visa here, I guess I would just have to give it up and head back home. I pictured myself getting off the plane in New York and creeping back, hat in hand, to my father's studio and I didn't like it.

The next morning I got on a bus to Hotel Street, Honolulu's main drag, where the British Consulate had its office on the third floor of a four-story office building. Inside, a middle-aged, bespectacled woman sat at a desk. Behind her I could see three smaller desks and some filing cabinets but only one other person working. It certainly was not the busiest consulate in the system. I explained my problem to the woman and she asked for my passport.

'There are no visas in this?' she asked, scanning it.

'I know. I haven't been to a foreign country yet.'

She took a form out of her desk. 'Fill this out and we will need two pictures. Do you have any contacts in Hong Kong?'

'No.'

'Why do you want to go there?'

I shrugged my shoulders. 'Just to visit.'

'How long do you plan to stay?'

'I would like to stay indefinitely.'

'Oh, in that case you will have to have a reason for going. Like a job or to attend the university and you must have a letter from your employer or your school in America. Failing that you must have positive proof of financial responsibility.'

'How much is that?'

'Enough to pay rent and board for a year. Approximately $5,000 dollars. Our embassy in Washington will have to have time to process your papers and that could take four to six weeks.'

'What about a tourist visa?'

'You must have $1,000 cash or traveler checks, a ticket and an onward booking on an airplane or a ship. A tourist visa of thirty days will be issued by our office in Washington so you must give us about ten days to two weeks.'

'Oh well,' I said, exasperated, 'forget it. I really can't understand why it's so difficult to get a little thing like a visa.'

'It's not a little thing. Hong Kong is on the border with China and it's a very sensitive place. You can't blame our government for checking carefully on everyone who wants to go there. Not pointing the finger at you specifically but we must be vigilant. You just got caught up in the system.'

'Well, I can't wait forever. I guess I'll just have to skip it. Thank you.'

Out on Hotel Street again I walked aimlessly, feeling sorry for myself. It looked like I would really have to give up this Hong Kong idea and slink back to New York.

I passed a travel agency with posters in the window advertising trips to the other islands in the Hawaiian archipelago.'

They showed beautiful scenes of tidy thatched roof huts, lush rain forests, and white beaches. I thought, 'What's there to lose at this point?' and went in to investigate.

An attractive Japanese woman greeted me with a beautiful smile. I must have looked as distraught as I felt because she looked at me and asked, 'What's the problem?'

I found myself telling her about my visa troubles, and how I was about to give up hope of ever getting past Hawaii.

She was sympathetic. 'How can I help?'

'I noticed your posters in the window. I was thinking maybe I could have some exciting adventure traveling around the Hawaiian Islands for a while.'

She paused, then asked, 'What's your name?'

'Marvin. Why?'

'Well Marvin, have I got a real adventure for you. We chartered a Pan Am Clipper to Tokyo to take a group of Japanese home for the Cherry Blossom Festival. They're leaving the day after tomorrow and I just had a cancellation. Would you be interested in taking the vacant seat? It's a one-way ticket to Tokyo and the price is fantastic. You would have to sit in the lounge, but you're young and you would be traveling with all Japanese people. Interesting, don't you think?'

She had my attention. 'But what about a visa?'

'You're an American. No problem. Give me your passport and I'll get you one.

'Japan,' I thought. What a fantastic idea. I gave her my answer quickly, 'Okay, I'm your man.'

I handed her my passport and she started taking down my details.

'The plane departs Thursday night at 10:30. You must be at the airport one hour before departure. Be back at my office tomorrow about 2 p.m. and I will have your passport with the visa and your ticket. Any questions?'

My mind was reeling. 'When do I pay?'

'Right now.'

Just 15 minutes ago I was headed home with my tail between my legs and now my life was completely changed. In a couple of days I would be in the Land Of The Rising Sun. I couldn't believe it. What extraordinary luck.

Our Clipper carried a collection of septuagenarians, octo-genarians and me, just short of my 27th birthday. Being the sociable type, I naturally wanted to talk with someone but nobody seemed interested. They almost acted as if I didn't exist. I figured they were shy, but it was a little disconcerting to make that whole trip without talking to another passenger. I had a seat in the lounge and ate the dinner with the tray balanced precariously on my knees. It was my first venture into the world of sushi and I became an immediate fan. A stewardess from Tulsa, Oklahoma handed me a copy of the Honolulu Advertiser and spoke to me from time to time and seemed to commiserate with my estrangement from the other passengers. But at Wake Island we changed crews and the next bunch was not inclined to make small talk.

Wake Island is a dreary little coral atoll right smack in the middle of the Pacific Ocean with more notoriety than its three-square-mile size would suggest. During World War II, the Japanese attacked Wake simultaneously with Pearl Harbor and occupied it until the end of the war. All that was there now was a Pan Am base for refueling and changing crews, a U.S. Air Force weather station and Black-footed Albatrosses affectionately known as Gooney birds because of the silly way they walked and bobbed their heads. Before we landed, my stewardess friend told me that after dark the crews that laid over and the weathermen went skinny dipping, had barbecues and played all sorts of games in the sand, so I guess it wasn't as dreary as it looked.

Our plane stopped for two hours, giving us a chance to stretch and tour the rusting remnants of war. Artillery pieces, landing craft and fighter planes lay derelict and disintegrated, partially buried in the sand. Ironically, the Japanese passengers pulled out their cameras and posed in front of these artifacts of the collapse of the Japanese war machine.

Airborne again, I looked down at the glorious Pacific Ocean. The Pacific is the deepest ocean in the world and covers more than a third of the earth's surface. From 25,000 feet, its majesty was on full display, deep blue broken only by coral reefs and tiny specks of white sandy beaches.

Winging over this wondrous scene I had time to think about the life I left behind. I never got very much out of school. My parents did their best to improve my appreciation for education. They took me out of a miserable public school and sent me to a military school in Georgia. After I was expelled from there they tried a private school in Manhattan in the forlorn hope that my work would improve. I was always getting into all kinds of trouble and never really settled down to study.

At the Franklin School, Truman Capote was one of my classmates and we became close friends. We were two misfits who never accomplished much academically, but were tolerated by the powers that be, probably because our education was being well paid for. After lunch Truman and I would sit on a park bench and wait for the afternoon session to begin. He told me stories of his high society friends and his childhood in New Orleans, some of which I took with a grain of salt. Once he showed me a story in The New Yorker magazine that he claimed he wrote. When I told him I couldn't see his byline he remarked that the New Yorker never gave credit to their writers, but I discovered that at that time he was actually an office boy at the magazine.

When our conversation got around to sex he told me he was bisexual.

'What is that?' I asked, feigning innocence.

'That means you can go to bed with boys as well as girls.'

'Oh,' I said, and left it at that.

He was only about 5 feet 4 inches tall, a very pretty little guy with a peaches-and-cream complexion and straight blonde hair. He spoke with a high-pitched voice and had extremely feminine intonations in his speech and girlish mannerisms. He pushed the sleeves of his angora sweaters up from his wrist to his elbows and wore long colorful scarves in the winter. He was different from everyone else in our school, but he was interesting and had a nice way about him and I liked him.

I remember boys from the school would stand on the other side of Central Park West during lunch break and wave hand-kerchiefs at him and whistle and shout nasty insults. He took it all with good grace and seemed proud of his sexual orientation. One time, one of them tried to provoke him by rudely waving his hands displaying a limp wrist and saying something inane, thinking he could get a laugh from his friends.

'Hi Truman. What are you doing tonight?'

Truman answered in his most girlish articulation, 'I'm busy, Irvine. Sorry.'

I slipped out of my reverie as the plane started its descent into Haneda International Airport in Tokyo. Though I'd never been to Japan I had the immediate feeling that I was home.

At the baggage carousel I picked up my knapsack and

rushed to get through the immigration and customs checks. My fellow passengers were packed onto special tour buses and whisked away and that was the last I saw of them. I'd spent the last 24 hours locked up with those people and not a single word passed between us. After paying the fare to the shuttle bus I was on my way into Tokyo.

3

THE GINZA BOYS

The bus from the airport arrived at the City Terminal and I became aware that all the shops had signs written in Japanese. It suddenly occurred to me that I might have difficulty making myself understood. I wanted to go to a famous hotel in Tokyo which all foreigners knew as the Imperial Hotel, but to the Japanese it was '*Teikoku*,' and that was the only name they knew it by. Designed by the American architect Frank Lloyd Wright it was the one structure left standing after the devastating earthquake of 1923. Tokyo is earthquake prone and they occur almost daily.

I got the cheapest taxi I could find. The meter read 70 yen and I told the driver the one Japanese word in my lexicon. He started racing through the streets at breakneck speed, dodging in and out of traffic, turning corners on two wheels and blowing his horn continuously. 'Honk-honk, honk-honk.' He was like a fighter pilot with all his machine guns blazing. I learned that those types of taxis were nicknamed 'kamikaze,' but I continued to fearlessly subject myself to their dangers because of the exhilarating ride, and the cheap price.

My eight-dollar room at the Imperial was a very tiny single but with all the necessary accoutrements. A bed, a small clothes closet, a chair, a dressing table with a mirror and a bathroom with a rarely seen European style sit-down toilet, and a bathtub which I learned was for the daily bathing ritual of '*ofuro*' (meant for relaxing, not washing). Everything was spotless.

I had slept a bit on the plane and had reached such a high level of anticipation that before anything I just had to walk the streets. In any case my strategy for beating the time lag was to force myself to stay awake the rest of the day and flop into bed about 10 that night, totally exhausted. Hopefully then I would sleep peacefully until the next morning and my time lag would miraculously disappear. That was my remedy, but I hadn't tried it out yet.

The young girl at the hotel desk directed me to the Ginza area, where many of Tokyo's celebrated attractions are grouped. I hadn't walked very far when I noticed a grassy strip on the other side of the avenue, ending in what turned out to be the Imperial Palace, home of the Emperor of the Chrysanthemum Throne. I was amazed because the location was right in the middle of the Otemachi banking district in downtown Tokyo.

The Palace was surrounded by high walls and a moat stocked with super-size carp. Japanese admire the fearlessness of the carp and its great power to swim upstream against the tide. On every Boys' Day, the Japanese fly cotton replicas of the fish from flagpoles, and 'it is hoped,' the saying goes, 'that every mother's son will grow up to be as courageous and powerful as the carp.'

I approached the palace, curious if I could join a tour. The palace guards seemed rather apologetic when they informed me that Emperor Hirohito, the Empress, and their son, Crown Prince Akihito received the public only on January 2 as well as the Emperor's birthday. At other times you were not permitted to enter the grounds so I had to be satisfied with just looking at the lovely setting from behind a fence.

I roamed the Ginza checking out department stores and restaurants for about an hour until I inadvertently wandered into a side street called Namiki Dori, crammed with upscale apparel shops, coffeehouses and private bars.

Private bars don't encourage foreign visitors. The price of the drinks is astronomical and Japanese business types don't want to be seen over-imbibing by *'gaijins'*—and they are known to over-imbibe. It is not uncommon to see a respectable-looking businessman in a three-piece suit being carried out of a bar singing Japanese folk songs at the top of his voice, or a couple of customers just lying in the grass in front of the club sleeping it off. The waitresses are similar to geishas but not so well trained in the Japanese arts. Most of them wear kimonos and can be seen lined up at the front door at closing time bidding the customers *'sayonara.'*

Companies defray the cost of the club for their executives, and also pay the executive's rent, his grocery bills and even his expensive suits. The firms can then legally write it off their taxes. It is a sort of perk with the government, in the end, actually paying all the bills. No foreigner could afford this high style of living enjoyed by 'cash poor' Japanese executives.

I was about ready for some refreshment and was looking around for a suitable spot on the Namiki Dori and my eye caught a coffee shop sign that read 'Café Julien Sorel,' a name I knew from a classic novel by the French writer Stendahl. It was a small place, had a coffee bar, a few tables and a jukebox and when I walked in there was only one other customer, and he turned out to be American.

'Howdy' he said. 'Welcome to Julien's.' He offered me a seat next to him.

'Are you the owner of the place?' I asked.

'No,' he laughed. 'Just a customer. But I hang out here all the time and know the routine.' I detected a New York accent.

'And what do you do in Japan?'

'I'm in the occupying army.'

His name was Lenny Green and he lived and worked from a room at the Osaka Hotel, an army hostel. He was a sergeant and handled air transport for army dependents. He was tall and slim with a pleasant, forthcoming way about him. 'I'm just an easy-goin' guy' was one of his favorite catchphrases.

He had a particular empathy for bartenders because he used to be one at a bar in Provincetown on Cape Cod in Massachusetts. He would bring them presents of cartons of cigarettes that he purchased for a pittance at the army PX. One of his other concerns was the welfare of bar girls. When one of them got sick he visited her in the hospital and brought her favorite comic books and candy bars. For this noble behavior he earned the sobriquet 'the kind man' and he was always handed his favorite drink, gratis, when he entered a bar.

Lenny had a beautiful and very tall girlfriend he had nicknamed 'Giant san.' Giant san made her living as a 'dancing girl' but was devoted to Lenny and was known to turn down big spenders that would have given her serious money for a roll in the hay, just to be with 'Green san' for no money at all.

Lenny more or less tolerated his army job as a necessary evil because it allowed him to stay in Tokyo and carry on his pub crawling activities.

'Where are you staying?' he asked.

'I'm at the Imperial. It's a very small room.'

'Probably one of those six mat jobs?'

'What do you mean by six mats?'

'The Japanese measure all real estate by the standard size of *tatami* mats. I guess the room you describe is about the size of six *tatami* mats. That's about as small as they get.'

I hadn't eaten since breakfast and I asked him if he knew a place where they served raw fish?

'You mean sushi. Yeah, I know of a spot just a couple of blocks from here.'

'Will you have the time to join me?'

'We could do that. There's no rush. Sit awhile and let's finish our coffee.' He was in no rush — ever — to do anything.

I soon settled into a fascinating life in Japan and thought less and less about my visa for Hong Kong. Lenny filled me in on the interesting places to go and I ended up staying for about three months.

In a city of extraordinary sights, the Queen Bee Dance Hall counted as one of the most memorable places that Lenny took me to. On my first visit I was amazed by its scale, as it covered an entire city block and employed more than one thousand hostesses. A huge neon sign of a queen bee with its wings in motion and the words 'One Thousand Hostesses' in Japanese ran across the top of the Queen Bee's three stories. With so many girls it was without a doubt the biggest dance hall in the world.

Inside, remarkably it was the size of a football field. Tables, booths and a stage for a 32-piece orchestra surrounded an enormous dance floor. The hostesses sat on the side, facing the customers with numbers attached to their chairs so the patrons could make a selection. There was even a section for kimono-clad ladies for the more traditional men. The distances in the Queen Bee were so vast that some of the nearsighted customers had to use binoculars to make their choice.

Cokes cost 100 yen at the bar, but drinks at the tables were 1,000 yen for a real drink for the customers and 3,000 yen for the girl's drink, which was only watered-down Coke. How much of an impression you made on the hostess could be ascertained from how fast she drank her first drink and ordered another. A popular hostess could make between 60 and 70 thousand yen on a good night and you could make a date to take the girl out after work if she was willing.

The Bee was starting to fill up when we got there and after a little while Lenny's friends the Ginza Boys arrived.

Ted Rausch was a German who had recently immigrated to the U.S. and been immediately drafted into the Air Force and sent to Japan. Ted was a blonde, Teutonic type with amazing dimpled cheeks. He wore a white turtleneck sweater and slacks so painstakingly pressed that he insisted on standing up all night so as not to spoil the crease. Richard Hughes was a balding, nervous type dressed in a three-piece business suit. His sparsely covered head and grave facial expression belied the fact that he was only 22 years old. Taking up the rear were Gerry Houk and John Marshall. These four made up the entire gang of skirt chasers that Lenny called the Ginza Boys. I marveled at how they cracked the businesslike personalities of the hostesses. Why these mercenary ladies were content to shack up with these penniless characters was beyond me.

During the evening I met Lenny's girl 'Giant san.' She was a looker and very tall for a Japanese, and she and Lenny seemed close. Tonight she told him she wasn't sure she could go out with him as she was with a group of high-powered business types who were going to a private bar and they wanted to take the girls along. It meant a nice piece of change for her. Lenny accepted it all in his stride. If she could be with him that was fine, but if she couldn't that was okay too. As he so often told me, he was an 'easy-goin' guy.'

Sitting at the bar I met Yoo Hee, a lovely Korean hostess in an extremely low-cut gown with a drop-dead figure. She spoke passable English and seemed very friendly, but her real passion was money.

'What you do in Japan?' she asked.

'I'm an art student,' I said, following the Ginza Boys traditional line. 'I'm studying industrial drawing,' I said, to make the lie more convincing.

'Why don't you buy me a drink?'

'I can only afford a Coke.'

'Come on. Don't be a Cheap Charlie, buy me a real drink.'

'Seriously, I don't have any money.'

Her lovely body was distracting but I wasn't ready to shell out 3,000 yen for that. The Ginza Boys had already warned me that once you paid for a real drink the girl took you for just another sucker and you wouldn't stand a chance of getting her into the sack unless you paid the going rate. 'Stick to your guns' was the advice.

'So you won't buy me drink?'

'I wish I could afford it, but I'm only a poor art student.'

You Hee looked closely at me and then walked away in disgust.

'I blew it,' I told Richard Hughes.

'Big deal. This is her place of business and she has to make money.' He shrugged his shoulders, 'So you blew it.' He couldn't care less.

Ted Rausch took a more balanced view. 'These girls are very smart. They know they can get nothing from us young guys, so they must take us only for our good looks. But you look like a business man and they figure you got money so you have no chance of getting a chick for free in this place.'

'Bullshit,' said Gerry Houk. 'That girl has no idea whether you have any money. Wait awhile, if she has no customer she'll be back.'

'Yoo Hee is in this country illegally,' Lenny offered. 'She got smuggled in on a ship from Busan. And she loves to drink whiskey, straight from the bottle. I nicknamed her 'Old Smuggler.' Give her a fifth of scotch and she's yours.'

John Marshall added, 'She's beautiful but very complicated.'

Everyone seemed to have an opinion on Yoo Hee.

'I like a simple, straightforward girl,' John continued. 'My woman puts on an evening gown and works here at night and in the daytime she's a telephone operator at the Matsuya department store.'

Lenny said, 'That's true. I call her 'The Operator'.' He seemed to have nicknames for everybody.

As matter-of-fact as these guys sounded about matters of the heart, Gerry Houk revealed a chink in the Ginza Boys' armor when he told me his own sad story of unrequited love.

'I was engaged to a beautiful hostess and a couple of weeks before the wedding she went to visit her family in Kyoto. While she was walking in the woods she heard a bird singing and saw in the mist an old man with a wispy beard playing a plaintive Japanese melody on a flute. She took that as an omen of some sort and asked the Shinto priests at her temple. They said it was a message from God telling her she shouldn't surrender her pure Japanese soul to a gaijin. When she arrived back in Tokyo she told me our marriage was off, and how miserable she was, but she couldn't ignore the word of the priests.'

About midnight, just before closing, Yoo Hee came back singing the same old tune.

'You buy me drink?' she asked.

'I told you I don't have any money.'

She looked exasperated, and after a few seconds said, 'Can you buy me coffee?'

'I think I can. I took some coins out of my pocket and counted them carefully. I think I can just about make it.'

Gerry was right. If you play them right and wait, they'll be back.

In the meantime the Giant had returned wearing her coat. She asked Lenny to slip out with her before her customer woke up to the fact that she was gone. So Yoo Hee, the Giant, Lenny and I went to an all-night coffee shop. I really liked the coffee culture in Tokyo. There were hundreds of coffee shops in town and they had a very relaxed atmosphere.

I was enjoying Japan. The only problem was that it was all play with me, and if I wanted to stay I had to get down to some serious thinking about my future and the money question.

It was just 9 a.m. on a Wednesday and raining. With nothing much to do at that hour I figured I could visit the British Embassy and try the probably hopeless exercise of applying for a visa to Hong Kong. I had the alternative of Japan now and it seemed an exciting place to hang out, so getting a visa didn't seem so important.

The visa office was in a building close to the Imperial Palace in Otemachi and I approached a pleasant, very English consul who sported a yellow wool tie while a Harris Tweed jacket hung on the back of his chair.

'What can I do for you on this miserable morning, old boy?'

'I am trying to find out what it would take to get a visa to Hong Kong, old chap.'

'Well, you've got to have $400 in cash or traveler's checks to establish your financial reliability.'

'That I have, and what else?'

He shook his head. 'That'll do it for a thirty-day tourist visa.'

I looked at him incredulously. 'You mean if I have $400 in cash or traveler's checks I could get a visa, no questions asked?'

'Oh you'll have to fill out a form and give us two pictures, but yes, that will be all that is required.'

'You mustn't mind my skepticism but I have found it very difficult to get a visa in the United States.'

He looked perplexed. 'The rules are the same worldwide for someone holding an American passport.'

'Well that's fine. I'd like one visa please.'

He gave me the form to fill out, I handed him my passport and two pictures. He told me the cost was $5 and the visa would be ready the next day. That's all there was to it. I was nonplussed.

'Will you be taking a plane?'

'What do you suggest?'

'If you don't mind traveling by steamship, Jardine has a freighter leaving on the weekend from Osaka. The trip would take five days and the cost is just US$99. You can get to Osaka in just six hours by taking the new high-speed train. If you went a day or two in advance you could tour Kyoto, a picturesque spot and very historic.'

I went directly from the British Embassy to the Jardine

shipping agent and booked a place on a ship called the *Eastern Saga*. What a name for the start of my Hong Kong adventure.

The die was cast. It was amazing: not even noon and I had a visa and reservations on a ship. I had made my decision to leave Japan without giving one thought to what I was leaving behind.

I treated Lenny to sushi as sort of a celebration and we ordered *sashimi*. It cost more than the standard sushi but as it was going to be my last meal of raw fish in Japan, I decided to pull out all stops. I selected fatty tuna – it was in-season at the moment – and I had them throw in a sea urchin and it was all served on a small wooden tray adorned with a kind of a fluffy green coleslaw and preserved ginger.

I was sitting there telling Lenny about my trip to Hong Kong, thoroughly enjoying the tender cuts of fresh fish, when I experienced my first Tokyo earthquake. The tremor was strong enough to shake the flimsy walls of the shop. I grabbed for my shuddering teacup and looked over at the manager and his helper who both stood very still, listening, probably expecting the train tracks to fall on them. In less than a minute it was all over and they returned to their work as if nothing had happened. Earthquakes are a common occurrence and every Japanese knows there is no security against them. They could be mild as this one or they could be wildly devastating. It was a matter of a lucky draw and the Japanese live in the expectation of that destructive force of nature that could wipe out everything. In 1923 an earthquake struck Tokyo measuring 8.3 on the Richter scale. More than 140,000 people lost their lives in that one and it, too, lasted only one minute.

4

HONG KONG AT LAST

As we anchored, cargo junks flying little white Jardine flags scurried up alongside the ship and unloaded teams of coolies who jumped on board and immediately started bringing up the cargo.

I packed my knapsack and was on deck ready to get a boat to shore. Jack and Anna Mills, the British couple, were on deck, too, being greeted by a couple of Jardine stalwarts. Jack was an export and shipping manager for Jardine Matheson, on his last 'tour of duty' before retirement.

'Well there it is,' Jack said, pointing to Hong Kong Island. 'And you arrived on the Queen's birthday. Should be a good omen.'

There was a piper band from the police force, dressed in kilts playing a familiar Scottish air at Queen's pier.

Jack was happy to be back and sang along with the music, 'Many's the heart that will break in twa, if ye ne'er come back again.'

He turned to me, 'We've come to the parting of the ways old boy. You have my card. What do you plan to do?'

I wasn't sure how to answer. 'I'm a freelance photographer,' I said impulsively.

'Is that right? Do you plan to go into China? Anyway, I'll probably be here another couple of weeks so if you have any questions about Hong Kong please call.'

I was watching their launch pull away when the other passenger, Dutchman Willem Kusters came up on the deck with his bags. Willem was a professional card player and had plans to take part in a big poker game in Macau.

'I am going to Kowloon. Do you want to share a water taxi?'

'Right now I don't know where to go. I want to get to the Foreign Correspondent's Club.'

'That's over on the Hong Kong side. If I were you I would check in at the YMCA on Salisbury Road, get a good night's sleep and tomorrow morning you'll be fresh and can make contact with the Foreign Correspondents' Club.'

'Thanks, I definitely will. The best of luck with your poker game.'

The crew was heading for Kowloon so I took up their invitation to join them in their '*walla-walla*' and we piled in and headed for Kowloon. As it neared the pier I turned around for one last look at the Eastern Saga. There were four junks alongside now, tied together and waiting their turn to load. They had installed a crane for the heavy cargo, which they were winching out of the hold and lowering onto the junks.

It seems that in 1946 the U.S. Navy and the Brits had a bit of a go at each other, nobody could remember about what, and the American navy were barred from going to Kowloon. So the peninsula always seemed a mysterious place just across the harbor. A place I could see but could never go to. But this was 1954. I was a civilian and Kowloon was wide open to me. I headed there for my first look.

I joined the crew at a Russian restaurant for a dinner of borscht, beef brisket with pickles and brown bread and a creamy dessert. Afterwards, they wanted to go to the Princess Garden for drinks and girls, but I passed on that. I just wanted to check into the Y and plan my next move. I bid farewell to the crew and watched them as they disappeared into the wilds of Kowloon.

The YMCA on Salisbury Road was typical of most Christian establishments. They had strict rules about not drinking, smoking or fraternizing, and there were Bibles in all the rooms. The bathroom was down the hall but the price of HK$13 (about US$2) for a single seemed fair. I was handed a slip of paper when I checked in telling me that there was a prayer meeting in the chapel at 6:30 every morning, which I chose to pass up, and breakfast served from 6 a.m. at the Jesus Coffee Shop, which I decided to accept. It was a pretty fair English-style breakfast for HK$5 with kippers, eggs, muffins and jam and hot milk tea.

After breakfast I called the Foreign Correspondent's Club from a telephone in the lobby and got the manager Mr. Tibesart on the line. I made a noise about being a photojournalist but he didn't press for details. He told me they had a room available and that if I would come over he would show it to me.

Crossing over to the Hong Kong side on the Star Ferry evoked old memories. From the deck I saw the Post Office, the Hong Kong Club, Queen's Building and St. John's Cathedral, all standing for almost a hundred years, and across Statue Square Park stood the headquarters of the Hongkong and Shanghai Bank and next to that the Bank of China. As

I stepped off the ferry I was ambushed by about 20 rickshaw pullers all competing for my business. Sadly for them, I had been advised to take a taxi up the hill, to 41A Conduit Road.

The driveway wound its way to a huge mansion of concrete and red brick with a spacious lawn in front. Built by a wealthy businessman back in 1888, the building had two floors with round towers at either end and a balcony on the second floor with a magnificent view of the harbor and Kowloon in the distance. Beyond the main building were the staff quarters and above that a concrete staircase that led up the mountain to a stone gazebo with a green-tiled roof.

The taxi stopped at a covered entrance where Mr. Tibersart was waiting for me. He was about 50 years old with thinning hair and a bit of a gut. He wore a light-colored tunic with several ballpoint pens jutting out of his pocket. He was personable and friendly and looked more like a newsman after a story then the manager of the club.

Mr. Tibersart led me up a wide oak staircase to the second floor and the six rooms they rented out.

'The large bedroom with the balcony and a private bathroom has been taken by Mr. Marius, a lawyer. The slightly smaller room is rented by Mr. Roads, the AP correspondent. For the time being we have four vacant rooms. They all have telephones and ceiling fans and are quite cozy.'

The rooms turned out to be nothing to write home about and were equipped with furniture that looked like it came from a secondhand shop. A bed, a cabinet for clothes, a bamboo desk with a cane chair and a small, bamboo sofa with soft pillows and faded covers. The bathroom was down the hall. A bit depressing, but it was the Foreign Correspondents' Club. I picked a front room that had the nicest view of Hong Kong, and in the distance, the hills they call the Nine Dragons. The price of the room was HK$400 a month.

Over tea Mr. Tibersart told me he had grown up in Tianjin where his father worked for a French sewing machine company. When the Japanese occupied the city his father was incarcerated with most of the other foreign men on the spurious charge of spying for the American army. Once a month his mother was allowed inside the prison for a half-hour visit, and she always brought a loaf of French bread, a sausage and a bottle of wine that they later discovered was confiscated by the Japanese guards. Tibersart's father was questioned unremittingly and several times they harassed him with a sword and threatened to chop off his head if he didn't confess. After a year of this treatment his father was freed for 'humanitarian reasons,' giving his failing health as the basis for his release. He never recovered from his ordeal and died soon afterward. Tibersart's mother died several months later.

After the Japanese were defeated Tibersart found work at a bank and married a French woman, an accountant he had gone to school with. But after a while the Chinese Communists came into power and made it difficult once again for foreigners living in China. Tibersart and his wife decided they'd had enough, and it was time to leave. It took them about a year to get exit visas. They sold their belongings to buy steamship tickets and discovered they had just enough money to get to Hong Kong, arriving in the colony broke.

He got a position working as the night manager of a hotel where he met Fred Hampson, president of the Foreign Correspondents' Club, who offered him the job running the club, and his wife came along as the club's accountant.

Tibersart's story was an entirely new one to me, but later I would hear many similar stories from people that were forced to leave China.

I had started my journey in New York with approximately $1,800 in my pocket and now I was actually sitting in my room at the Foreign Correspondents Club in Hong Kong. It was a dream come true. I had exactly US$280 left after deducting the month's rent, and I realized I had to take especial care of my tiny treasure trove until I found work.

5

THE TIGER STANDARD

The next morning I slung my Rolleiflex around my neck, made an effort to look professional and started canvassing the news agencies – UP, AP, Reuters and Australian Associated Press. They all told me the same thing. If I got any pictures I considered newsworthy I should bring them in and they would look them over. They paid HK$50 for any picture they accepted, but that of course, didn't offer much hope for my future. The AAP bureau chief, Graham Jenkins came up with an idea.

'Try the English language papers,' he told me. 'Forget the photographer pitch and see if they are interested in reporters or copy editors. News photography in Hong Kong is a non-profession, but the reporters are mainly Chinese and have a poor standard of English. If you want to work in the news field that would be the way to go.'

I took his idea and started making the rounds of the newspaper offices. *The South China Morning Post*, *The China Mail* and finally the *Hong Kong Tiger Standard*, and there I hit pay dirt.

The Hong Kong Tiger Standard was housed in a four-story building in the middle of a slum area on Wanchai Road. The top floor was given over to the manufacture of Tiger Balm, a cure-all menthol used for headaches, rheumatism, measles, chicken pox, the common cold, cuts, bruises and snake bites.

The English language *Tiger Standard*, its sister paper the Chinese language *Sing Tao* and Tiger Balm were all owned by the fabulously wealthy Aw Boon Haw. According to conflicting legends, Haw had risen to great wealth from simple beginnings as either a coolie or a rickshaw puller in his native Burma when he stumbled on the formula for Tiger Balm. Either way he was now a rich man and his whole empire was accommodated in this insalubrious little building that smelled of menthol and printers ink.

The Haw family lived in Haw Par Mansion, an ornate structure right in the middle of what they called the 'Tiger Balm Garden,' a sculpture garden featuring the most grotesque collection of statuary in existence. Brightly painted tigers, snakes, rabbits and characters from Alice In Wonderland sat alongside sculptures of Buddhist Hell showing people having their guts ripped out, decapitations and gore everywhere. The garden was open and free to the public and there wasn't a television network that hadn't reported on this monstrosity at some time or another. To top it all off the Singapore side of the family boasted a much larger and even more grotesque Tiger Balm Garden.

Along with the garden, the Haw family's home was also open to tourists as it hosted one of the most extraordinary jade collections in the world. A guide would lead groups through the house at all times of day. Even when the family was having dinner, groups would come shuffling through and the guide would point out each family member individually.

'That's his daughter who runs the *Tiger Standard* and *Sing Tao* newspapers,' said the guide, 'and the one on the end of the table is his wife and the lady dipping her chopsticks into the vegetable dish is his niece who lives here in the mansion, and the other lady on the opposite end of the table is another niece who is visiting from Singapore.' The family kept right on eating, paying no attention to the crowds sweeping through their dining room. Only Aw Boon Haw himself never made appearances for the public.

To get a job at the *Standard* I told the editor a totally made-up story about my education as a journalism major at Stanford University, which just happened to have one of the best journalism courses in the United States. He naturally looked very impressed, but then I wonder if it made any difference. They had already been looking, in vain, for a sub-editor when I happened along. Leslie Sung, the editor, was tall, quite good looking and looked like a college professor with his spectacles. He hired me almost as soon as I entered his office.

'We need a sub-editor very badly,' he admitted. Sung spoke impeccable English.

'Well I'm your man.' I said, thinking a sub-editor was like the right-hand man to the editor-in-chief.

'Up 'till now I have been subbing all the copy myself and now I can hand it over to you. What a relief,' he said, thankful for his newfound support.

What did he mean, 'subbing copy'?

'So, what will my duties be?' I asked, scrambling.

'Checking for mistakes in English and punctuation and occasionally rewriting parts of stories to make it more interesting. I think in America they call it a rewrite man.'

'Oh, a rewrite man. I didn't quite know the term sub-editor. They don't use it in the States.' I didn't know if they did or not.

'What's the salary?'

He knew but he wasn't going to tell.

'All of the business side is handled by the GM,' he said.

'The GM?'

'The general manager. Sally Aw Sian, daughter of the old man. Come on Marvino,' he called me, companionably, 'I'll introduce you.'

He peeked in at Miss Aw's door, told her what job I was applying for and then took off. She sat behind a desk in a surprisingly small and very cluttered office. She seemed too young to run a newspaper. The *Tiger Standard* had been running at a loss for years but the *Sing Tao Evening News* had always been a financial success with 30 to 40 pages of advertising every day. I wondered uncharitably if her youth was the reason the Standard had been in the red almost since its inception.

Miss Aw was about 26 years old, wore glasses and, for all her apparent wealth, wasn't a fashion icon. On our first meeting she wore a frumpy pink frock with a high collar. Every morning she went to work accompanied by a coterie of ladies, including her mother, in the family Rolls Royce. She seemed to be pleasant enough but she was very shy and had difficulty looking me straight in the eye. That might have been a good thing, what with all the lies I had made up about myself. She didn't ask to see my diploma from Stanford either so we were off to a good start.

'Mr. Sung explained what we will expect of you?'

'Yes ma'am.'

'The position pays $600 a month. We pay half of that every two weeks.'

'That's in Hong Kong dollars?'

'Of course. I know that is not a very handsome salary and if you cannot accept it I will understand, but that is absolutely all we can pay.'

'I'm a photographer, too. What if I took pictures on the side for the paper?'

'That would be very generous of you. But we cannot give you more than the $600.'

'And if I wrote stories and submitted them to the paper?'

'Actually we would expect that, but there will be no extra pay for it.'

My god. 'What would my hours be?'

'Five p.m. until 9 p.m., six days a week, Monday through Saturday.'

The hours seemed convenient. Just the pay was painful.

'I have to tell you I expected a higher salary in that position.'

'We have another American working here as a reporter, and he only makes $350 a month.'

'Can you tell me why you pay such low salaries?'

'It's a Chinese custom,' she said.

From the impatient look on her face I realized I had to make up my mind immediately.

'Okay. I accept.'

And that's how I began my short but eventful career with the *Hong Kong Tiger Standard*.

My job at the *Tiger Standard* was fairly interesting and the hours suited me, only I did have to eat dinner at the office. I had just enough money to fill my stomach with dumplings from the Mei Li Kin restaurant just down the street. I ordered 10 steamed and 10 fried dumplings at a cost of 10 cents apiece and dipped them into a sauce of black vinegar and ginger, all delivered right to my desk at the Standard for no extra charge. I drank strong tea that tasted like sewer water, brewed by one of the reporters in the men's room and served in a chipped cup, black with tea stains. I existed on this diet for the first month of my employment at the Standard but by the end I couldn't look a dumpling in the eye, so sometimes after work I went with some of my fellow newsmen to the restaurant itself and had a whole chicken roasted in soy sauce for HK$4.50. Luxury.

Our chief, Aw Boon Haw, was one of those great men who had achieved success in the face of adversity. There were conflicting reports about his beginnings. Some said he started in his native Burma as a rickshaw puller, and others said he was a coolie when he stumbled onto the formula for Tiger Balm. Though the efficacy of his medicine was always suspect it received wide usage and he received great distinction (and lots of money).

I remember seeing him only once. He came to the *Tiger Standard* office on a hot summer day dressed in shirtsleeves with wide, green suspenders — or, as the British call them, 'braces' — holding up his trousers. He wore an irritated look and proceeded to switch off all the lights and berate Leslie Sung for wasting electricity when there was bright sunlight coming in the windows. He swept through the building like a general inspecting his troops, followed by a cluster of his directors.

His daughter was by his side during the visit and was not exempt from his disagreeable behavior either. She didn't speak, just listened and shook her head in answer to his questions in the obedient fashion of a respectful Chinese offspring.

He toured both of his newspapers and his baby, the fourth-floor Tiger Balm factory. He asked about the number of employees needed to run his empire and was very interested in electricity costs. He wanted to know if anything was being done to prevent the workers from stealing toilet paper and towels. The toilets could have used a good cleaning but he never mentioned that. He ended his tour by giving the GM a list of ways to save money.

With his penurious ways one wonders why he endured the huge financial losses made by the Standard year after year, or why he would continue that eyesore, the Tiger Balm Garden, to which he added grotesque and costly new exhibits from time to time.

The next time I encountered him was just a few months later, at his funeral. The staff of his three companies gathered outside the building in Wanchai and the cortege stopped. He was a Buddhist and a group of monks chanted the funeral service as musicians with tom-toms, eerie-sounding horns, a trumpet and a clarinet played a mournful dirge that sounded something like 'My Old Kentucky Home.' We had to bow three times toward the coffin and then the procession of his family and paid mourners, clad in white, moved on.

The close of the remarkable life of a simple, illiterate patent medicine man who proved that, as the saying goes, 'If you build a better a mousetrap the world will beat a path to your door.'

6

AND THE BAND PLAYED ON

My job was to correct the stories the reporters filed, some of them written in almost indecipherable English. By the end of the day I often found I had rewritten a large portion of the paper's news and feature pages and I hadn't needed a degree in journalism to do it. The reporters never complained; they just handed in their stories and I interpreted them the way I pleased. Leslie Sung had his own troubles editing the paper so he left all of the rewriting in my supposedly capable hands.

The only colleague whose work I didn't have to touch was Norman Denny, an American reporter who had come all the way from Europe on his bicycle and was paid the niggardly sum of HK$350 a month. He knew more about writing for a newspaper than I did but he never grumbled about my getting more pay. In fact he helped me out quite a bit in deciphering the hieroglyphics of the other reporters.

A tall, gangly guy he had a very pleasant way about him. He came from Gloversville, New York where his father was a minister in the local church and Norman had obviously learned about ethics there – he'd never allow anyone to pick up his check. When I mentioned his miserable salary he told me it wasn't so bad, and that six months ago he had actually gotten a very generous raise of $5.

Saturday was race day at Happy Valley and I went with Didi Ismail, the Standard's sports editor, to cover the races. The Happy Valley cemetery was across the street from the entrance to the track. The mourners wore white, music played and there were ovens where paper effigies were burned of the many good things the departed person could look forward to in their heavenly existence. The fires devoured paper like-nesses of race horses, servants, cars, clothes, houses, jewelry and huge wads of hell money.

Didi Ismail was half Chinese and half Pakistani and a devout son of Islam. He observed their strict dietary laws and gave his blind support to Muslims in whatever they did; right or wrong. Despite his uncompromising politics he was very affable and we got on extremely well. We watched the races from the press enclosure and Didi wagered small amounts on each race. He tried to explain all the important features of the horses to me. I listened but I didn't get it.

'Let's go down to the paddock and see the horses for the next race,' he said. 'We can have a word with the jockeys.'

Didi explained that these were gentlemen jockeys, mostly well-to-do businessmen, who rode for no pay. Their status notwithstanding, they were not above conspiring about which horse should win the next race. Fixing was against the rules but it did happen occasionally so if you were 'in' with the tack room you could make some money.

'Meet Marcel Samarq,' Didi said, introducing me to last year's champion jockey. Marcel was a bit taller than I would have expected a jockey to be and wore a yellow silk shirt with huge blue polka dots, white jodhpurs and the regulation black riding boots.

After a few minutes of chatter Didi casually said, 'You're riding *Cheerful* in the next race. What are his chances?'

Marcel ignored the question and said quietly, 'I hear that *Apple Pie* can't lose,' and with this bit of information dispensed he went to get weighed in.

'Did you hear that?' Didi asked me excitedly, 'He says *Apple Pie* can't lose. What do you say we split a bet on *Apple Pie*? Say $2.50 each. Just for fun.'

'Okay,' I said reluctantly. 'But just this once. For fun.'

What can I say? *Apple Pie*, an extreme long shot, won the race and paid the magnificent sum of $525 for each $5 bet. I couldn't believe it. I was hooked. I started betting $5 a race on my own and just bet on what Didi called 'cold ponies.' They were the ones which appeared not to have a chance, but if they did win they paid a huge amount. I guess the handicappers had it right because over a long period of time I never won another race. But that night I went back to the paper with $250 burning a hole in my pocket.

It was 9 p.m. when I finally left the office and headed off down Wanchai Road. When I got to Johnston Road it was aglow with neon signs and bright lights from the shops. Rickshaw pullers were vying for business among the hundreds of people passing by. The squeak of the wheels of the double-decker trams as they moved over the rails to Kennedy Town in the west, and Shaukeiwan in the east, added to the cacophony. It was a lively scene that I couldn't imagine seeing anywhere else in the world. On Queens Road I passed the darkened Hongkong and Shanghai Bank building and headed up the steep hill at Ice House Street and proceeded to Conduit Road. The streets lamps gave off a soft yellow sodium light which only added to the atmosphere.

Saturday night was usually busy at the Foreign Correspondents' Club. Light blazed from the main building, cars crowded the parking lot and more overflowed onto the driveway. The band was playing dreamy dance numbers and the floor was spilling over with people tripping the light fantastic. Some folks gazed out over the front wall at the exquisite night view of the harbor and serious drinkers piled up three deep at the bar.

I decided to jump the queue at the bar, managing to slip through the crowd and make my order. I thought I'd got away with it but a red-faced young man sitting at the bar and well into his cups, observed me.

'I saw you,' he said teasingly. 'Sneaking in to get served, eh?'

'I just wanted to order the drink. I'm going now,' I reassured him.

'Are you a member of Her Majesty's army?'

'Not very likely, I'm an American.'

'So you're an American. So what? What do you have against the British army? What's wrong with us?'

'Nothing.'

'We drove in all the way from Sek Kong to enjoy Saturday night and we don't have to put up with any insults from some goddamned American.'

'Look, I didn't mean to insult you. I think the British are wonderful people.'

'Yeah, what's so wonderful about them?'

'I have only been in Hong Kong a short time but I am very impressed with way the British are handling the government here, and I am sure the army is doing its part.'

'What makes you so sure?'

He lifted his voice in an aggressive manner and began to shout. At this point his wife, who was sitting on the stool next to him tried her best to shut him up.

'Take it easy Randy. No need to get upset. We're all friends here.'

Another Brit sitting on the end of the bar was drunk as well, and he looked like he was itching to get into the argument.

'I'll tell you what's wrong with the Army,' the stranger said in a loud voice. 'They don't do a goddamned thing except march their soldiers up and down a couple of hours a day and spend the rest of their time playing football and drinking beer.'

'And what makes you so smart, wise guy. I'll bet you're in the navy.'

'You got it mate,' he said pointing his thumb at his chest. 'We do all the patrolling and the dangerous work like looking for illegals and searching Chinese junks for contraband.'

The atmosphere was growing belligerent and Randy's wife was visibly irritated.

'Come on, can't you guys talk together like grown men. What do you have to fight about?'

The navy man looked incredulous.

'Who wants to fight? We're just discussing things that's all.'

'Yeah,' said Randy. 'Hey Yank, how's about taking my wife for a dance so we can discuss the matter at hand without a woman sticking her nose in?'

'You don't have to get rid of me,' his wife said. 'I just want you to behave like a gentleman that's all, before we get thrown out of here.'

Randy seemed fed up. 'Look Yank … er, what's your name?'

'Marvin.'

'Okay Mar-whatever-it-is. Will you take my wife for a dance? I want her out of my hair for a little while.'

'If she wants to I'd be delighted.'

'Well, don't get too delighted. Just take her for a dance that's all.'

'Of course.'

His wife got off of the barstool and she appeared very pleased at the prospect of getting away from husband for a short while. The band had started to play 'On A Little Street In Singapore.' She put her arm through mine and we walked outside to the dance floor on the lawn.

'I'm really fed up with that guy,' she told me. 'He always starts fights with strangers. Sometimes we get thrown out of bars. Very embarrassing. Oh it's such a relief to get away from him for a few minutes.'

'But you seem so patient,' I said, complimenting her. 'Anyway, I'm glad he suggested this dance.'

'Do you mean it?' she asked, squeezing my arm hard.

'I do.'

She thought a second. 'Did you particularly want to dance?'

I shook my head. 'Whatever you say?'

'Why don't we take a walk?'

She led me straight to the parking area.

'Oh, this is our car,' she said as though surprised to see it. She opened the back door and ushered me in. In a flash she was in my arms and before I knew it we were kissing each other passionately. I thrust my hand down her open-necked dress and discovered that she was one of those liberated women whose breasts were braless and when she lifted up her skirt I found that she didn't wear any panties either. She was a rather large woman and moved like a freight train and her heavy breathing resembled the whistle on the engineers cabin to warn other trains that we were coming through.

Realizing our time frame was short we made ardent love without dawdling. The windows began to steam up, but due to the limited time we had to spend on the actual deed I couldn't afford to take notice of many other details. As it happens we were in luck as no one passed by. When our brief encounter was over we adjusted our clothes as quickly as possible, she put on some lipstick, ran a comb hurriedly through her hair and we returned to the bar. I delivered her back to her husband somewhat disheveled, although he didn't seem to notice, just as the band was playing the final notes of 'On A Little Street In Singapore.' I excused myself and went up to my room.

I never saw them again and I don't think I would have recognized them if I had passed them on the street.

7

THE SHANGHAI CROWD

Abysmal accommodations aside, I actually liked living in the Foreign Correspondents' Club, or as everyone called it the 'FCC.'

I met a lot of interesting folk at the club such as Saul Marius, a brilliant young attorney who occupied the big room with the balcony. He was just 25 years old and was in town with a team of high-powered Wall Street lawyers to take on the Chinese government.

Communist China was still a relative newcomer on the world stage and the British didn't have a clue how to deal with it, so their philosophy was not to upset the apple cart. Saul and his partners had an uphill pull, especially as their client was a nationalist Chinese company which had recently arrived in Taiwan having narrowly escaped the Communists on the mainland.

With his curly hair, blue eyes and straight teeth, Saul could easily have been mistaken for a movie star, yet he was a seasoned lawyer working with others more than twice his age. They were in Hong Kong fighting a case for the ownership of Holt's Wharf on the Kowloon waterfront.

'What is Holt's Wharf?' I asked him when we met at dinner one evening.

'It's a warehouse complex on the Kowloon waterfront. Right now it's filled with aircraft parts and engines that belong to our clients, the Civil Air Transport, Incorporated of Taipei. They own the whole works, the equipment, the land and the buildings.'

'So the Chinese want the equipment?'

'They want everything, lock, stock and barrel. The Communist government's case is that CATI is a fugitive company that doesn't exist anymore, and therefore China owns all of its assets.'

'It's a British colony that's true, but Communist China looms large in the picture. Do you think you have a chance of winning?'

'There is still the rule of law here, and that is what we are banking on for our clients.'

Saul told me about the company's hair-raising escape from Communist China. CATI had been launched in Shanghai by a group of aviators after Claire Chennault's Flying Tigers disbanded and they started flying routes commercially around China. When the Communists were approaching Shanghai the company's leaders realized their business would be a target due to their close relationship to Chiang Kai Shek and they had to get out and fast.

They flew all of the aircraft to Taipei and then bought an old LST, christened it The Buddha and loaded it with all the equipment from their workshop. They sailed out of Shanghai, south to Canton keeping just ahead of the Communists. When the Reds were pressing Canton the plan was to take the ship the 90 miles to Hong Kong, but without the present captain who was considered too much of a Chinese patriot to trust. He got wind of the sailing though and with his cabin boy they fixed the electric wiring so that everything shorted out and the ship couldn't be moved.

Meanwhile the Communists were edging closer to the city so the loyal members of the crew jury-rigged the electrical system just enough to get it out of China before the Communists reached Canton. They proceeded down the Pearl River at a speed of only two knots and somehow made it to Hong Kong and felt safe at last. But it wasn't to be.

The British were going to recognize the Chinese Communist regime the following day and they were warned that if they were still there the ship would have to be confiscated. They didn't have time to fix the wiring so they sailed out of Hong Kong harbor as was and prayed. They made it into international waters with truly only minutes to spare.

Then in the Formosa Strait they hit a violent storm and the ship pitched and rolled and aircraft parts were thrown everywhere. The crew thought it was the end, but somehow they limped into Keelung harbor in one piece where they burned joss to thank the Enlightened One for their escape.

'They have their aeronautical workshop set up again and it is in operation. Now we have to get everything else that belongs to them,' Saul finished.

'Do you have a secret strategy for winning the case against China in a Hong Kong court?'

'The case will be tried under British law. A country that takes great pride in the rule of law, and still prizes the freedom and dignity of men.' Saul winked at me. 'And that is our ace in the hole.'

A footnote to this story. Saul and his group of legal eagles won the case.

As the Communists tightened their grip on the reins of power in China, many people uprooted from their homes came to settle in Hong Kong, but few with such pride and self-esteem as the 'Shanghailanders'. Every morning from 10 to 11:30 this elite group met at the Gloucester Lounge for coffee and a gab session where eclectic topics were discussed and women were mostly absent. Shanghai was remembered with a bitter tear.

The Shanghai crowd was dominated by Europeans. Shanghai Chinese were invited, but most chose not to attend. They had worked with Europeans in Shanghai, and their ideas didn't always jibe. The European businessmen considered themselves the big guns of Shanghai business and it gave them little to participate in tedious conversations where only English was spoken. Notwithstanding, both Chinese and European 'Shanghailanders' considered themselves superior to their Hong Kong counterparts in education, intelligence and business acumen.

One of those Shanghai Europeans, Bob Godkin, had called Shanghai home for the last 30 years. He and his wife, Charlotte, ran a company called Titan Steel that acted as the middleman between steel manufacturers and the buyers. In his late 50s, Bob was always neatly attired in a dark business suit, spoke English with a slight, nondescript European accent and was fluent in Russian. He was usually together with his wife and she was the only woman to break the unwritten law restricting these morning sessions at the Gloucester Lounge to men only.

Charlotte was Bob's right hand in the business. She had a very pretty face and was tall and full figured. Born in Dalian in northern China, she spoke English with a very thick Russian accent. In 1937 she escaped to Shanghai to avoid incarceration by the Japanese and there she met Bob. They were my ticket to the Shanghai crowd's morning nostalgia sessions.

'What ever happened to John Holland?' Marco Jesu asked, opening up the day's session.

Marco was an unusual commodity, as he was actually born in Shanghai. He had Italian parents, and had inherited a thriving family business. He loved his Italian heritage and was a superb cook and often prepared feasts of spaghetti and meatballs.

'John was a character. Do you remember he lived in that huge apartment on Nanking Road?'

Marco said.

'Can I ever forget?' Sam Tata reminisced. 'It was way above his means and he went as much as a year without paying the rent. I remember he used to pick up prostitutes from the bars, bring them home, and when he was finished passed them on to his friends, much to the disappointment of the ladies because nobody ever paid for their services. One guy told the girl that the next one would pay, and so on down the line until she was out in the street with nothing.'

John Holland made his living by covering news events for various newspapers but most times he was broke and existed only by borrowing money from fellow journalists, which he did with impunity. Then the day came when he couldn't borrow anymore, so he left the apartment without leaving a forwarding address. His landlord swore that he would find him and collect the 12 months back rent, with interest.

'Do you have any contacts in the garment industry?' Eric Gabriel asked me. 'We make top-of-the-line knitwear and I am sure there would be a big market for our products in the States.'

Eric was from Shanghai originally, but moved to Israel where he joined the Stern Gang, 'freedom fighters' who used heavy-duty tactics to expel the British from Palestine. Several years ago, for business reasons, he had left the violence behind and come to Hong Kong with his wife Riva and their two daughters.

'Knitwear,' I said. 'I'll have to think about that.'

Monya Kaner, a jovial, chubby salesman was telling a story of how he discovered the lost tribe of Israel in China.

'I was driving around the north, selling piece goods when I came to a city called Kaifeng and what do I see but a building with a Star of David on the front door. A Chinese rabbi with a long flowing beard was conducting services in Hebrew, to a Chinese congregation. After the service I went in and introduced myself to the rabbi. He wanted to know if I was Jewish? I told him I was, and he looked at me uncertainly and said, "That's strange, you don't look Jewish."'

'Very comical,' said Harry Odell, the impresario who introduced symphony orchestras to Hong Kong.

'You mean you don't believe me?' said Monya. 'Check it out. Kaifeng is southwest of Peking and has an active Jewish community, made up of mainly Chinese. Although since the Communist takeover I wonder if all that hasn't changed?'

Then somebody asked Ray Bede if his champion racehorse, Firefly, stood a chance in Saturday's race meeting.

'Don't bet on him,' Ray said. 'He's running strictly for the exercise.'

That was true in many cases, but I never heard an owner admit it, openly.

'My bank is paying a lousy six percent on my U.S. dollar time deposit,' Bob Seligman moaned.

'We can give you seven-and-a-half percent,' said Solomon Saul. He handled foreign exchange for the Kadoorie bank.

'Really. When?'

'Anytime you say.'

'What about right now?'

'Give me a check and I'll take care of it when I get back to the office.'

'I'll give you $100,000,' Bob said as he wrote a check in U.S. dollars.

'Any amount,' was Sol's answer. Shanghai businessmen talked big bucks.

'Did you hear that Jim Shashoua was playing hanky-panky with Riva Gabriel?'

'Tell me something I didn't know,' said Harry Odell.

Charlotte leaned over and whispered in my ear, 'How about coming up to our apartment on Sunday afternoon at five for high tea?'

'Great.'

I didn't know exactly what 'high tea' was but anything to get away from the FCC where my tab was growing to dangerous proportions.

'We live at the Peak Apartments, flat 2A. It's the very last stop on the Peak Tram.' Charlotte said.

8

THE PEAK TRAM MURDER CASE

The Peak Tram ran from Garden Road to the exclusive residential district at the top of Victoria Peak, with five stations along the way that were so steeply inclined they required the skill of an aerial artist just to alight from the tram.

The 15-minute ride in first class cost HK$1.50, but they also had a second class car tagging along that you could ride for only 50 cents. The last stop was Lugard Road, a two-mile country path that encircles the Peak. A wonderful place to view all of Hong Kong on a clear day, but when it was foggy and deserted it was a great place for a murder.

On the evening I went to the Godkins' it was dull and misty and there weren't any sightseers on the tram. Bob and Charlotte lived in a large apartment with an excellent view of the city and huge rooms, tastefully decorated and filled with souvenirs they had brought from China.

They had another guest for tea, a French client visiting from Tokyo. His party trick was cutting pieces of chicken away from the bone using only a knife, and not his fingers. Very fascinating, but I couldn't quite master it. He also whined about the high taxes in Japan, which he blamed on the policies of the occupying American army.

'The war is over,' he said. 'The Japanese have learned their lesson; why not leave them alone and stop imposing crazy business restrictions on them? Especially taxes on the import of steel.'

'I don't care for the Japanese,' Charlotte interjected. 'They are shifty and treacherous and whatever happens to them is just retribution for the way we were treated during the war.'

'Live and let live I always say,' countered the Frenchman.

The look in Charlotte's eyes were evocative of her terrifying experience with the Japanese.

Her guest took the hint and changed the subject.

At 9:30 that night, both the Frenchman and I left the Godkin abode. He took the tram down but I decided to take a walk on Lugard Road. The fog was eerie but I enjoyed it and made the complete circuit in just under an hour. When I got back to the tram station a European police inspector and two Chinese constables approached me and asked where I had been.

'Just walking around the Peak.'

'Why were you walking around the Peak?'

'I just came from dinner at a friend's house and thought I would take a walk. Is there any law against it?'

'It's not a good night for walking. Not much to see?'

'Well I'd never been up here before so I thought I would

take a look around. I enjoy the fog.'

'Okay, let's get into the van.' He shoved me not too gently toward a police vehicle.

'Why?'

'Because I said so,' the inspector demanded. 'Are you going to give us any trouble or do we have to handcuff you.'

'What?' I said, completely shocked. 'What the hell is going on here?'

'You tell us.'

'I don't know what you are talking about.'

'Did you have a girl with you on your walk around the Peak?'

'No. I was alone. Where would I get a girl?'

'Just answer yes or no to the questions.'

At that moment I saw two constables come out from Lugard Road carrying a stretcher with what I took to be a body covered with a sheet.

'Oh my God.'

'As far as we know there wasn't anyone out on this path tonight except you … and that girl,' he said pointing to the body on the stretcher.

'Hey, now wait a minute. I didn't see any girl. I didn't see anyone. What are you trying to pin on me?'

'We're not trying to pin anything on you. Just trying to get at the truth.' This made him sound like the detective in a 10-cent novel.

'What are you talking about? I had nothing to do with this. You can check with my friends.

They'll tell you I was at their house for dinner and I didn't have a girl with me. They're Bob and Charlotte Godkin and they live at the Peak Apartments. They can vouch for me.'

'Get them and bring them to the station,' he instructed one

of the constables.

'Jesus. I go for a little walk and I get accused of murder.'

'We didn't accuse you of anything yet. We just want the facts. That's all.'

At the station house Bob and Charlotte were distraught. They swore I couldn't have done anything to anyone. When I left their apartment I was alone. They were sure I didn't know the girl, whoever she was.

The tram driver and the ticket taker from the Peak Tram were being questioned, too. The driver didn't remember seeing anyone but then the ticket taker came up with a startling revelation. He said that he thought he remembered seeing a girl with a young Chinese man. Because of the nasty weather it was a quiet night on the tram and he recalled seeing the same young man coming down about two hours later. Alone.

'There,' I said. 'I wasn't the only one on the Peak and the other guy had a girl with him, and he was alone when he went down. Any fool could work that out.'

'You're not in a position to make comments on my intelligence. The testimony of the ticket taker doesn't completely exonerate you. It's a little hard for me to believe that you just went walking around the Peak in the fog. Perhaps you were an accomplice?'

The guy was incredible. 'Look, I just went to the Peak to have dinner with friends. I took a walk in the fog because I enjoy doing things like that. I didn't know the girl or the guy and I have absolutely nothing to do with this case. I am merely a victim of circumstances; that should be plain to see.'

Finally the inspector seemed to have second thoughts.

'Just give us your address and we will be in touch.'

'Then I'm free to go?'

'We will want statements from you and your friends first.'

We gave our statements and they released me without bail and I promised that I would be available for questioning at anytime. I went back to Bob and Charlotte's apartment again for some hot chocolate and to calm my nerves.

'Thank God that ticket taker remembered the couple on the tram. I hope they find the guy.'

'Oh, they'll find him' Bob said, 'but they'll have only circumstantial evidence.' Bob was talking like a lawyer. 'They'll have to prove first that he was actually on Lugard Road and second that he committed the murder.'

'Well, I think I have convinced them that it wasn't me. Do you think I'll have to testify?'

'No doubt about it,' Bob said.

'I'm sorry they had to drag you out of your house in the middle of the night.'

'We wouldn't have missed it for anything.'

Without the ticket taker's evidence I might have spent the next couple of weeks in jail and in the worst scenario, I might have been hanged for a crime I didn't commit. It sounds crazy but it just might have happened. That idiot 21-year-old police inspector was convinced I was the murderer.

It seemed that the Chinese boy was the dead girl's boyfriend, and by making inquiries among her friends they tracked him down. He willingly admitted he had gone to the Peak with her but said he had never gone to Lugard Road. They had sat at the Peak Café and talked for more than an hour. They had an argument when she told him she was pregnant and wanted to know if he was going to marry her. He told her that at just 20 years old he was too young to marry and maybe he could think of an alternative plan, like an abortion. All distraught she left the café by herself and he claimed he didn't know where she went. The boy stayed at the café for a short while and then went straight from the restaurant to the tram and left the Peak, he said. In the subsequent autopsy the authorities established that she had not been pregnant after all.

The boy was defended by one of the colonies leading criminal lawyers, the brilliant Marcus Da Silva, a man small in stature but great in his knowledge of the law—and of what he could get away with. He had a wealth of coal black hair that always seemed tousled and he dressed in an expensive three-piece suit. One of his prized possessions was a gold watch on a silver chain which he absentmindedly kept turning over as he listened to the prosecutor's case.

Da Silva told the jury that the girl had left the Peak Café alone, apparently very annoyed by the defendant, and probably took the walk on Lugard Road to cool down. Part way down the path she was accosted by a party, or parties unknown, who for some unknown reason strangled her, and left her in the bushes on the side of the road. Probably robbery was their motive. His client had a slight build and a gentle manner and was incapable of carrying out such a brutal act.

'My client,' he said, 'waited for the girl to return to the café. He thought she might have taken the Peak Tram down herself. After a while, when she didn't come back and unaware of the horrendous events that occurred on Lugard Road, he took the tram down. The police have no proof, except very weak circumstantial evidence to implicate this boy.'

When it came my turn to give testimony, forensic evidence was presented that proved the crime was committed while I was still having high tea at the Godkins. If it wasn't the boy who committed the murder it was someone else on Lugard Road but it certainly wasn't me.

Meanwhile, Marcus Da Silva concentrated on his client's alibi. According to several witnesses the boy hadn't left the Peak Café until he went to take the tram and when he rode down he was seen and positively identified by the ticket taker. Marcus changed that damning piece of evidence into points for his client. The boy said that he never had been to Lugard Road in his life and according to Marcus it was not for his client to prove that he wasn't there but for the prosecution to prove that he was. He told the jury it was true that in some cases you could convict a person of murder merely on circum- stantial evidence but Marcus warned them they must take extreme care in reaching a verdict. His client was 20 years old, at the beginning of his adult life. He was innocent of the crime he was charged with, but the jury could snuff out his young life with a guilty verdict. A girl had been brutally murdered and someone had perpetrated that dastardly deed but it wasn't his client. If there was any reasonable doubt in their minds they must find his client not guilty.

'Remember,' he said, enunciating carefully. 'Any. Reasonable. Doubt.'

After hearing Marcus's summation I found doubts creep- ing into my own mind as to the boy's guilt. I really didn't know how I would have voted if I were on that jury, but now, after years have passed since the Peak murder, it seems likely that the boy had chased after the girl to continue their argument and then in a fit of frustration strangled her. I was sure the boy was guilty but Marcus, clever devil, knew that the courtroom atmosphere is electrifying and when you are depending on ordinary people to bring back a verdict you must play on their conscience as well as their sense of duty.

Sentencing a young man to 'hang by the neck until dead' is not easy for an ordinary person. So the jury brought in a verdict of 'not guilty' and went home and slept peacefully that night. To this day the case of the Peak Tram Murder has never been solved.

9

ANYTHING FOR A SQUARE MEAL

With the Peak Tram Murder behind me and no further diversions, I began to ponder my debt to the FCC. I had run up a tab of over HK$5,000 with no means, at the present time, of paying. The club committee said they could wait for the room rent but I still needed to eat, and so in order to keep my tab from growing too fast I devised a plan. I would cover little stories that came onto my desk of luncheons at the Rotary Club and dinner parties celebrating the opening of the primary school ballet season. Anything to get a free meal.

Working on one of these stories I wound up in trouble with Jean Bateman who ran the leading ballet school in the colony. After putting away a delicious four-course dinner, compliments of the Societé du Dance de Hong Kong, I panned their dance recital of 'Peter And The Wolf.' Jean took especial offence at my article as the dancers were only seven and eight years old and although they tried their best, she had them playing 'cutesy' for the proud parents and I couldn't stomach it, so I took it on myself to punish them with a bad review. I felt slightly guilty later, but the story was released so what could I do.

Jean Bateman had a fierce adversary in a Russian

woman named Dorothea Ivanov who ran a rival ballet school. After my review came out, Ms. Ivanov phoned me to compliment me, saying my article had showed great courage and could she meet me in person? She invited me to join her and her mother for dinner at their home on Village Road in Happy Valley.

Dorothea Ivanov was about 30 and not bad looking, but her mother Irena, though not unattractive for her age, was a bit pushy and I began to suspect they had asked me to their house to make a match between me and Dorothea rather than to discuss their dispute with Jean Bateman.

Actually, Dorothea was Irena's stepdaughter as her real mother had died some time ago and her father had a drinking problem but no apparent interest in his daughter. Irena had raised Dorothea and they got on splendidly.

They served me a really grand Russian dinner with fish soup, beef stew smothered in sour cream and plenty of pickles and black bread. At dinner Dorothea told me how she was excluded from the Societé du Dance because she was an open rival of 'the great' Jean Bateman, and I felt the palm of her hand run daringly up and down my thigh under the table-cloth. I was happy to agree that she had received grossly unfair treatment from the Societé du Dance. On a tour of her studio she continued her bold display of affection and took my hand and squeezed it close to her body.

Dorothea was tall and her hair was a dirty blonde color. She was my idea of a typical Russian peasant, strong a bit heavy in the bosom; the toes of her muscular dancers legs were permanently pointed in the fifth ballet position.

They originally came from Vladivistok where her stepmother had made a living giving ballet lessons. The winters were very cold and ballet lessons didn't bring in enough to sustain them so one day they got on a train and headed for China, where they settled for awhile in the Manchurian city of Shenyang. The winters were no less harsh and the people very poor, and as Mrs. Ivanov found precious few students interested in dance, they packed their bags and headed out once again, looking for richer pickings. This time they landed in Hong Kong where they discovered many young girls were pressed by their doting mothers to learn ballet.

Dorothea started teaching and from the tender age of 17 and with the supervision of her mother she gradually took over the classes. They made out fairly well financially but from the start, the big thorn in their side was Jean Bateman, the undisputed 'queen of ballet' in the colony who wanted to rule absolutely. The Ivanovs refused to fall in line and were ostracized by the elite of the dance community, which was the reason they liked my bad review of 'Peter and the Wolf.' They also appeared to crave attention, other than from their students and their adoring mothers.

I found their apartment very cozy with many pictures of their home in Russia and as Dorothea was acting very tenderly to me I got the idea that it would not be difficult for me to push my designs on her a bit further. As a classical dancer she took romance as a natural part of her artistic life and had no compunctions about acting spontaneously. Once in the bedroom I put my arms around her from behind and kissed her neck. She responded passionately, and in no time at all we were on the huge bed rolling around, touching and kissing. We were lost in each other's arms and I didn't hear

Mrs. Ivanov enter the room. I finally noticed her standing at the edge of the bed staring at us and I jumped up.

'Take off your shoes young man,' she told me. 'You don't want to dirty that pretty satin cover, do you?' With that she yanked off her dressing gown under which she wore only a slip and climbed onto the bed. I was confused about what my next move should be, so I looked over to Dorothea. She continued to be loving and paid very little attention to her parent who had by this time established herself under my left shoulder. Taking the hint I threw all caution to the wind and indulged myself in this delightful situation.

The daughter took off her clothes and Irena, her stepmother, removed her slip under which she wore absolutely nothing. I also disrobed and in a minute we were all three lying there totally naked. I had heard tales of mothers and daughters enjoying one man but this was the first time I had experienced it.

Dorothea had a well-developed, muscular body with large and firm breasts while Irena had curves in all the right places, although she was a little bit on the flabby side. After the first revelation of the situation began to wear off, I started to romance both the daughter and the mother. We remained there playing on the bed for close to two hours and I congratulated myself for finally finding a way to zip up the older lady's mouth. When we were finished Irena went into the kitchen and returned with three small glasses of vodka and in a totally Russian manner we toasted our joyous 'coming together.'

I wondered if I had compromised my professional standing by playing into the hands of these two formidable women. I pondered it for a couple of seconds and then let it drop. And I also wondered if I might eventually find it difficult to extricate myself from the clutches of those dear souls? But why would I ever want to disentangle myself such a delightful relationship — especially one that involved such wonderful food.

Unfortunately I hadn't got any farther on the trail of additional income and was becoming increasingly nervous about my debt to the FCC when I met Guy Searls, the CBS radio correspondent who very kindly gave me some advice.

'Nobody else in town is shooting newsreels,' he said. 'I would say moving pictures are the way to go.'

He told me that the UP bureau in Hong Kong had a 16mm movie camera, donated by their headquarters in the hope of getting some TV news footage from Asia, but so far nobody had used it. I strolled over to the UP bureau and suggested to Bud Merrick, the bureau chief that he loan the camera to me, and he straight away pointed to the shelf.

'Take it. And the film, too. It's been wasting valuable space.'

I didn't realize it at the moment, but I was starting a career that would carry me to the four corners of the earth and last me the rest of my life.

With the old-fashioned wind-up Bell and Howell camera, I filmed about 22 stories that launched my new career. A mud slide in Sau Mau Ping that buried 25 people, a priest who made noodles on a homemade machine, and a mucky squatter area where 6,000 people lived in horrifying squalor in rickety huts made of scrap wood and cardboard boxes. The first month I had the camera UP/Movietone used 21 of my stories. I was on my way.

I made over a thousand U.S. dollars and was able to pay my bill in full at the FCC. With my job as sub-editor at the Standard and shooting newsreels on the side I was set financially, but Leslie Sung pulled the carpet out from under me. The GM wanted me to come in an additional four hours in the morning, with no additional pay, and said that if I refused I would get canned, plain and simple.

'Lincoln freed the slaves in 1865,' I told him and was fired on the spot. I figured they could take their lousy HK$600 and shove it.

UP added a beat-up old sound camera to my inventory and I was really in the newsreel business.

My first sound story was about the brother of a Bishop Walsh who was under arrest in Shanghai, accused of being a counterrevolutionary. His 66-year-old brother came all the way from Yonkers, New York for a measly half-hour visit. The press conference was a really emotional account of that visit.

'What were your last words to the Bishop?' asked one of the reporters.

He looked at the assembled newsmen with tears in his eyes. 'I could only say 'goodbye.' I remember clearly that he stood at the door, looked at me silently for a fleeting second and answered, 'Goodbye Jerry. I'll see you in heaven.'"

Those were troubled times and in the course of my newsreel work I met a fair of share of priests but one I will never forget was Father Poletti, nicknamed 'the border priest.' He had a church at Fanling in the border area between Hong Kong and mainland China and it was one of his duties to pick up nuns and priests expelled from China. He never knew when one was coming so he was there at the crossing on the Lowu railroad bridge every day. He was a colorful figure, speeding along the Sheung Shui road on his Yamaha motorcycle with his straw hat strapped under his chin and wispy beard and white cassock blowing in the breeze.

I used to stop at his church for a cool drink and a chat. He owned a myna bird that he called Tommy who answered knocks on the door in perfect Cantonese. '*Wan bin goh*, aack, aack, *wan bin goh?*' it said. And '*Ave Maria* aack, aack *Ave Maria*.'

Father Poletti's great object of devotion, second only to God, was his hat collection. Straws hats, a velvet fedora, an English bowler and numerous baseball caps. On one visit he told me that one of his parishioners had stolen a hat from his collection.

'Yesterday I put a hat on that chair and a farmer, he come to talk to me,' Father Poletti said in his thick Italian accent. 'His family is in big trouble he says. Begged for my help. I left the room for one minute, just one minute and he stole my hat.'

'Why would anybody want to steal a hat? Maybe you made a mistake. Perhaps you mislaid it?'

'I don't make mistake. These people are not honest. I live here for over twenty years. I know dem.'

'So what did you do with the guy who stole your hat?'

'I kick him on his ass.'

Each day trains and ships came loaded into Hong Kong with people expelled from China. Some were like American entrepreneur, C.V. Starr who had arrived in China three decades ago, penniless and left as head of one of the great multinational corporations. But there were many more who after many years spent building a life had to leave everything behind and start again.

When supporters of Chiang Kai Shek put up flags in Hong Kong to celebrate the Double Tenth National Day, Communist sympathizers tore them down. It started with name calling and then shoving and then fist fights and in very little time there was full-scale rioting. The Garden Bakery in Sham Shui Po was set ablaze, cars were burned and over a hundred people died on that day, October 10, 1956.

A Dutch diplomat and his wife thought it would be fun to take a few snapshots of the action. At the first sight of the angry mob their taxi driver was too terrified to go on but the couple cajoled him to go just a little farther. They thought that if they stayed inside the taxi they would be safe. When the police arrived on the scene an hour later, they found the taxi – and the diplomat, his driver, and his pretty young wife— burned beyond recognition.

One day on the way back from covering a story at the border I stopped for gas in the small farming town of Sha Tin. Rummaging through my pockets I realized I didn't have any money. The owner of the station said that I could pay him later and asked me to join him for lunch in his tiny restaurant next door. It was an accepted fact that in most cases foreigners could be trusted and their bills would always be paid.

'What do you do?' he asked as we ate.

'I'm a cameraman. I've just been up to the border covering a story of Fulbright scholars expelled from China.'

'What do you mean 'covering a story?''

'I film them crossing the border and then I get a sound interview. I will write a description of the film and drop it off at the airport. They will have it in Los Angeles by tomorrow morning and it will air on the morning news on a hook-up to New York.'

I took a mouthful of fried rice.

'Do you have much gasoline business on this road?'

'Not too bad. I own most of the land around here. The farmers don't have much cash so they pay their rent with rice.'

I tried to picture the farmers paying their rent with 100 pound bags of rice.

'Do you have a family?'

'Just a baby son.' He paused a moment, 'My wife died about four months ago giving birth. She was just twenty-three years old.'

I drove all the way back to Sha Tin the next morning to pay what I owed the good fellow.

The person in charge told me that Mr. Wai had gone to the hospital with his baby for a routine checkup. Nothing serious, just a routine checkup.

10

CATHAY GOES DOWN

I was at the UP office, checking the printer for a story when Peter Sum shouted at me from across the room: 'A Cathay Pacific plane carrying passengers just crashed into the sea on the way here from Bangkok.'

Peter was from Shanghai. A tall, slim man with knife-like eyes and a 'nose for news,' he was clever and fearless and had the making of a great reporter.

'There's a plane from the Clark Air Force Base in the Philippines picking up survivors,' he said as I grabbed my camera and we made rapidly for the door.

We boarded a walla-walla that took us through the harbor directly to the airport. No one was staffing the check-in area so we walked behind the desks, through the door and out onto the tarmac. We had an excuse ready in case anyone asked what we were doing, but there was so much confusion nobody questioned us.

Outside, a Cathay spokeswoman was filling people in on what had happened.

'A DC-4 passenger plane crashed into the sea, east of Hainan Island with sixteen passengers and six crew on board. A U.S. Navy Grumman Albatross from Clark Air Base is expected here at any minute with survivors.'

'How many fatalities?' Peter asked.

'At this point we don't know. But the captain and first officer were among those rescued.'

The tarmac was crowded with the families of the crew of the
ill-fated aircraft, the American military attaché who supplied
the rescue craft and the airport ground staff. The Cathay
spokeswoman said that it was the first serious accident in
the company's history and that was all she could tell us at the
moment.

About 15 minutes later the rescue plane arrived. Survivors,
covered in yellow dye shark repellent, climbed down the ladder or were carried off on stretchers. They were loaded into
waiting ambulances and when Peter and I rushed over to
interview them the spokeswoman blocked our way.

'No interviews,' she said.

'Why not?'

'Because they need medical assistance. Now, please step
back.'

'Some of them looked okay to me,' Peter said. 'Let's see if
they are in condition to be interviewed.'

'I said no interviews and I mean it,' she said, raising her
voice. 'If you persist on trying to interview them I'm going to
have to call airport security.'

We didn't want that, so we reluctantly backed off.

One distraught-looking woman asked the surviving stewardess if she had seen Stephen Wong, the radio operator.

'Oh, I think he's dead,' the stewardess answered, not aware that the woman was his wife.

The woman stared at her for a few seconds in disbelief then suddenly her hands went up to her face. She started crying uncontrollably until she fainted into the arms of a medic and was taken to an ambulance.

'I know how upset you must be,' the spokeswoman said to the stewardess, 'and you didn't know who the lady was, but please don't talk to anyone. Refer them to me, please.'

Philip Blown, the captain of the aircraft seemed to be alright, but they got him to lie down on a stretcher and wheeled him straight into an ambulance. The Cathay PR department was definitely not being cooperative.

'Why are you hiding everyone from us?' Peter was exasperated. 'The captain was able to walk on his own, so why the stretcher?'

'That's routine. He might have internal injuries. We just want to find out what caused the plane to crash. Was it engine trouble? The captain would know.'

She evaded the question. 'We don't know anything yet,' she said, but we sensed she was concealing something.

'Could it have been sabotaged?'

'We don't think so.'

'So sabotage is a possibility?'

'I said I didn't think it was.'

'Well, was it shot down?'

'Why did you say that?'

Peter had simply been working down a list of possible reasons for the disaster.

'Well was it?'

'I am not at liberty to give you reasons for the crash right now.'

It seemed that Peter had unwittingly stumbled onto the truth.

'Then it was shot down? By the Chinese Air Force?' he speculated.

'I will definitely not confirm your speculation so don't print it. I will say it is a lie. You'll have a statement when Cathay Pacific is ready to make one.'

'This is unbelievable,' Peter said not listening to her protests. 'The Chinese Air Force actually shot down a passenger plane?' He was incredulous.

'I must have a statement from you right now. I am not going away. This is big news.'

'Look, we know as much as you do, until we speak to the captain.'

'Okay, then when can we speak to the captain?'

She looked flustered. 'We'll arrange a press conference later.'

The ambulance carrying Captain Blown drove away.

'We've got as much as we're going to get here.' Peter said. 'Come on let's go file the story. What a scoop!'

'But she's going to deny the whole thing.'

'How could she deny it? It's the truth, and we've got an exclusive. First we file the story and then we go to the hospital and interview Captain Blown.'

But if we were going to get into Captain Blown's room, we'd need a disguise. At the hospital we slipped into the doctors' changing room.

'If we get caught stealing a doctor's coat we'll really be in trouble.' I said.

'Two doctor's coats. And we are not stealing, just borrowing.

We have to get to Captain Blown and if we walked around the hospital wearing civilian clothes chances are we'd get thrown out. Don't let it trouble your conscience; we're just doing our job.'

We purloined a couple of identification tabs to pin to our coats, and Peter finished off his disguise with a stethoscope he found in one of the doctors pockets. I, on the other hand, was very noticeable with my big camera bag on my shoulder.

Peter wasn't worried. 'It could be a doctor's treatment case. Just look like you belong here and nobody will notice the difference.'

We took an elevator to the floor with the private rooms and found Captain Blown's name chalked on a blackboard outside the door. When we entered we saw the captain sitting at a table reading the paper and sipping tea, and looking perfectly fit after his terrible ordeal.

'Hi, Captain Blown. My name is Peter Sum and this is Marvin Farkas. We're from UP and we wanted to have a word with you.'

The Captain chuckled. 'You're not doctors then? What about our PR people? Shouldn't they be in on this?'

'Your PR people don't know anything. We have a deadline and we couldn't wait. The news of your crash has already been broadcast. It'll just take a minute. The world is waiting to hear your story about this vicious attack.'

I took out my camera and turned on the main light in the room. I didn't have the time to take a light reading so I speculated on the exposure and just shot, recording the sound on a separate tape recorder.

'Can you give us a few details of what happened?'

'Well, we were headed to Hong Kong from Bangkok when we were deliberately attacked by these two Chinese Air Force fighter aircraft.'

'How did you know they were Chinese?'

'They had big red stars on their fuselage and red noses. They attacked us from both sides, using 50 caliber shells and blew holes a foot and a half wide into the fuselage.'

'Were you off course?'

'Definitely not. We were eighty to ninety miles off the coast of Hainan in the international air corridor regularly used by all civilian aircraft.'

'So what was the reason for the attack?'

'Search me, it was entirely unprovoked. As soon as it began I took immediate evasive action swinging back and forth, but what could I do against highly maneuverable fighter aircraft, armed to the teeth. They hit us with volley after volley and then they went around and came at us again with their guns blazing. We were like ducks in a shooting gallery. They hit one of our engines, and it caught fire. We started losing altitude. They came around again and again and didn't stop firing until we were down to about 1,000 feet and heading for a watery grave. Then they just flew off, like nothing had happened.

'Stephen Wong, my radio officer was badly wounded and was lying propped against a bulkhead, shouting into his microphone 'Mayday, Mayday.' I had to try to ditch into the ocean so I pulled with all my might to get the plane level. I managed by some miracle to make a pretty fair belly landing on the water. I knew we had to evacuate the plane fast as it wouldn't stay afloat long. Cedric Carlton, my first officer, and I got out through the front window. The radio operator and engineer must have been washed away by a sudden surge of water in the cockpit. One of the two stewardesses was dead and I don't know how many other people.

'There was chaos and blood all over. It was like a nightmare, but I didn't have time to assess the scene. I pulled the surviving passengers onto the rubber dinghy and instructed them to use shark repellent as the blood would attract sharks.

'Thank God Steve Wong's Mayday transmission got through. It was heard at Kai Tak airport and a search and rescue operation got under way. After floating around in a rubber dinghy for what seemed forever we saw an Albatross aircraft coming in for a landing on the water. I counted the survivors. There were only eight of us. I still can't believe it happened.'

'What the hell is going on here?' came a voice from the door. It was the Cathay spokeswoman accompanied by a few doctors.

'What gives you the right to come barging in? I told you I was arranging a press conference.' She was furious.

Peter didn't even try to explain the intrusion.

'Sorry but we had a deadline. We couldn't wait for your press conference,' he said, somewhat contemptuously.

'I know where you come from and I will certainly lodge a complaint with the police. This is a private hospital.'

'Listen, you can't hold back a story like this for a more convenient time. This is bigger than Cathay Pacific. This story belongs to the world, and you can report us to whoever you want.'

Before she knew what was happening, we were out of there.

Peter filed Captain Blown's interview way ahead of the competition and received kudos from the New York headquarters. I sent the silent film of the Captain and they played that together with a tape recording of his words. They tell me it had a very dramatic effect and for the interview along with footage of the rescue plane landing with survivors I got an extra $50 for submitting the best film story of the week. The PR lady didn't bother reporting us to anybody.

11

TWO GUNS COHEN

The Hong Kong of 1954 hadn't changed much from the place I knew back in '46. The Star Ferry, the railway station, the clock tower, the ever-present rickshaws and the last two sedan chairs waiting for customers at the bottom of Wyndham Street were still there, along with buildings dating back to the turn of the century. The city had an ageless quality that I hoped would never change. Of course, I realized it must fall victim one day, as we all do to the relentless passage of time, but recording it with my camera was exciting and I felt that I had finally found my niche in life.

A regular stop on my daily search for stories was the railway station coffee shop. One day I found a small group of local newsmen waiting for the train from China to arrive. I asked Bobby Liu, a reporter from of the South China Morning Post, if anything was up.

'Did you ever hear of Two Gun Cohen?' he asked.

It sounded like a joke.

'No. What's the story about this guy?'

'Two Gun is the only *gwailo* who is welcome both in Red China and Taiwan. He's arriving on the 11 a.m. train.'

Bobby used the term for foreigners, the somewhat

derogatory '*gwailo*' which translates to 'foreign devil.' The word has ceased be offensive, in fact some foreign devils actually allude to themselves as *gwailo* in polite conversation.

Sounded good enough to me, so I settled in with a cup of coffee and Bobby told me his version of Two Gun's story while we waited.

'Two Gun Cohen had been a prizefighter back in Liverpool, England. He wasn't the greatest fighter of all times, so he decided to give it up before his brain got too addled. It wasn't easy to find work in the U.K. for an ex-fighter with no education, so he moved to Canada to try his luck. At first he engaged in some dubious activities, but he managed to get along.

'He ate his meals in a Chinese take-away and one night two tough-looking guys came in toting pistols, demanding money from the cashier. Without a second thought Two Gun jumped up, went over to the cashier's cage and cracked the heads of the robbers together and knocked them out cold.

'The restaurant owner was so grateful he told him that he would never again have to pay for a meal in his restaurant and Two Gun Cohen became a hero to the Chinese community.

'When Sun Yat-sen was due to make a fund-raising tour of Canada and the U.S. they asked Two Gun to be his bodyguard. He accepted the job, and at the end of the trip Sun asked him to come back to China and stay on as his bodyguard.

'There are a lot of stories about his exploits. Once in Canton he helped defended Sun's compound against attackers along with a troop of trusted bodyguards, laying on his belly and firing two guns at the same time. From then on he was known, as 'Two Gun Cohen.' They say that his aim was so accurate he could keep a coin spinning in the air for a whole minute by firing at it with both of his guns. Some of the stories are too fantastic to believe, but it was true that Sun made him the first

European general in the Chinese army. It was also rumored that he was the only *gwailo* to belong to the Tsing Chung-Hui triad, but they are a secret society, so who can say if that is true?

'When Sun Yat-sen died in 1925 there were provisions in his will for Two Gun and he goes to China every year to collect his stipend and is received with honor by government bigwigs. They believe that he has connections around the world with important business people who can do them favors. At the same time he is honored in Taiwan by big shots, as the close friend of Sun Yat-sen. That, as I know it, is the story of Two Gun Cohen.'

Later I learned that no two stories about Two Gun Cohen seemed to be the same. At 11 a.m. we went to meet Two Gun's train, along with some friends of his from the old days in Shanghai. He wasn't very tall but he was beefy and tough looking and his scarred face bore mementos of his prizefighting days. Nattily dressed in a gray suit he wore a felt hat with part of the brim turned down. A monocle on a silver chain hung round his neck, and he carried a black lacquer cane with a silver ball on the top. He gave all his attention to his friends and ignored the members of the press. Our ranks had swelled in the meantime from four to about 16 reporters. We followed him into the street but the newsmen were a bit squeamish with their questions as he had the reputation of being a curmudgeon. I started shooting from the moment he came off the train.

'What are you doing?' he asked, looking at me angrily.

'Just getting some shots of you, Two Gun.'

'Well stop it this moment.'

'Aw, come on, Two Gun,' I cajoled and kept right on shooting.

'I said stop shooting,' he raised his cane menacingly in my direction. He was really angry. 'And give me your film.'

'Nothing doing,' I said and kept right on shooting.

'Don't let this gray hair fool you son,' he said, doffing his hat and pointing to his rather sparse silver tresses.

'Now give me your film.' He kept his cane with the solid silver top raised.

On the street he saw a couple of gendarmes and shouted to them to come over. The police didn't know who he was, but he was a foreigner with a commanding tone of voice and that was enough. By this time a crowd was following us and the reporters had a story they hadn't figured on.

'I demand that you take this man into custody,' he blustered.

'Oh yeah, on what charge?' I asked.

'Invading the privacy of person.'

'What kind of a cockamamie charge is that?'

I kept right on shooting. Now he was really mad.

'Seize that man,' he shouted.

The policemen were perplexed. Two Gun's loud voice intimidated them. I guess they figured he was important with all the press photographers around him and in any case I was just a cameraman, so they followed his orders and seized me.

'P.C. get the shot,' I shouted at P.C. Lee, the Standard photographer that was on the scene. He got what became an historic photograph of one of the policemen grabbing me by the collar and the other with a steel grip on my arms. They marched me, with the huge crowd following, up the hill to the marine police station.

We crowded around the sergeant's desk. Me, Two Gun and his friends, the two police constables, all 16 reporters and a small crowd of spectators drawn in by the commotion. Everyone was shouting at the same time until Two Gun raised his hand and took control of the situation.

With all attention on him he explained his complaint to the desk sergeant, and while nobody was looking I removed the film from the camera and put in a fresh roll and hurriedly put the roll I shot into my camera bag.

'I understand your circumstances very well sir,' the sergeant said sympathetically to Two Gun. Then he addressed me.

'What right have you to take pictures of a person that doesn't want to be photographed?'

'We were in a public place and the law says that I can shoot anything that comes into public view.'

If Two Gun could make up his own laws then I could make up a few myself.

'I want his film,' Two Gun said.

To satisfy the desk sergeant and take the responsibility off of myself I suddenly became conciliatory.

'Just to show I am a good sport and to end this farce I will destroy the film in front of everybody. Will that satisfy you?'

I opened up the camera, took out the film I had just loaded and ran the whole 100 feet into a trash can. First I feigned a look of resignation and then when I finally finished piling the new roll of film with no pictures on it into the rubbish bin my look turned to one of sad condescension.

'So you win,' I told Two Gun.

'No hard feelings,' he said. 'I just wanted to teach you a lesson. You don't have the right to invade a person's privacy without their permission.'

The crisis over, we walked down the hill and back onto Salisbury Road. The whole party kept walking toward the Peninsula Hotel where Two Gun was staying.

'Mr. Cohen, would it be alright for me to film you walking down this street,' I queried most respectfully.

'Certainly,' he replied magnanimously.

What an asshole.

When I sent the story with all its comic ramifications to UP Movietone I won kudos for my quick thinking in preserving the film. They asked me to get a sound interview with him discussing his colorful career and some of his adventures protecting Sun Yat-sen. With the help of Harry Odell, who was an old Shanghai friend of his, I located Two Gun at a reception at the Jewish Club. He remembered me well and was very friendly but was not going to grant me an interview.

'I've given the 'X' (meaning 'exclusive') to NBC. It's a shame but in the future watch your manners. Remember, you can get more flies with honey than with vinegar. Now let's have a glass of wine and put our unpleasant experience behind us.'

I hung around Two Gun for a good part of the evening but he wouldn't bend to my pleas for an interview. Harry Odell even put in a few words for me.

'You really ought to help out this nice Jewish boy.'

Two Gun looked surprised. 'He's Jewish is he? That accounts for his arrogance.'

But he wouldn't change his mind and kept repeating that he had given the X to NBC. Harry Odell told me later that Two Gun had told him confidentially that he promised the Chinese authorities that he wouldn't talk to anybody about his experiences with Sun Yat-sen.

12

WALKS ON THE WILD SIDE

For all its glamour and beauty, Hong Kong also had a dark side. I got a glimpse of it when I was given a breather from my sub-editing duties and spent a short time covering the law courts.

Lee Hop Kee was an entrepreneur of sorts. An illegal street hawker, he was an expert in the art of making '*chau doufu*'—a deep-fried and very strong-smelling tofu. When he arrived in Hong Kong from his native Taishan, he acquired a cart with a charcoal burner, a couple of jars of cooking oil, a supply of the bean curd, and he was in business. You could pick up the odor of Lee's 'stinky tofu' from three blocks away, but rather than fleeing in the opposite direction the people of Hong Kong followed the smell straight to Lee's cart. The price for four pieces, wrapped in brown paper with a special chili sauce was HK$1. Of course his business was illegal as he had no license, so to keep ahead of the police he regularly changed street corners. But alas there was no way to disguise the pungent odor, so he was picked up several times by the cops who confiscated his cart and fined him.

Still, he made enough money to consider this legal hazard a business expense and even with the fines he cleared a hefty

HK$1,500 to $2,000 a month. He had intended to follow this line of work indefinitely until one day his cunning sister-in-law approached him with a new plan for making money.

She and a girlfriend planned to run a figure-drawing art school using live nude models. The friend had a two-room flat they would use and the two girls themselves would do the posing. The charge would be $1 for each 'student' for a 10-minute class and they would be given a sheet of paper and a pencil to confer an appearance of legitimacy.

Lee went for the idea immediately. They constructed a stage in the friend's apartment, and the girls would come out in the buff and strike suggestive poses. After 10 minutes the students left and they would be replaced by other students, and so on, for the rest of the day. Lee supplied the capital for paper, pencils and the renting of folding chairs. He played the art teacher, collected the money and made sure that the men didn't get carried away.

Word spread about the 'art school' and the 'students' came in droves. Lee and his partners made scads of money. Then, one day two undercover cops and an undercover fireman came to the school and the next day Lee and his partners got a summons for running a school without a license and creating a fire hazard. They were brought before the court, fined and forced to close up shop.

However, they discovered that if they had less than 10 students at a time it wouldn't constitute a proper school, and therefore no license was required. The fire regulations could be circumvented if they had 'no smoking' signs displayed and fire extinguishers installed, and very soon they were back in operation. They had large groups on the stairs and in front of the building, but inside they followed the law meticulously and had only nine 'students' attending the class at one time.

Well, the modified art school carried on for almost six months without any interference from the police. All this time the government was trying to figure a way to put an end to the 'art schools' now proliferating around the colony. They finally settled on a comprehensive ruling that no school, no matter how small could operate without permission of the education department. So Lee Hop Kee and his two partners were shut down and fined again. Only this time they were totally out of the art school business.

His inventive sister-in-law came up with another surefire plan. A man could get his shoes shined by a naked lady for HK$1. But the police found an old statute against that, and Lee and his partners were out of business and fined once again.

Her next idea was to have a naked lady press your pants for HK$1 but the police said that the fact that a man had to disrobe in the same room with a naked lady constituted a lewd performance, so they banned and fined that, too.

Their next scam was for a naked girl to comb the customer's hair while he sat in a barber's chair, but the government, in exasperation, made a blanket ruling that any type of performance by a nude person attending to a customer in any way, shape or form was against the law.

The three offenders stood contritely before the magistrate with their heads bowed. He said that this time, in admiration of their entrepreneurial skills, he wouldn't impose a fine. However, he warned that if they engaged in another of these nefarious enterprises he would lock them up and throw away the key.

Hong Kong is the place for innovative business and the magistrate, it seemed, was sympathetic to their cause and wanted to see them succeed in a way. It's just this sort of entrepreneurship that which makes Hong Kong what it is. Hard work and pioneering ideas are the name of the game. But the law is the law and the magistrate had to uphold it.

Lee Hop Kee's capers seemed almost innocent compared to my next unexpected foray into the Hong Kong underworld. One cool summer evening I was eating dinner alone on the porch at the FCC when a young English lady came up and spoke to me.

'Mind if I join you?' she asked.

'Certainly not. I'm Marvin Farkas.'

'Lois Mitchison,' she said, extending her hand.

Lois was English, in her early 30s, stockily built and attired in a dark masculine-looking suit. She wore her short hair straight with a part down the middle, no makeup, and a pair of spectacles. To my mind, she was definitely the intellectual type.

'You must be a journalist,' I said.

'You guessed right. I'm going into China to do a series of economic stories for the *Manchester Guardian*.'

'Lucky you. Americans can't get into China these days. We are called 'China Watchers' and have to do our reporting secondhand. When are you going in?'

'The day after tomorrow.'

She hesitated a moment and looked at me thoughtfully, wondering if she'd found the right person for what she wanted.

'There is one thing I want to do while I am in Hong Kong.'

'What's that?'

She got directly to the point.

'Do you know a place I can smoke opium? I understand that journalists know about those things.'

'Are you serious?'

'Very serious. I really want to try it while I am here.'

'Well the only place I know for sure is the Walled City.'

'What is that?'

'It's a sort of enclave that belongs entirely to China. It's on the Kowloon side and the Hong Kong government has no jurisdiction over it. As far as I know it's wide open. Drugs, prostitution, gambling and anything illegal you can think of. The police only go into that area on very rare occasions to capture a criminal and then they don't linger.'

'Sounds interesting. Do you know how to get there?'

'Yes, but I've never actually been in.'

'Would you take me?'

'To smoke opium?'

'Yes.'

'Tell you what. I'll make you a deal. I do newsreel coverage for UPI and I'd like to do a story on the place. So if I take you there, would you let me shoot a few scenes of you smoking opium? It wouldn't be a story of you. You would just be a part of my description of the Walled City.'

'I don't know. Where will it show?'

'In the States. Are you worried about a friend seeing you?'

'Oh, no. Most of the people I know in London would be envious if they saw me. But my mother is a member of Parliament and it might not go down too well with her constituents.'

She thought a moment.

'Okay. If it doesn't show in the U.K.'

I didn't promise her anything. 'You have only the one day, so if you really want to go it'll have be tomorrow.'

'That's fine. Do I have to wear any special clothes? You know, sort of go incognito?'

'No, nothing special. It's supposed to be quite dirty so I wouldn't get too dressed up. And don't worry about being incognito, you'll stick out like a sore thumb anyway.'

About 2 p.m. the next day we found ourselves at the entrance to the Walled City: Lois, me and Y.B. Tang who came along as our interpreter. On the outside it didn't look like anything unusual, but as we made our way down an old, cracked concrete staircase to enter, the sun disappeared and we emerged into a dark, grimy and mysterious place. My imagination was working overtime, and I would describe it as though we were entering Hell. The sun shone brightly outside the walls, but in those dank and sinister alleyways the sun had disappeared and there was a boding, evil sense about the place. The houses were two and three story buildings mostly made of bricks encrusted with the dirt of centuries. Here and there were rickety wood structures that seemed to defy nature by even remaining to stand.

'Where do you think the opium divans are?' Lois asked.

'Search me.'

'Do you think we ought to ask?'

'What do we ask? Where we can find the nearest opium den? I say we walk around a bit and get the feel of the place. I've been told that the streets where drugs are sold are right out in the open so let's see if we can find them on our own.'

We had entered the Walled City through an archway which connected to a series of cobblestone-paved alleys. Rivulets of muck ran between the uneven stones. We passed a woman sitting on the steps of a tenement sticking a long, needlelike contraption into live ducks one at a time, letting their blood flow into a bucket.

We came into an open area with vendors selling small packages from a few kiosks. We took the merchandise to be drugs as the customers resembled images I'd seen of Nazi death camp prisoners with emaciated bodies. Shaking off feelings of hopelessness, I hoisted my camera to my shoulder. I was a little nervous to start filming there, but it was what I had come for. I looked over for a nod from Y.B. It was his first time here also, and he couldn't tell me if it was safe or not so I held my breath and started rolling.

I took shots of the street and the kiosks and then moved in for close-ups of the packets of drugs. The man who ran the kiosk ignored the camera but one of his customers didn't take too kindly to being photographed. His eyes were bulging, and his rib cage seemed to protrude out of his body, he had on filthy trousers and no shirt and as I shot he came over and hit my camera hard with his hand and shouted at me something unintelligible, in a loud, angry voice.

Y.B. quickly intervened, speaking quietly to the man in Cantonese. It didn't work. The guy pushed him and another one came over to join the fracas. I started to raise my fists in an attempt to simply frighten them away, but Y.B. warned me off. Serious heroin addicts are so frail that a single blow could kill them. After awhile he managed to calm them down and seemed to reach an agreement of some sort.

'They told me where we can find an opium smoking place, but they want to go there with us and they want us to buy them opium.'

'Can you ask them what opium costs?' Lois asked. She was close to her goal and excited.

'A dollar a pipe.' Y.B. used the jargon of the opium smokers.

'A pipe is equal to one dose. It's a deal.'

We followed our escorts through the squalid streets and past several menacing-looking characters, but nobody threatened us. I guessed our escorts were our ticket to safe passage, but I was uneasy. We followed them through a doorway and up a set of rickety stairs to a large room lit only by a couple of florescent lights. A negligible amount of daylight came through two windows which looked as though they had never been washed. Men with jaundiced skin reclined on sagging cots lining the walls while an attendant passed out the oil lamps used to light the opium pipes. The den came right out of what I had seen in old movies. Y.B. asked permission of the man in charge to start shooting, but only after we told him we were going to buy a pipe for everyone in the place and showed him the money, compliments of Lois Mitchison.

Each addict had a small vial in front of him containing liquid opium. Using a long pin, they dipped in, extracted some of the solution and then solidified it with the flame from the lamp. They'd move the pin back and forth until they had extracted all the opium from the vial and had a solid mass on the edge of the pin. Then they would force it into a small hole at the top of the pipe, lay back on a hard lacquer pillow (to avoid a feeling of vertigo), put the pipe next to the lamp, take a long, deep puff, close their eyes and go into a trancelike state.

'Do you want to back out now that you've seen it?' I asked Lois.

'No. Definitely not. It looks an astonishing place.'

'Well, pay the man the $30 and let's get going.' I started running the camera. It took Lois a little while to get into the correct posture on the cot – a sort of fetal position. The servant helped her with forming the opium ball and inserting it into the pipe. Then she lay down, put the pipe next to the lamp to light it and put it up to her mouth and puffed. I couldn't help thinking of the many mouths of grimy opium addicts that had already sucked on that pipe.

It took her a while to do it right. Then suddenly her pupils dilated and her eyeballs seemed to dance around dizzily, but she didn't fall into a trancelike state like the addicts. After waiting a moment for the drug to take full effect she sprang up with a giddy feeling, her heart beating extra fast. I filmed the whole episode.

'Let's get out of here. I feel terrible. My head is spinning. I've got to have some fresh air,' she gasped.

We helped her as we headed for the door. Once out on the street Lois leaned against the wall of the building to steady herself and threw up. She just wanted to get away from the Walled City as fast as possible. In a taxi heading home she claimed she was glad to have had the experience, but once was definitely enough. She wondered how the addicts got any pleasure from opium. Her headache and dizziness hung on for the rest of the day but she slept exceptionally well that night.

We couldn't complain. Lois got to try opium in a real opium divan, I got a colorful story and those drug addicts got a fix for free, so it was a successful trip for all concerned. When my assignment editor in London realized who Lois was he wanted an interview, but I didn't even bother to ask. I think I had got all I was going to get out of Lois Mitchison.

13

A TRIP TO INDONESIA

My first international trip as a news photographer came when I had been in Hong Kong for about six months and CBC producer Donald Brittain contacted me to shoot scenes for a documentary called 'Fields of Sacrifice.' He wanted footage showing the graves of the Canadian soldiers who had been wiped out, to a man, by the Japanese at the battle of Wong Nei Chong Gap during World War II.

Donald in turn introduced me to Michael MacClear who produced CBC Newsmagazine and needed film from Indonesia, and Michael asked me to contact Bill Stevenson their Southeast Asia correspondent in Hong Kong for details.

'It seems there was a dispute over the ownership of a remote section of the country known as Irian Barat,' Bill told me. 'The Dutch who were the former rulers of Indonesia annoyed President Sukarno when they refused to leave.'

The Dutch had controlled all of Indonesia's business and trade for 200 years — right up until World War II. The Japanese invasion of the archipelago effectively ended Dutch rule and then with the subsequent defeat of the Japanese, Indonesian independence leader Sukarno proclaimed the Indonesian state. But the Dutch wanted to reinstate their rule and stubbornly held onto Irian Barat (West Irian or Dutch New Guinea) as their bargaining chip. This move infuriated the Indonesians and they threatened to fight to regain their territory until the Dutch finally had to back down. But while the dispute raged, Sukarno expelled all Dutch nationals that remained in the country. The expulsion of the Dutch was the story that CBC wanted us to cover.

'Great. When do we go?' I asked, eager for my first trip away from Hong Kong on a news story.

'We'll take a flight at 7:30 tomorrow morning.'

I loved the immediacy of news work. Here today and away on a plane tomorrow. Early the following morning Bill picked me up in a taxi and we headed for Kai Tak airport and Garuda Indonesia Flight 236 to Jakarta.

Bill Stevenson was actually an Englishman who had made his home in Canada. He was employed full time as the Far East correspondent for the *Toronto Globe and Mail* newspaper but made himself available to the CBC for coverage in Asia.

'We must somehow get an interview with Sukarno. We'll work it out once we get there,' Bill said. 'I want to get scenes around Jakarta and show the Indonesian lifestyle as well as what they can expect after the Dutch leave. We want shots of the Dutch packing up and leaving and if it's possible, some interviews with them.'

'Sounds interesting. I don't foresee any problems.'

Our first problem occurred before we even got out of the airport in Jakarta. The customs officials didn't know what to make of all the equipment we brought.

'You want to bring all this gear into the country?'

Bill ignored him and said quietly, 'Let me speak to the head customs officer, please.'

'You can speak to me,' said the officer brusquely.

'We have official authorization to shoot here and have permission to bring in our equipment,' Bill said, in an imposing tone. 'I want to speak to the head customs officer who has a cable from your consul general in Hong Kong informing him that we are coming.'

The officer backed down. 'Okay. You can find him in that office over there.'

He waved his hand in the direction of a glass door with some Indonesian writing on it.

'Should I come with you?' I asked Bill, ready to do battle with the authorities.

'No. Just wait here and watch the equipment. I can handle this alone.'

I waited, watching Indonesian customs at work while Bill waved his hands at the official behind the glass door. At customs, a Chinese man approached with a large valise. The customs inspector opened the case, took out a whopping handful of lipsticks, put them under the counter and then waved the Chinese man on. He had obviously passed inspection.

In about 15 minutes Bill came out of the office together with the head customs officer who spoke to his man in Indonesian and cleared the way for us to pack up the equipment. We were free to go.

In the taxi I asked Bill about how he worked it.

'In Indonesia, money talks' was all he said.

The traffic in Jakarta was sheer chaos. We were stuck, what seemed inextricably, at several intersections while I conjured up visions of being trapped there for the rest of the day. Policemen wearing snug-fitting uniforms were stationed at each crossroads, blowing whistles interminably. It harmonized nicely with the cacophony of car horns, but none of it seemed to have any effect on the traffic.

Our taxi driver expertly maneuvered his way through the knots of tooting horns and ringing bells and we were soon in the Indonesian countryside with its endless groves of oil palms and coffee trees. After about an hour of traveling we got to the Transaera Hotel.

The Transaera was a middling hotel in the old Dutch style. It had large, comfortably decorated rooms though everything looked a little timeworn. My room was outfitted with soft double beds, a dressing table, ample cabinet space for clothes, and a very noisy air conditioner that blew out warm air. I set up a corner for charging camera batteries and then peeled off my sweating clothes and headed for the bathroom.

The bathroom was equipped with a shower in a large open space with a wooden mat on the floor. When I turned on the water, a great swarm of mosquitoes came charging up at me like the Jakarta Luftwaffe out of the porous wooden mat. I grabbed a wet towel and started swatting them as I headed for the safety of the bedroom. After a few minutes I ventured cautiously back to the shower and found that the running water had dispersed them, somewhat. A sign over the sink in Indonesian and English read, 'Do not waste water,' but made no mention of the menacing mosquitoes or the fact that the only water available was cold.

The heat of the day kept us from getting too hungry and I drank lots of iced water with dinner. Bill didn't trust the water and preferred beer. We ordered *gado-gado*, an Indonesian salad made with a variety of fresh vegetables and lots of crunchy peanut sauce and served with crispy prawn crackers called '*krupak*.'

After the meal we went to the hotel garden and had a cup of very dark coffee that was the best I had ever tasted. The night was fairly cool for Indonesia and we sat there, with a giant coil of mosquito repellent smoking under our table, comfortably talking.

About 6:30 the next morning a room boy woke me by shaking my pillow with such vitality that I reckoned an earthquake had struck. He brought me a cup of that delicious coffee and let me know in sign language that he would be back in a little while to make the bed. I asked in vain for a pitcher of hot water for shaving. Later that day I made a point of learning the words for hot water — '*air panas*'.

Bill was waiting for me in the lobby, anxious to rent a car and get the proper press credentials. It seemed that in Indonesia you must inform the ministry of information, the police and the military about what you are doing and get a raft of press passes from each of them. They made it as complicated as possible, but Bill sailed right through with cash payments. The windshield of our car was so plastered with official stickers that we could hardly see out.

Corruption is a way of life in Indonesia. Businesses deliberately set aside a part of their income for bribes. High government officials in charge of huge contracts were paid so poorly that their families would starve if they weren't on the take.

You could buy almost anyone. It was ludicrous, but this was their country and the giving and taking of bribes had been worked out to an exact science. Who were we to say if it was right or wrong, all we knew was money really smoothed the way if you wanted anything done in Indonesia.

With enough press passes to cover the walls of a 20-floor apartment house we were ready to begin. The information ministry tipped us that President Sukarno stopped by for an informal meeting once in a while with foreign journalists in the international press center of the Merdeka Palace and we might have a chance to talk with him there.

The Istana Merdeka was an impressive maze of white plaster buildings with marble staircases, highly polished floors and bigger than life Greek statues. Smartly dressed soldiers guarded checkpoints at all the entrances and after being stopped 46 times to have our bags inspected we finally reached the international press center and there we met several old friends.

'Bill Stevenson, what brings you to Indonesia?' asked Bernie Kalb of the *New York Times.*

'We're working on the Dutch expulsion story for CBC.'

Noticing our sound camera he said, 'You're expecting to get an interview here with the *Bung?*' He called Sukarno by his sobriquet *'Bung'* which means 'brother.'

'Well, we're going to try.'

'He likes to talk with foreign journalists and he's charming, but he doesn't like impromptu filmed interviews. Though don't take my word for it. You may get lucky.' Bernie shrugged, He obviously didn't think much of our chances.'

'What about the Dutch and West Irian?' Bill asked.

'West Irian is mostly jungle, but it's part of the Indonesian motherland and so according to the government there is absolutely no position for negotiation,' Bernie said. 'I believe the

Dutch government doesn't understand this country so they naively gave their military orders to hold out. You'd think after two hundred years of pillaging the place they would know better.'

At that moment the door opened and Sukarno walked in with a couple of military officers. He looked cheerful and exactly as I remembered him from newspaper pictures. He was not tall and had a slightly pockmarked face. That day he wore dark brown military trousers, a white shirt and on his head, his trademark, a velvet *peci*. He obviously liked talking with members of the foreign press and he greeted the New York Times correspondent like an old friend.

'Bernie. What have you writing about me?'

'Nothing inflammatory ... I hope.'

'Nothing inflammatory? Just that I was dead.'

'Oh, I'm sorry about that.' Bernie smiled uneasily. 'Our wireless operator in Singapore misread what I wrote. He doesn't speak English very well. But in any case the story never went out. It was just a mistake.'

'Obviously. I don't look dead, do I?' He snickered. 'That mistake may get you expelled from Indonesia for awhile.' He made that quip with a half-smile on his face so I couldn't make out if he was joking or not.

He looked around the room and spied our sound camera.

'What's this?' he asked, looking straight at me.

'I'm Bill Stevenson from CBC,' Bill said, intervening. 'We just arrived in town. We're here to cover the Irian Barat story and I thought we might get a few words from you, on camera.'

He came over and shook hands with Bill. Bill introduced me and he shook my hand as well.

'Look Bill, Marvin, I can't do an interview without prior warning. I must have time to think over the answers. You understand?'

'Of course I understand, sir. We brought the sound camera along just on the off chance that you might consent to an interview on the spur of the moment. I know you are a master at speaking your mind and are never at a loss for words,' Bill said, trying flattery.

'That's not entirely true. You shouldn't let my informal behavior fool you. I am a little bit anxious in front of a camera and I feel more comfortable with some preparation. Get in touch with Mrs. Saleh at the Information Ministry and she might be able to arrange the interview. Then when we do it, it'll be in my office with official flags and presidential seals on the wall. How does that sound?'

'It sounds perfect, sir.'

It may have sounded perfect but Bill didn't particularly like the phrase 'Mrs. Saleh might be able to arrange.'

Peter Kerr of the *Sydney Morning Herald* asked, 'Is there anything further on the expulsion of the Dutch, sir?'

Sukarno glanced around the room. 'That is already old news,' he said, chuckling. 'I have differing opinions from my cabinet on throwing those damned Dutch out. Some believe that we are biting off the nose to spite the face. 'What about the Dutch business?' I am asked. So what about them? We can take over their businesses and learn to operate them better, without the Dutch. We didn't fight a dirty guerilla war just to give away part of our country. If we stumble at first, that is our prerogative, but we know that eventually we will be able to replace the Dutch in whatever they do.'

'Does that mean you're rethinking the expulsion of the Dutch?' asked Charley Smith of UP.

Sukarno answered irritably. 'Are you listening to me Charley? There is no question. We want every Dutchman and his family out of Indonesia. It is not their country and this is not negotiable. My government stands by me in that, to a man.'

'The expulsion goes through as planned,' said Francis Lara of Agence France Presse. 'Will it be okay for me to file that statement?'

'If you want to file it, feel free to file it, Francis. It may not be important, but I'm afraid you don't have this exclusively. I had a similar talk a short while ago with members of the local media but you foreign newsmen are not competing with the local press are you?'

'No, of course not,' Peter Kerr replied. 'But I wanted to ask you one or two more questions related to this subject.'

'You can get all the information from Mrs. Saleh. Now I must go.'

And with that farewell and the wave of his arm he left abruptly.

'That's Sukarno,' said Charlie Smith. 'He gives you a story and then he tells you it has already been handed to the locals. The rest of you guys may not be in competition with the local press, but we are. A couple of them are my customers.'

In the meantime Bill hired an interpreter who also was a fixer, sound engineer, gopher and all-around assistant named Mohammed Anwar. He came highly recommended by Charlie Smith as being shrewd and resourceful and he felt he would make a useful addition to our crew.

We spoke to Mrs. Saleh at the Information Ministry and she told us she couldn't confirm an interview with Sukarno at the moment.

'We got sort of a promise when we saw him at the press room this morning,' Bill said.

'I know' said Mrs. Saleh apologetically. 'But he is scheduled to fly to Surabaya tomorrow morning to address 20,000 workers at the stadium.'

'Can we get him before he leaves or when he gets back?'

'I'm afraid not. His schedule is very tight so he really has no time for interviews right now.'

'Well how about if we went along with him to Surabaya?'

'There is no room on his plane, but you are free to take a commercial flight if you want to. I must warn you though that his security in Surabaya will be very tight. I don't see how we could even get near him. It would probably be a wasted trip.'

'He told us that you could arrange something for us. It's very important that we have the interview for our story. There is no, er, little thing that we can do to facilitate,' Bill said, shaking the coins vigorously in his pants pocket.

'Absolutely not,' Mrs. Saleh said, crossly.

'Oh, I didn't mean it that way.' Bill smiled, but he was well aware that he had committed a faux pas.

'If things change all of a sudden please let us know.'

In the meantime, we interviewed Vice President Juanda and he told us that in the matter of Irian Barat he agreed with the president 100 percent. Except, granted the Dutch were high-handed and arrogant and Indonesia had enough of them, but was it a good idea to get rid of them so quickly? Was the decision of the president a little too hasty?

What he said didn't add up to anything new, but Bill reminded me that having the vice president of a country as remote to Canada as Indonesia on camera would always impress the viewers.

Strangely the Dutch people we interviewed didn't blame the Indonesian government but were quick to blame the intransigence of the Dutch for their expulsion. A Dutch businessman told us,

'Irian Barat is after all an integral part of Indonesia and yet the Dutch government stupidly refused to give it back, or even to discuss it with them, until they were eventually forced out.

And now we have to leave and the Dutch government can take the blame for that too.'

'We've lived all our lives in Bandung,' his wife said with tears in her eyes. 'And we thought we would die in this country but the government gave us just one day to pack up all our belongings and get out.'

The story was repeated by almost all the Dutch we spoke to. They seemed sympathetic to the Indonesian point of view and mostly blamed the Dutch government for holding onto that useless bit of territory. These interviews were very significant but what Bill really wanted was Sukarno on film speaking on the subject. It was like an obsession with him.

'Okay, Anwar,' Bill said to our interpreter. 'Get us three round-trip tickets on the plane to Surabaya tomorrow morning as early as possible. We need that interview and we are going to get it one way or another.'

14

ATTEMPTED MURDER AT THE MOSQUE

The night before we left on our trip for Surabaya I asked Anwar to show me a little of Jakarta's nightlife. He took me to a small café in downtown Jakarta called The Cozy Corner. It was surrounded by food stalls and as we approached the door we were ambushed by a score of three-wheeled *bejacs*, pedi-cabs, each of which carried a pretty girl soliciting business. One particularly attractive *bejac* girl began tugging at my arm.

Anwar pushed them out of way, saying, 'That's a banshee, a boy that dresses like a girl, if you're interested?'

'Not so much,' I said.

'Well some guys like to try to banshees. I was working for NBC and their English soundman always took a banshee. He was married with children but he wanted to try one and he liked it, so he always took a banshee.'

The Cozy Corner consisted of a tiny bar, a few booths, a jukebox playing Indonesian songs and a number of large fans. Strings of colored lights gave it a festive air. Anwar took a beer and ordered me the non-alcoholic specialty of the house, a guava juice concoction with chunks of coconut meat mixed with extract of vanilla.

'So tell me the story of these banshees,' I said after we got comfortable.

'I thought you weren't interested?'

'I'm not, as a date, but what sort of body do banshees have? Do they cut off their manliness in exchange for female organs?'

The banshee that had latched onto me looked like a girl in every aspect. He had a young and cheerful face with no semblance of a beard.

'There are no doctors in Indonesia to do that sort of operation,' Anwar said. 'The banshees take hormone injections to make their breasts large, like a girl and I think it makes their hips bigger too. They are female in every way, except for what they have under their skirts.'

Anwar reminded me we had to be at the airport at 4:30 a.m. When you flop into bed at 1 a.m., no one likes getting up at 3 a.m., but at the appointed time Bill was already awake and rapping at my door.

Despite the early hour the airport was roiling. A huge crowd spilled over onto the road outside of the terminal. As soon as we got out of the car I found myself fighting off would-be porters wanting to carry our equipment into the building. I didn't want to let any of the stuff out of my sight so I declined the offers. I almost came to blows with a group of them but after a couple of minutes of persuasive discussion they seemed to get the picture. I was sorry to deprive those poor souls of the chance to make a few rupiahs but I had to take precautions, and not letting the equipment out of my hands was high on my list of priorities.

The three of us pushed and shoved our way through the crowds until we came to the long line at the check-in counter. The single open counter was handling about 20 domestic flights going to various parts of the country and they all seemed to be leaving at the same time. There was such pandemonium that I wondered if we had enough time to complete the formalities before our plane was due to take off.

Anwar took control. He told the waiting passengers something in Indonesian and they stood aside and made a clear path for us, right up to the counter where we immediately got into an argument with the ticketing agent who insisted we put all the equipment into the baggage compartment. But Anwar had already warned us about that. He said they threw the bags in there helter-skelter and the lenses or the camera could easily get damaged and almost certainly some of the film would go missing. Bill dealt with the agent in his usual persuasive manner — a thousand rupiah note. In record time we had been checked in, handed boarding passes and hustled over to the waiting area.

'What did you tell those people on line to make them step back?' I asked Anwar.

'I told them, almost, the truth. I said you were a TV crew that had come all the way from Canada to film President Sukarno in Surabaya and we were in danger of missing our flight, and would they mind letting us go first. The Bung is a very popular man and it's like they were doing him some honor to give up their places to you.'

About 6 a.m. we finally boarded the aircraft. It was a two-engine DC-3 and the passenger cabin was in dire need of repair. The foam cushion in my seat was bursting its seams and the carpet was worn right through to the steel floor in several places. The whole inside of the aircraft looked so shoddy that if we were in our right minds we would have gotten off and taken the train.

We took off and immediately began a precipitous climb through the mountains. The early morning mist created some light turbulence but it was secondary to the view. The approaching dawn painted a superb picture as the sun broke up the dark shadows and spilled rapidly over the valleys, colliding with the mountaintops.

There was only one stewardess on our flight and about 15 minutes into our journey she laid out a huge banana leaf — that was our table cloth — and then served us a thick slice of white bread smeared with something I took for lard. As Indonesia was a strict Muslim country it couldn't have been pig fat but it sure didn't taste like butter. On top of that she added a coating of chocolate sprinkles and then stabbed a fork right in the middle. Our breakfast was completed with a paper cup of tea, a banana and a bittersweet chocolate bar. The chocolate was delicious and I guessed chocolate making was one skill the Indonesians had picked up from the Dutch.

Surabaya, the capital of East Java, lies to the southeast of Jakarta and is Indonesia's second largest city. After the Japanese were thrown out at the end of the war the city was incorporated into the Republic of Indonesia. It had a population of almost 2.5 million and a very strong labor union movement, but was a rough place and Anwar warned us to watch our tails.

It wasn't 9 a.m. when we arrived in Surabaya but Bill wanted to get right to work and film around town in preparation for Sukarno's speech, scheduled for 2 p.m.

We hired a 1947 Oldsmobile that the driver assured us was perfectly sound and as up-to-date as any car we could find in Surabaya. He spoke a little English and when he found out we were TV newsmen he was delighted and suggested places to film. We began at the main mosque where we arrived just before the start of the second prayer session.

The mosque was a magnificent structure with minarets and a huge rotunda prayer hall. Call to prayer was given by the muezzin and I was determined to film the whole procedure while Bill and Anwar waited in the car. After shooting exteriors of the building I went into the rotunda to film the prayer meeting and met with some disagreeable stares. I tried smiling back to show I was a friendly guy, but when I started the camera rolling during the actual prayer service, they lowered the boom.

A gigantic man, about seven feet tall with a huge beard grabbed both my arms. He took me by the belt of my trousers and the scruff of my neck and marched me to a little office. A couple more bearded men were waiting. I tried to explain myself in English, but they must have figured I was insulting them and one of them hauled off and slapped me in the face a couple of times. I could taste blood on my lip. I tried to pull away from them and succeeded only in ripping my shirt. They forced me into a chair while one of them went out and returned with a fourth man who spoke a little English.

'This is sacred temple of Islam. You no take picture here,' he told me, menacingly.

'I realize that and I am sorry, but I am a stranger in Surabaya and I didn't mean any offense to Islam.' I took out my press pass with trembling hands and showed it to him.

'I have permission from the government.'

He took the bits of paper, gave them a cursory review and then threw them on the floor.

'You think these paper give you the right to violate holy place?'

'No, I don't. I am sorry, sir.' I was really frightened.

He glared.

'You no welcome here, get out.'

With that he gave me a shove toward the door, so forcefully that I fell down and dropped the camera.

'Yes sir. Thank you, sir. I really didn't know what I was doing.'

I have learned that in tight situations when you don't know what to do it often pays to just grovel. I had got down on my knees to pick up the camera and press passes, when one of the bearded ones gave me a sharp kick in the behind and sent me sprawling. The group of bearded men got a great kick of that. I regained my feet and quickly went out the door and half walking, half running I got back to the car. I examined the camera. It was built like a Sherman tank, and it would take more than a knock on a concrete floor to harm that little Bell and Howell.

When Bill and Anwar heard my tale and saw my swollen lip and torn shirt they shook their heads in mock commiseration but did not show me much sympathy.

'Serves you right. You should have known better than to shoot in a sacred temple without permission.'

'I am sorry I didn't tell you,' Anwar said. 'These people are very sensitive about infidels walking around taking pictures inside their mosque.'

'Can you beat that, I'm an infidel.'

I tried to put the incident out of my mind, sucked on my bloody lip and asked Bill what the next item was on the agenda.

Bill turned to Anwar. 'Anwar, tell the driver I want to go to a really depressed area. I want to show misery and gloomy scenes of destitution. People in real need, living in tumbled down houses, you know what I mean?'

'Yeah, but showing a country's weaknesses like that is difficult to film. We don't want a repeat of what happened at the mosque. This time we shoot from the car.'

'Let's see what's there and then we'll discuss how we're going to film it,' I said.

The driver found a community of dilapidated dwellings constructed of tin scraps and old wooden packing cases adjacent to the railroad tracks. Flies swarmed the food hawkers' carts and dirty, naked children darted around unpaved roads. I shot a mother rocking her baby in a swing made from an old sarong in front of a wretched hut. It was the perfect place, but I needed to get out of the car to shoot it properly.

'I think it's safe,' Anwar said, looking carefully up and down the street. 'I'll go with you. But don't force it. If you see trouble just back away. I'll talk to them.'

I shot a wide view of people sitting around the hawker's cart, eating colorless dishes with their bare hands. I asked Anwar to get permission to go inside one the shacks.

'Can't you just get the shot from the street?'

'No. I have to go inside. The woman seems friendly enough. Come on, let's try?'

Anwar spoke to the woman and she agreed. I pushed aside a dirty tarpaulin and entered a kitchen that had a broken window, black with soot from cooking fires. A carelessly placed flame could have set the structure and probably the entire squatter area ablaze. A roughly hewn bed made of discarded wooden boxes with a straw mattress sat on one side. The woman, her husband and their three children all slept in that one bed. In another corner a comb with several teeth missing and a broken piece of glass which served as a mirror lay propped on a small table. There were no closets and the washing hung near the hut's only window. The woman told us her husband was out looking for work and her two sons had gone to a junkyard to pick up what they could find. When I finished filming at her house I told Anwar to ask for directions to the junkyard.

It was a shocking sight. People and rats searched for food and salvageable scraps in a filthy garbage dump covering about three square city blocks. The odor was overpowering.

I was getting the footage I came for when, all of a sudden, a young man dressed neatly in light-colored slacks and short-sleeved shirt came up and angrily asked what I was doing. A crowd of locals joined him and they seemed more hostile than curious. Anwar told them we were newsmen and were trying to tell the real story of Surabaya's poor people.

'Are you trying to make these people look foolish?'

'No, no. We are just trying to help them by showing their story.'

'If you want to help them, give them money.'

Anwar told Bill quietly, 'I think we ought to give them some rupiahs before this guy starts a riot.'

Bill took several thousand rupiahs notes from his pocket. 'Will this help?'

It was what we needed to extricate ourselves from a very sticky situation. You never know what a mob will do if they are provoked and the young man looked very belligerent.

15

THE GREAT MAN SPEAKS

From the junkyard, we headed for the government houses in an upscale neighborhood. Banyan trees fronted great old Dutch houses with tiled roofs and fine lawns. The scene stood in stark contrast to where we'd just come from. On our way from the junkyard, we had driven past canals running right through the center of town that had originally been built by the Dutch to beautify the city but now served a dual purpose as open-air sewer and laundromat.

From the junkyard, we headed for the government houses in an upscale neighborhood. Banyan trees fronted great old Dutch houses with tiled roofs and fine lawns. The scene was in stark contrast to from the one we had just left.

One house in particular had a heavy military presence. 'This house of chief general in charge all Surabaya,' our driver told us as we observed heavily armed soldiers in military vehicles parked out front.

When I tried to film the general's house an unsmiling group of soldiers approached. Flaunting their weapons, they inspected my camera thoroughly and then ordered us to leave the neighborhood straight away.

'We have press passes that were actually issued by the army, so where do they get the authority to order us around?' I said to no one in particular.

One major with an AK-47 rifle thrust his weapon into my face with his finger on the trigger, looked pointedly at his weapon and said in perfect English, 'This is my authority.'

We got into our car and drove off to lunch.

'Well at least it didn't cost us anything this time,' said Bill smiling. 'I wouldn't have been surprised if he took that AK-47 and put a few rounds into you Marv. He'd probably have gotten a medal for it.'

'It's just past noon and a soldier threatened my life, those worshipers in the mosque were prepared to kill me and that guy at the garbage dump was about to start a riot. What else is going to happen before this day is over?'

Before going to the stadium where Sukarno was giving his speech we took time to lunch, *al fresco*. We shared a delicious '*soto madura*,' a curried lamb soup with fresh squeezed lime, a *satay* of goat meat (a dish we could have passed up) and the biggest avocado I had ever seen.

Appetites sated, we were ready for Sukarno. The stadium was newly constructed and spectators filled every one of the 20,000 seats. Many more stood in the aisles. As 'Bung Karno' was introduced a colossal roar went up from the crowd and they didn't stop cheering for almost 10 minutes. Sukarno stood on the podium smiling and he raised his hand several times for silence. Anwar translated.

He said he was deeply touched by their show of high regard for himself and his policies. He spoke about his agreement with the Soviet Union which had supplied experts and made a loan of a US$100 million. He welcomed their assistance, but he said he welcomed the Americans' assistance, too. He showed no discrimination to any country that sincerely wanted to help rebuild Indonesia after a disastrous 200 years under colonial domination.

He said that when the Dutch came to their country, they treated the Indonesian leaders with contempt and took what they wanted. They stole land from the Indonesian peasants. They enslaved the workers and left the mass of the people uneducated and in abject poverty. The only thing the Dutch gave them was disrespect. Then after the war they had the impudence to want to return and take power again, but the Indonesian people drove them out, forever.

Anwar went down to see if he could get a copy of the speech, but it seems that Sukarno was speaking, as usual, off the cuff. While engaging in small talk with the official, Anwar discovered that Sukarno was going to stay the night in Surabaya at the Hanuman Hotel. Bill decided that we should stay there as well. He was on the trail of his interview, but I just wanted a good meal and a comfortable bed.

The Hanuman Hotel was an old, two-story villa that had been taken over by the Indonesian government when the Dutch left. The rooms were large, comfortable and beautifully provided with quaint Dutch style furniture. We were proudly informed by the management that Sukarno and his party had taken the entire upper floor, so we booked the remaining three rooms on the ground floor.

After a shower we met in the bar. It was dimly lit and appointed with huge leather chairs and paintings of old Dutch scenes giving it the cozy atmosphere of a private residence. After some strategic talk about how to snare the interview we adjourned to the dining room, hoping that Sukarno would show up there. The manager told us it was very unlikely as the hotel had a large kitchen on the second floor and Sukarno had a personal chef traveling with him.

After putting away a delicious Dutch *rijsttafel*, we went back to the bar and were feeling very sorry for ourselves when the great man himself walked in. He had an entourage of military men with him and as they took a table near ours, Sukarno seemed to recognize us.

'You're from some TV network?' he asked, looking at Bill.

'That's right, sir. I'm Bill Stevenson from the CBC. We met you yesterday at the Merdeka Palace.'

'Oh, that's right. So what are you doing here? Is it a coincidence or are you still looking for an interview.'

'Well we actually covered your speech at the stadium this afternoon. I understand it was very inspiring.'

'But you are still looking for that interview?' he asked.

'Well, as a matter of fact, yes we are.'

'Well, as a matter of fact, the answer is still the same,' said the Bung, laughing. 'Oh excuse my rudeness, won't you and your friends join us?'

We were overjoyed. It was quite a thrill sitting there having drinks with a world leader.

'So you're not going to give up on that interview?'

'I hope I don't have to, sir,' Bill replied. 'But it's all up to you, if you want to do it or not.'

'That's not a hundred percent correct. As the president of the country I have many people to answer to. I cannot make a move like that unilaterally. For instance these men here are part of my problem. What do you say gentlemen. Are you for or against my granting the CBC an exclusive interview?'

One general feigned seriousness and said, 'We'll have to take it under advisement.'

'You see it is not me that says no,' Sukarno said, smiling.

All of a sudden, the all-powerful leader of 200 million Indonesian people stopped what he was saying and a hostile look came into his eyes. He was looking across the room at a group of six Europeans talking quietly.

'Hey,' he shouted. 'Hey you! Are you Dutch?'

The people looked at each other in surprise before replying.

'Why yes,' one of their group answered.

'Pay your bill and get out,' the president commanded.

'We were just sitting here and talking.'

'Are you deaf?'

'No.'

'Then get out. Now!'

They called for the bill and the waiter told them it was waiting for them outside at the desk. They got up as fast as they could and left. I wondered how they felt getting kicked out of the bar by the great Sukarno himself.

'I don't want any Dutch people near me. The sooner they are all out of this country, the better it will be for the country.'

All of his generals surrounding him agreed, as generals do. The rest of the evening with Sukarno was very convivial. He only insisted on one thing—that we didn't discuss politics. And Bill reluctantly consented not to mention the interview.

'Have you seen the new miniskirt fashion?' Sukarno asked changing the subject.

'Oh yes, it's very popular in the United States and is beginning to catch on in London.'

'What about Canada?'

'I'm afraid Canadian women are behind the times,' Bill said, shaking his head. 'They are a bit backward in fashion. What do you think of miniskirts Mr. President?'

'I think they're outrageous. They show too much of the legs. They should absolutely be banned. I am sure that they will never catch on in Indonesia.'

'Why is that Mr. President?'

'Because Indonesian men wouldn't stand for it. They like their women obedient and would strongly object to seeing them in miniskirts. Anyway, Indonesian girls are very modest and respectable and would never appear in public in such outrageous clothing.'

'Ah,' said Bill remembering, but not mentioning, Sukarno's renowned womanizing.

'That's men, but women have their own minds, especially about fashion.'

Sukarno shook his head with a shudder.

'That is the problem with Western men. They have no control over their women. The women act anyway they please and wear anything they like and the men dare not say a word. That's why western society is on the decline. The men have no backbone.'

'I see what you mean. I guess you're right.'

Actually Bill didn't agree, but you don't argue with the president in his own country.

'Certainly I'm right,' Sukarno said.

One of his aides reminded him, 'I think it's late and we must be up early tomorrow morning.'

Sukarno agreed. 'Yes. We must go now. It was very pleasant talking with you and I hope I will see you back in Jakarta.'

'We have really enjoyed talking with you this evening, Mr. President,' Bill said for all of us.

A moment after he left it was like waking from a dream. Had we actually spent the evening chatting casually with the president of Indonesia?

The following day we had a plane reservation back to Jakarta at 5:30 p.m. We slept late, ate an early lunch and spent what time we had left touring around the Surabaya waterfront looking for shots. The harbor area is enclosed by breakwaters and contains floating docks, piers and warehouses. Bill would have liked to take a couple of scenes there but again we came up against the military, so we just left and passed the time riding around town.

The time had finally come for our departure from Indonesia. For all our disappointment about not getting an interview with Sukarno, it turned out that the CBC didn't think the interview was crucial anyway. The great star of our story was Indonesia: a country of 187 million who lived spread out on 13,000 islands and spoke over 500 different dialects. At that time they were just emerging from more than 200 years of foreign domination and were struggling to catch up with the rest of the world. For all the hardships they faced they were a single nation and had made a start. It was a tribute to the significance of Indonesia that when CBC Newsmagazine aired our story, it played alone, over the entire half-hour show.

16

THE ACUPUNCTURIST

The FCC had been a good place for getting a start in Hong Kong. I had met some great people and enjoyed some terrific food, but I needed a real home and found a one-bedroom flat in Causeway Bay on the northern shore of Hong Kong Island with a view overlooking the tram tracks. I decorated it with inexpensive bamboo furniture and my 'piece de resistance'—a custom-made bed seven feet long and seven feet wide. I put in a large dresser, a few chairs and tables and lots of photos of friends and relatives on the wall.

Next, I had to supplement my sporadic freelance news work. Television was new in Hong Kong and for the moment not an overly popular advertising medium. Companies didn't want to waste their meager advertising budgets making black and white TV ads when movie seats cost only a couple of dollars and were very popular. Theater ads were definitely the direction to go for me.

The Metro motor car company had HK$5,000 to squander and I landed a 60-second advertising film of the new Austin Mini. I couldn't move them on the budget, but in the end I accepted. I figured that money was not the most important thing on my first advertising film.

I hired a 35mm Mitchell camera along with a studio cameraman. The great American harmonica virtuoso Larry Adler happened to be passing through town, and for HK$500 he played his famous Genevieve Waltz on the soundtrack. With the cost of renting the camera, buying film, processing, editing, putting on a soundtrack and titles and paying off Larry Adler I cleared about 16 cents on the job. The sponsor was crazy about it though, and we had a sample of our work showing at 11 theatres simultaneously.

I followed that up with commercials for Watson's, the soft drinks manufacturer, Formica, Brylcreem and Pepsi-Cola. I wrote ridiculous little jingles like, 'Watson's Orange gives no trouble, snap off the cap and watch it bubble.' I was the only one in Hong Kong making commercials, so business was good.

On the way home from work one night I stopped in for a bite to eat at a tea house where I struck up a conversation with an elderly gentleman sitting alone with his pot of tea. His name was Holly Wong and he said he was an acupuncturist. The practice of acupuncture in China dates back over 4,000 years. According to the theory, vital energy flows along certain 'meridian' spots in the body and diseases are caused by interruptions to the flow of these energies. Inserting and manipulating needles restores the normal flow.

At any rate, Holly was close to 60, had lived in Paris for more than 20 years and spoke English with a mixture of Chinese and French accents. He had a rasping voice and a funny little laugh and when I met him he introduced himself as Dr. Holly Wong. He had come to visit one of his patients who suffered from migraines, he said. She lived just across the street, a young lady named Chen Yuk Soi and while we sat in the restaurant he told me the interesting story of her life.

Miss Chen had been raised on a fishing junk, anchored at an island called Tai O. She didn't have any education and could neither read nor write. Her father was a fisherman and had been renting a junk from an old merchant and paying for it with part of his catch. One day, a violent storm broke off a large section of the mast and Mr. Chen was seriously injured. The old merchant went to see the boat first, and then he went to the hospital to see Chen. He told Mr. Chen that he had been very careless, and as a result, the boat had sustained serious damage and he would have to pay to have it repaired. So while Mr. Chen lay there in pain, the old miser toted up the bill. It came to HK$8,000.

Realizing it was more than Mr. Chen could ever pay, the old man came up with an alternate solution. He would be willing to accept one of Chen's daughters in lieu of cash. He was fond of 10-year-old Yuk Soi, and she could assist his three wives with the cooking and housework. As girls had little status in a typical poor Chinese working family, the fisherman gladly swapped his daughter to cover the debt. No signing of papers, no court orders, not even a handshake. Yuk Soi packed up her one *sam fu* and a pair of tattered shoes, moved into the old man's house, and never saw her family again.

In old China girls were often viewed as having little value. When they grew up, girls would marry and leave the family, but boys shared the work and had an obligation to stick with the family and look after the parents when they were old and most importantly, pass on the family name to their offspring. Selling girls happened often.

When she was 14 years old there was no hiding the fact that Yuk Soi had blossomed into a beautiful young woman. It did not go unnoticed by the old man who took her to his bed and brutally violated her. As a result of this encounter the girl, who was not yet fully developed, hemorrhaged and her life hung in the balance. She managed to survive and when she was well the old man took her as his third wife.

They had a wedding in the traditional Chinese style. She wore a brocaded wedding dress and rode to the ceremony in a sedan chair covered with red muslin, and held a veil to her face to prevent her from seeing inauspicious sights. She was carried into the house on the shoulders of the bridesmaids so that her feet would not touch the ground and leaped over a ring of fire to prevent evil spirits from entering the house with her. A great feast was held and according to practice the old man was presented with a roast suckling pig with a bloody handkerchief in its mouth to prove his wife was a virgin.

One night he ordered her to sleep with him and when Yuk Soi refused, he beat her. She ran away, stealing a large sum of money from the old man's cache. She hired a sampan to take her from the old merchant's home on Cheung Chau Island to Hong Kong where she found this room. She suffered frequent migraine headaches which had brought her to Holly Wong.

Holly told me in a whisper, 'You know, she is anxious to make love with a foreigner, and I would like to introduce you.'

It was so sudden, coming from a man I hardly knew.

'But she doesn't speak English,' I said, sputtering. 'I wouldn't know how to start.'

'I think you do,' said Holly in his crafty French way. 'Just play the part of lover. All women will understand.'

'Are you sure?'

'*Absolutement*, I guarantee it. I am her confidant and know everything about her.'

Holly called her to come over for tea. She was really lovely, but seemed uneasy. Holly was of no help, he just paid the bill and left. Ignorant of each other's language there was nothing we could say, so after a brief period of just sitting there feeling embarrassed, we went to her room.

She lived in a single room, decorated with a cheap-looking imitation leather sofa and a chair also covered with imitation leather. She had a collection of Chinese comic books on a table next to the bed, and a shrine to the Goddess Tin Hau, the patron saint of all fishermen.

Once in her apartment Yuk Soi started to take off my clothes. This was no wild scattering of garments in the heat of the moment, but a careful and neat disrobing. She took off my tie and my shirt, then my trousers and she folded them very neatly and put them on a chair, and then she started to remove her own clothes. Article by article they were folded neatly and put on the chair next to mine.

When she finally came to bed, she looked straight ahead and put her arms rigidly by her sides. Her body was thin and her breasts were almost non-existent. I could see she was petrified and I couldn't wrest her arms from their position. I don't know if she was frightened of me because I was a foreigner, or was just fearful of the act we were about to perform, but I decided I should be as considerate as possible, keeping in mind she did have a history of brutal treatment. She didn't seem an old hand at making love, but for my part I enjoy all women, stiff and inflexible notwithstanding.

The next morning I received a telephone call from Holly.

'Did you enjoy last night?'

'She was lovely.'

'What did you give her?'

'Well, I don't know. I think she enjoyed it.'

'I mean, did you give her a present?'

'Well, no. Should I have?'

'Of course.'

'I didn't think it was that kind of a deal.'

'Of course not, but she would have appreciated some sort of present. It didn't have to be money,' he said exasperated. 'Oh, you don't understand Chinese women. Cantonese women. She would have put much more value on your lovemaking if you gave her a present.'

'Well I am going back tonight and I will bring her some flowers. Do you think that will do the trick?'

'I was thinking about something more substantial, like a piece of gold jewelry.'

'Look Holly I can't afford to give her jewelry, I believe flowers will be enough. I would like to think she made love with me because she cared. What you tell me comes as a big blow to my self esteem.'

'I should have mentioned that she would expect a present.'

That night I went back to visit Yuk Soi armed with a bouquet of peonies, which I understood were a particular favorite of Chinese women. A young Chinese man opened the door. I checked the number to make sure I had the right place.

'I was looking for Miss Chen?'

'She's taking a bath. Who are you?' He looked at me inquiringly.

'I'm just a friend. I saw these flowers and they looked so pretty I thought I'd get some for her.'

'You don't have to wait. I'll give them to her.'

'Excuse me a minute, who are you?' I said, beginning to get annoyed.

'I'm her boyfriend. We have a date so if you don't mind leaving just give me the flowers and I will make sure she gets them.'

'I'm not sure I like this.'

'Did you have a date with Chen?'

'No. Not exactly. I did say I would see her tonight.'

'In English? She doesn't understand English.'

'Oh, is that right? And how long have you been her boyfriend?'

'What does that matter?'

'I just want to know.'

'Since … this afternoon.'

I was skeptical. Since this afternoon? If it was true, she certainly worked fast. I threw the flowers into the room. Holly was right. I didn't understand Chinese women. It was a great blow to my masculine pride. She had dumped me without even a *joi gin*.

17

THE MONKS OF BANGKOK

After a few months, I hit a dry spell in my TV and theatre commercial business. Some of the budgets offered by potential clients were too small to be believed, so I gave up the business temporarily. I started taking still pictures and with that I enjoyed immediate success.

We made a poster of a sampan girl for Cathay Pacific Airways which won first prize at a poster competition, and they hired us to do all their publicity photography. They didn't pay is in cash, but in 'contra.' Contra translates to air tickets in return for work done and after a short while we amassed about HK$100,000 worth of it and I had to figure out how to use it profitably. When business was slow I used a tactic I learned from my father. I phoned my old friend Lindy Johnson, managing director of Mandarin Textiles and made up a story.

'We're going on a trip to Bangkok and Singapore with three models for a client who is paying all the fees and expenses,' I told him. 'I got to thinking we could do you a favor and photograph the same models wearing Mandarin Textile garments. You would have to pay only HK$500 for each of the garments we photograph at temples in Bangkok, the waterfront in Singapore. All exotic Asian locations to show your garments, and worn by Hong Kong's top models, at negligible cost to you.'

'It sounds okay if there are no strings attached?'

'No strings. The only problem is that we're leaving the day after tomorrow, so I must have an immediate answer.'

'You say there would be a charge of $500 for each piece you shoot and we aren't responsible for any of the expenses?'

'Correct.'

'Well, if that is really the deal then I'm in.'

'That's great. How many garments can I count on?'

'We have, let me see, four spring dresses and ... six ... seven ... eight summer dresses. All together twelve items.'

'Fine. I'll come over tomorrow morning to pick them up and we'd like a check for half of the fee. The final payment when we get back with the finished work.'

I managed to snare two other dress manufacturers and then I hired the models at HK$1,500 each. That was a fraction of their regular fee, but I played up the fun — the all-expense-paid trip — and they bought it. Mei Ling Chan was Hong Kong's top model. The other two, Cora Yeung and Mandy Kwok were not as experienced but they were lovely and had perfect figures. The story I told the clients was not all together true but we were giving them something great, at bargain prices, so what's a little fib between friends?

The first stop on our itinerary was Bangkok where I fixed up free rooms at the Erawan Hotel by promising to take pictures of our models around the swimming pool in scanty bathing suits.

The morning after our arrival we jumped out of bed at 8 a.m. and the girls tried on the garments, stripping down to their bras and panties. I learned right from the outset I was going to have to get used to seeing scantily clad ladies as part of the job.

Bangkok has more than 500 Buddhist temples and we planned to do our initial shooting at one of the most lovely, the Marble Temple.

The responsibility of every Buddhist is to support the community of monks and every unselfish act earns merit. As we drove up to the Marble Temple we saw a family standing beside a table set with a large bowl of rice. Standing silently in front of them was a line of barefoot monks that had come on their 'alms rounds' with their 'begging bowls.' The father filled the bowls with rice, the daughter added some vegetables, the mother handed out long-stemmed lotus flowers and envelopes with money, and then the whole family bowed their heads and clasped their hands in the manner of prayer. Such scenes were common in Thailand. The food the family served was sufficient for the one meal a day a monk eats and it is written in Buddhist scripture that it is a transgression, if by nod or gesture, a monk shows that he anticipates or accepts a gift.

The Marble Temple has a roof of shiny orange and green tiles and tiny bits of glass inlaid in the alabaster structure that sparkle in the sunlight and give the building a rich, shimmering quality. I chose to set up shop just inside the temple (or 'wat') entrance in a courtyard where the monks came to sit on the stone benches and meditate.

We photographed Mei Ling and then Cora and just about the time we got to Mandy a group of monks appeared on the scene. All males in Thailand must enter a monastery sometime in their lives, shave their heads and dress in saffron-colored robes. The group that came to watch us was comprised mainly of young boys but I managed to persuade three of them to pose with our models. We were having a lot of fun and everything was going extremely well when an old monk appeared from across the iron bridge that led into the temple. He was fuming.

'Who in charge here?' he exclaimed, out of breath.

'I am,' I said, surprised at the interruption.

'Don't you know you must have permission to take this kind of picture here?'

'Oh, I'm really sorry. I didn't realize it.'

'And doing these dirty things.' He said with a shudder pointing to Mei Ling who was partly in and partly out of a dress and exposing a perfectly flat bare tummy

'I had no idea that anybody would be offended.'

The young monks crowded around and got a great kick out of the old guy haranguing us.

'It's my mistake asking these girls to change dresses in public like this. Would it be alright if they used the ladies restroom to change?'

'But you do not have permission of Abbot to take picture here.'

'Can you give us permission?'

'Oh no. You must get permission from Abbot.'

Just then Mei Ling came up and spoke to the monk in perfect Thai. I was shocked.

'Where did you learn to speak Thai?'

'I lived in Bangkok for eight years. My father had a business here.'

When I got over my surprise I asked her, 'Do you think you can talk this guy into letting us continue our shoot?'

'I'm afraid this man wouldn't dare assume the authority. But Buddhists are very reasonable, I think you have a good chance if you talk with the Abbot.'

She instructed the other girls to move all of the dresses to the ladies room, and she and I went to take on the head man.

The Abbot was very cordial. He spoke to Mei Ling in Thai and she straightened the matter out in a few minutes. He said we could shoot the remaining shots at the Marble Temple but we shouldn't use monks in the pictures. In any case, we had enough shots already with the monks.

After finishing at the Marble Temple we shot on the Chao Phraya River. We hired a peculiar-looking motor boat with a propeller shaft about eight feet long and a tiny propeller. It had a narrow hull and looked like an elongated canoe, but it moved very fast.

We stopped at a coal storage depot on the river where the coolies worked. We gave each one 20 baht to pose with our models and, covered head to toe with black dust, they made a stark contrast to our brightly colored garments.

Then we spent several hours shooting at the floating market where women sold fish, pork, fruit and vegetables out of small boats.

'The beers are on me,' I announced after the boatman had dropped us off and I had paid him 300 baht for almost five hours of taking us up and down the river. I picked out a picturesque restaurant on a houseboat that had huge windows overlooking the river. The walls and floors were a dark, polished mahogany and everywhere was the fragrance of fresh-cut flowers. Mei Ling excused herself to phone a friend.

The restaurant's scenery was augmented further by our waiter—a transvestite wearing a loose-fitting house dress, his long hair uncombed and the stubble of his beard just beginning to show through his makeup. He had slap dashed on some lipstick that wasn't fooling anyone and he gave me the impression of someone who went to a hell of a lot of trouble to look like a woman and didn't quite make it.

'Can I take your order?' he said with a high-pitched falsetto.

'Start us off with four big bottles of Singha and we'll order food later.'

Mei Ling passed the waiter as she came back up the stairs. She had returned with a European monk in white robes.

'This is Pra John,' she said making introductions. 'He tells me he is a monk with no fixed abode, am I right?'

'I'm actually a monk without portfolio,' he said with a perfect New York accent.

'A New Yorker?' I asked in amazement.

'An Italian from the Bronx, Pelham Parkway.'

'Will wonders never cease. What the heck are you doing in this part of the world?'

'It's a long story, but briefly, I was an MP in the Air Force stationed in Udorn. One day I detained a couple of monks who had strayed into an off-limits revetment. It was all very innocent and I interceded with the commanding officer for their release. They were grateful and invited me to their wat and we became good friends and over time I developed an interest in Buddhism. When I was going home to be discharged the monks persuaded me to stay in Thailand and become a monk.'

'Why the white robe?'

'For some reason, known only to them I couldn't be ordained a full monk and wear saffron-colored robes, but I was allowed to wear white robes. I can't be connected to a wat on a permanent basis so I move around from wat to wat. Sometimes I stay at the homes of devout Buddhists I meet. Right now I'm sleeping on the floor of a Scottish girl's apartment. She's planning to become a Buddhist nun.'

'You're living with a girl?' I was astounded.

'What's wrong with that?'

'Nothing, in my view, but what about your vows of chastity?'

'I respect the laws of the monkhood and I abstain from any sexual contact.'

'I don't understand. What is your job?' Cora asked, perplexed.

'Well, I have some money from my family and I travel around Laos and Cambodia and Thailand collecting Buddhist artifacts.'

'What do you do with them?' I asked.

'Most I keep to add to my collection, but to sustain myself I have to sell some of them. Usually to Chinese Buddhists.'

'Why Chinese?' With the mention of Chinese, Mei Ling instantly became interested.

'For many years the Chinese have dominated the economics of this country, so they have all the money. It's as simple as that.'

Pra John had a long, lean body and a beard and looked like a lot of artist renderings of Jesus Christ. His white robes were slightly frayed and could have used a good run through a washing machine. I invited him to have something to eat but he declined, saying that monks eat only one meal a day, but he consented to have some ice cream.

Out of his robes he started pulling small pieces of bamboo

fastened together with a string going through a hole at the top. He had about 30 pieces in all and on each one there were tiny words in an unfamiliar script and miniature colored drawings.

'This is one of the things I collect. It's actually a very old book written on bamboo and tells the story of Buddhism. It's not the whole story but I can give you a brief idea of what is written if you are interested.'

'I am very interested,' Mei Ling said.

'The words are written in Sanskrit and they recount the story of Siddhartha who was a prince of a warrior caste twenty-five hundred years ago. He grew weary of the opulence and decadence of the royal court and one day he set out wandering in the wilderness to find the true meaning of life. He shunned all worldly goods, dressed in rags and lived in poverty.'

'Something like you,' Mandy said, slightly callously.

'Yes, something like me,' Pra John said, smiling graciously at Mandy.

'In his travels he came upon a doddering old man, another man who was terminally ill and finally a dead body. At that point he realized that suffering is the common lot of human-kind. He forsook wealth and power in his quest for truth. He was an oral teacher and left no written work, but his thinking and way of life were put in writing by acolytes many years later. Through the centuries they have built shrines of incred-ible opulence to the poor, barefoot Lord Buddha.'

Pra John added, 'Not long ago they discovered a golden Buddha, over seven hundred years old and made of almost six thousand kilos of pure gold.'

Mei Ling was fascinated. 'May I get a closer look at your little book?'

'It is written in the classic language of India where Siddhartha was born,' he said, giving the book to Mei Ling.

'Here,' he said, 'keep it.'

'Oh, I couldn't accept it. It is such beautiful piece of art.'

'I want you to have it. It pleases me to know that it gives you pleasure. Please take it.'

'Thank you Jo ... Pra John. I will treasure it.'

For dinner we had *tom yum goong*, a spicy and sour soup laced with green and red chilies and chock full of fresh prawns and lemon grass. Once you got used to the hot spices and could taste the soup, it was delicious.

When Cora saw the little chilies floating around in the soup she declined her share.

'No, no. It'll give me *yit hei*.'

'*Yit hei*' is a malady that seems to strike only the southern Chinese and whose symptoms include headaches, discolored skin and pimples. It supposedly is caused by chilies, bread, cookies and a myriad of other foods and the only known cure is '*leung cha*,' a horribly bitter tea that the Cantonese swear by. Leung cha is served at special shops from great, ornamental copper cauldrons and they do a thriving business, but I have never known it to cure anything.

Just as we finished dinner Sarah, the Scottish 'girl friend' of Pra John, arrived. She taught English to young monks and lived just across the river in Thon Buri. I wondered how she could teach English with such a thick Scottish brogue. She wore no makeup, had a few freckles and dressed in a blouse that was opened at the neck and a skirt that came just slightly below her knees.

'What made you want to become a Buddhist nun?' I asked.

'I have a dream of liberating the exploited women of the world. Asian women, for instance, have always endured a lower status than men and have suffered the worst kind of oppression. Nuns have been made to play an inferior role to monks in the religious life. They wear white robes, so you can't mistake a nun for a monk.'

'You mean you couldn't tell the women from the men if they had the same color robes?' Mandy asked.

'Not always. They both shave their heads and Thai men often have very fair, soft skin like women. Nuns are assigned demeaning tasks like cleaning temples, eating mostly left-overs from the monk's meals and are not allowed to make alms rounds to get food and money. Besides a desire to live a spiritual life, I have strong feelings about the discrimination against women, and I want the opportunity to help the nuns achieve a more equitable status.'

Suddenly we heard a voice call from the stairwell.

'Where can I find Mei Ling Chan?' All heads turned.

It was Rolf Schneiter, a Swiss friend of Mei Ling's who worked for the well-known Swiss trading company Diethelm and Company. He was about 28 years old, six feet tall, and dressed in a flamboyant sport shirt with a huge flower pattern and a pair of light-colored slacks. He had a well-tanned, hand-some face and thick blonde hair, lightened by the sun.

'Here I am.' Mei Ling ran to him, kissed him on both cheeks and then introduced him around.

'How's business over at Diethelm?' she asked.

'Everything's fine, but let's not talk business. Night is the time for fun and Bangkok is the place for exciting nightlife. But tell me first, what brings you to the city?'

'I'm on a modeling job.' She indicated our group. 'These are my colleagues.'

He took a healthy swig of beer and addressed the whole group.

'In honor of Mei Ling Chan, my old carousing buddy, we are going to do some interesting things tonight. Is everybody game?'

'Thank you, no,' said Pra John. He and Sarah weren't interested in experiencing Bangkok's infamous nightlife.

After Rolf finished his beer, we piled into his car and headed for the Charvalat Club which was nothing but a high-class massage parlor. Not for massages as you would traditionally think of it, but Bangkok-style, which revolves around cheap and tawdry sex.

18

THE CHARVALAT STREET OF DREAMS CLUB

From the outside, the Charvalat looked garish. It was flanked by tall pillars and lit up with blazing lights and an enormous neon sign. In contrast, the interior lighting was so dim that it took our eyes several minutes to adjust. A floor manager with a flashlight greeted us and led us to plush, cushioned seats. We sat facing a glass enclosure filled with scantily clad females with numbers pinned to their bras.

'What are those girls are waiting for?' Mandy asked.

'They are waiting for us to pick out one of them and then they bathe and massage you,' Rolf said.

'Only girls? Don't they have men?' Cora asked with a skeptical look on her face.

'No, only girls, but they handle women customers, as well. I know Swissair stewardesses that come here and enjoy the service very much.'

'What is the service?' Cora asked.

'Anything you can think of.'

'I'm not interested in any hanky-panky with girls,' she said, holding her arms tightly.

Rolf called for number nine, his favorite, while I fancied number 14.

Mei Ling looked over the field and picked number six who, she observed, was quite cute.

'A good choice,' said the floor manager. 'Number six will give you excellent service.'

The manager suggested numbers 23 and 24 for Mandy and Cora, as they were especially for ladies. They were reticent.

'Oh, don't be so prissy,' Rolf said. 'It's just for fun. Nobody will tell your mother.'

The manager called the numbers into his walkie-talkie and the hostesses came out of the glass cage. It reminded one of an Arabian slave market where partially clad girls were sold to the highest bidder.

Rolf turned to Cora and Mandy and said, 'Have a drink, loosen up. Nothing here to get nervous about.'

A third round of drinks seemed to take the modesty out of everybody and Rolf announced that the time had come to move out. Each hostess picked up a wicker basket with soap and towels and we headed to our assigned rooms. They were a bit larger than the standard bathroom and the lighting was a dim, pink color. In the center of the room was a bathtub and massage table. The hostess stripped off her garments, started the water running and instructed me to take off my clothes and get in. She washed me thoroughly with a soft sponge and then asked me to get out and lie on the massage table with my entire body covered with soap suds.

Another girl came into the room, removed her clothes and lay down on the tiled floor and was soaped thoroughly by number 14. Then she returned the honors until both their bodies were swathed in suds. Then one of them got under me face up, and the other one got on top of me, face down. They both started moving rhythmically, very slowly, undulating their soapy bodies against mine. They didn't use their hands, only their legs and shoulders. They massaged my back, my neck and parts in-between. They kept up the erotic pressure on my body for more than 30 minutes and then it was finished. The second girl disappeared rather quickly and number 14 washed away my suds, dried my body and helped me on with my clothes.

Just about that time Rolf appeared at my door with a towel around his middle.

'What did you think of the sandwich gig? I set it up for you,' he said with a roguish smile.

'It was an experience I won't soon forget.'

A few minutes later the girls joined us. They looked fresh and clean — and not about to give us any details — so we walked to the desk and Rolf paid the entire bill with his Diethelm credit card.

'We have to be up early tomorrow morning so how about calling it a night?' I said, explaining that the girls needed to get their beauty sleep.'

'Where you will be in the early afternoon? Maybe we can connect up?'

'Yeah, that sounds like a good idea. We'll call you.'

The next morning we phoned Sarah, the wannabe nun and she and Pra John took us to a *wat* where we could photograph Buddhist nuns with our models. A natural, brilliant light came in a huge window and while our girls struck sophisticated poses in the foreground, the nuns performed their menial tasks in the background. Sarah was pleased and felt that we somehow brought out the inequalities of the male versus female syndrome, by showing the nuns doing their work against the backdrop of high fashion.

At 11 a.m. we called Rolf and told him to meet us at the Reclining Buddha Temple. Mandy had somehow sprained her ankle and Pra John recommended a monk at the temple who, he said, was a world renowned healer. I thought we could kill two birds with one stone, get Mandy healed and some colorful shots.

The healer's methods certainly weren't standard. He blessed the sore spot with a femur from a skeleton, waving it over Mandy several times like a band leader's baton. He put an assortment of ingredients into an old earthenware bowl and boiled them on a charcoal fire. Then he said some words over this elixir and dabbed the mixture on her sprained ankle. After the hocus-pocus was over, the monk said there was no charge, but it was usual to make an offering of 300 baht to the temple. We had to carry Mandy back to the car with no discernible difference in her condition, but we did get some excellent shots.

Rolf arrived and drove us to our hotel and we took a few shots of the girls in swimsuits around the hotel's elegant pool, a little more upscale than the canals or '*klongs*' where the poor folk swam. In the old days almost all of Bangkok's roads were canals, but they were gradually filled in to make more room for the burgeoning population. Cars took the place of boats and, as a result, Bangkok had one of the worst pollution problems in the world. The *klongs* that remained were filthy, but naked children still frolicked in their murky waters, dodging motor boats while their older sisters skillfully bathed underneath their sarongs without revealing much of anything.

We took to the streets and posed the girls alongside policemen directing traffic and wearing handkerchiefs tied over their noses as protection from the pollution. The pictures were fine, but the girls, after exposure to the exhaust pipes of hundreds of cars, trucks and *tuk-tuks*, spewing poisonous carbon monoxide, came off the location wheezing.

Rolf suggested we go to a Hungarian restaurant he knew for dinner and we all trooped off to catch a 'water bus.' The water buses were a cheap and easy form of transportation but you had to be ready to jump because the boats hardly spent 10 seconds at the pier. The coxswain docked and then sped away almost immediately, narrowly missing other vessels chugging more slowly up the river. If you didn't move quickly enough you'd end up in the canal. The boat had seating for 40 people, but if you wanted a little excitement you could hold on to a pipe rail, mounted on the gunnels, inches from the water.

Irene's Hungaria restaurant was picturesque with a lawn out front and a huge garden in the back with large mosquito repellent coils under each table. Rolf suggested we leave it to him to order and as we sat over a dessert of apple strudel I was thinking the meal wasn't bad but not exactly like mother used to make.

After dinner Rolf suggested we go to Patpong Road to continue the fun. At these words Pra John and Sarah jumped up and said they had to leave. All too soon we found out the reason. Patpong Road is the most infamous street in Bangkok. At the time it was particularly sordid, squalid and sometimes dangerous place full of pimps, prostitutes, transvestites, gay boys, lesbians, go-go girls, seedy massage parlors. And every one of the night clubs was a clip joint.

Patpong Road first achieved fame as a cheap entertainment venue for American GI's, but its notoriety spread and now included foreign contract workers and assorted European types. During the day it was a respectable section of Bangkok with banks, office buildings, a supermarket and a good bookstore, but at night it changed face and became a lowdown, vice-ridden area. The general consensus among the foreign population was that it was a fun street, but the 'virtuous' Thais would never be seen on Patpong Road. They felt it was better-suited to the prurient tastes of the barbaric 'white man.'

Clubs on Patpong have names like Hot Stuff Lovers, Fine Cat and Pussy Galore. We went to Whiskey A Go-Go where they sold cheap Thai whiskey at exorbitant prices, and had a team of tawdry, scantily clad go-go dancers with names like Lu Lu and Lollypop and Noy and Toy cadging 'whiskey' that purported to be the real thing, but was actually nothing but cold tea. We almost got slugged for refusing to pay for drinks foisted on us by the management. Rolf agreed to shell out the cash just so we could get out of the place in one piece.

After our experience at Whiskey A Go-Go, we wanted to leave the infamous street, but Rolf convinced us to go to just one more place that he said was 'a load of laughs.' It was a private peep show with any combination you wanted. Man and woman, woman and woman, man with two women, man and man. Well if you think watching an emaciated middle-aged man getting it on with a plump woman with varicose veins on a broken-down filthy bed is entertainment then you may be as sick as we felt.

'Oh my god,' Cora shrieked, speaking for all of us. 'This is really disgusting. Let's get out of here.'

Rolf regretted his mistake, but Patpong Road aside, he was generous and gregarious and we had a great time with him. He came to our hotel to say goodbye and disappeared into the bar with Mei Ling. I shouted after her that we were meeting at 8:30 the following morning for our 11 a.m. plane to Singapore.

19

COLLYER QUAY

The morning after our arrival in Singapore I met the girls for breakfast in the Tiffin Room at the Raffles. The three Sarkies brothers started a hotel in 1886 called the Tiffin Room and that establishment eventually became the Raffles Hotel, taking its name from the first British explorer to discover the island, Sir Stamford Raffles. Other than the name change the hotel hadn't changed much in the last 70 years. Sure, it sagged a bit around the edges and I spotted the occasional cockroach, but it retained a certain colonial opulence with turbaned Sikh doormen, little touches of the old days and the Long Bar—reputedly the longest bar in the world and home of the famed Singapore Sling.

The Tiffin Room featured an amazing circular skylight about 40 feet straight up with the walls and ceilings painted in light blues and tans that gave the place a feeling of a bright summer morning. Tiffin translates as 'luncheon' in the Hindu dictionary but at Raffles the Tiffin Room served breakfast as well and I ate a traditional English breakfast of kippers and milk tea while we discussed the day's agenda.

Mei Ling took over the dress selection and when all was ready girls and garments piled into a cab and we told the

driver to take us to Collyer Quay, close to the center of town
and near the Singapore River. Sailors of all countries disem-
barked at the pier there so we thought there would be some
interesting scenes to photograph.

But we hadn't gone far when we came across a large group
of leftist students from the Chung Hwa Middle School pro-
testing against the authorities in Singapore. They wore school
uniforms, white open-necked shirts emblazoned with white
ducks and the name of the school. They looked harmless.

The police had set up a road block at an intersection and
the protesters shouted, raising their fists, demanding to be let
through. We needed to get through so I got out of the taxi and
asked the policeman in charge how we could get around the
crowd.

'No can do. The barricade is to contain this mob and it stays
in place,' he said.

The girls followed me out of the cab to see what was going
on and Mei Ling walked up to the barricade. Suddenly, all
hell broke loose. The kids on the other side started pushing
and shouting and made a grab for her. I pulled her out of the
way and the whole barricade caved in and I found myself in
the midst of screaming, clawing Chinese youths. My shirt got
ripped up the back and then a group of them came at me,
knocked me to the ground and started pummeling me with
their fists. Escape was out of the question, there were just too
many of them. I tried hitting back but that just brought more
attackers. Then on a word from their leader, a group of them
held my arms and pinned me to the ground. He signaled for
silence as he spoke to the police.

'We want to continue our march. If you use tear gas on us
or your batons we will not be responsible for what happens to
this man. If you allow us to carry on our demonstration we
will disperse and free him when we get to Orchard Road and

we want those girls and the taxi out of here. Now.'

'Wait a minute,' Mei Ling complained.

The leader pointed his finger threateningly.

'Get out,' he shouted.

They quickly got into the taxi, the driver spun the car around and exited the area with all haste, leaving me behind with the mob. There I was, pinned to the ground by a group of teenagers, my nose was bleeding and I had cuts on my face and my arms were scraped from being dragged along the pavement. I had planned a pleasant day shooting fashions and now was held by a screaming pack of leftist students. I was in very real danger. My only hope was the police standing by. They tried to reason with the students to release me but they wouldn't hear of it.

'Look,' the chief inspector said, a tanned Englishman, dressed in the standard Singapore police riot gear, short khaki pants with a black steel helmet on his head.

'I cannot negotiate with you while you are holding a hostage. Release the man and I will let your march continue to Orchard Road.'

'Liar,' screamed the leader. 'I don't believe you.'

'We don't want any harm to come to an innocent person. You just want to carry on your protest march to Orchard Road, and that is okay, but you must release this man first.'

'Why must you have so many police here? I want them to pull back.' The student leader started dictating terms.

'Okay. Anything is possible, but first release the hostage.'

The mob in the throes of victory became so involved in the conversation between their leader and the police inspector that they loosened their hold on me, for a split second. The police, looking for just such an opening, rushed in and started to assault the students. They beat them over the head, mercilessly with their batons, clobbered them across their backs, and ruthlessly thrust the hard rubber missile into their stomachs. They fired tear gas into the crowd at the rear that was surging forward. The police grabbed me and pulled me out of harm's way and then opened up full force on the students.

There were smashed eyeglasses scattered everywhere in the street and many bloodied faces in the crowd. A crowd of policemen surrounded the students and made them lie, face down, on the ground. The advantage had shifted rapidly to the police.

'Are you alright?' the chief inspector asked me.

'Just scraped elbows and my face feels like it has been stepped on, but I guess I'm okay.'

I looked at the students, now completely cowed.

'What are you going to do with them?'

'We're going to take them to a prison compound and then I am prepared for the school principal and their irate parents to lay into us for using excessive force on their children.'

'Do you need my testimony?'

'No. There are plenty of witnesses. We have them on incitement to riot, holding a hostage and several infractions of the new laws to control violent protests. I would charge them with attempted murder if I thought it would stick. These kids are dyed in the wool Communists and I don't think they would have hesitated to kill you if they felt it was to their advantage to do so.'

'Well, thank god for the police.'

'What are you doing in Singapore?'

'We are here from Hong Kong, doing fashion photography and had hoped to work on Collyer Quay today. Getting mixed up in the politics of Singapore was not our intention.'

'In a short while this road will be opened so you can go to Collyer Quay without a problem but you look a proper mess. I will send you back to your hotel in a police car.'

The three girls were waiting for me in the lobby when I arrived, all battered and bloody with my shirt in shreds. Singapore hadn't seemed to us such a violent place but later we learned that Bob Symonds, the UP bureau chief, had been killed that very morning in another section of town by a different mob of teenagers.

The girls were very solicitous attending to my wounds, and then left me there to rest until lunchtime.

That afternoon, we tried again and this time we made it to Collyer Quay, an old covered pier in the heart of downtown Singapore. And we had a double treat. The Russian navy was in port and so were the Americans. We got representatives of each to pose with the girls in full uniform with the pier and boats as background. We also got a couple of seamen wearing sarongs from the wooden sailing ships that came from the Indonesian Spice Islands. The girls had to make use of an insalubrious ladies room to change clothes though. They were all for changing behind one of the billboards but having been a sailor myself I thought it best to keep them away from the prying eyes of the navy.

At the conclusion of the shoot I treated everybody to drinks. The Indonesian sailors hardly spoke at all. They drank a couple of beers and went on their way. The Russians couldn't speak one word of English, but the Americans hung around and succeeded in making dates with the girls for later that evening. Then we took our bundle of dresses and slack suits to a site on the Singapore River about 10 minutes from

Collyer Quay. We crossed the old Cavenagh Bridge, standing since 1867 to commemorate Singapore's founding as a British Crown colony. We set up headquarters at a dockside warehouse or 'godown' and while the girls changed I explored the location.

The street was cut down the middle by the river and it had a profusion of godowns on both sides of the road. The area was aptly named by the Chinese, Bu Ye Tian or 'place of ceaseless activity.' The street was loaded with photogenic action and I found the citizens of Singapore very friendly and interested in what we were doing.

Coolies, hauling 100 pound bales of raw latex, their muscular bodies shining with sweat, were fabulous subjects for our pictures. We photographed truck drivers supervising the loading of their lorries and a group of men weighing cane rods on an industrial scale. The models came up with great poses to set off the action.

When we had finished, the warehouse boss invited us to have ice cold coconut milk with a shot of sweet mint juice. He furnished us with an electric fan and conversed with the girls in Cantonese. The mob of spectators just stared at the girls and followed us around noiselessly until we climbed into a taxi and headed back to the Raffles.

20

BUGIS STREET

With the three models dating the American Navy for the night I was free to do as I pleased, and I had a fine roast beef dinner at the hotel. After dinner I sought out the Sikh doorman, the supposed expert on such matters, to ask his advice on what to do with the rest of the evening.

'What do you mean, Sahib? Girls, I guess? I have telephone numbers I can call.'

'No. No. I am looking for a different kind of fun. I'd like to see some of the lowdown joints.'

'You don't want to meet high class ladies sir, that you can take dancing?'

'Oh, definitely not. I just want to see what a Singapore red light district looks like. Just to see it, you know.'

'Oh.' It finally got through. 'I see what you mean. If you want to see some very interesting red light place you should go to Deska Lane. They have many girls there, but it not a clean place. Girls cost you $10 Singapore money for short time. But don't tell people at front desk I send you there.'

'Of course not. But that sounds exactly like what I want. Is it far away?'

'Only about eight minutes in taxi.'

Was I ever that good looking? I had the third lead in a Broadway show called 'Pick Up Girl,' a moderate hit in 1944. But World War II ended my Broadway career when I was drafted into the Navy.

Aboard the USS Norris DD859 with shipmates in 1945. At exactly the middle of the Pacific Ocean we received word from the captain that the war was over. I'm second on the right.

Filming junks in Aberdeen, after my move to Hong Kong. I'm on the far left.

Famed shot of me being dragged away by Hong Kong police, at the insistence of Two Gun Cohen, Sun Yat-sen's former bodyguard.

Morris 'Two Gun' Cohen served as an aide-de-camp for Sun Yat-sen and, later, a series of southern Chinese leaders. He did not like being filmed.

An American friend with one of the 'sisters' of Singapore's infamous Bugis Street, famed for its nightly gathering of transvestites.

Ah Mary. She was a rare beauty, back when we got married in 1957.

Behind the camera on location in Singapore.

I hovered at 95 feet to get this picture of Hong Kong's World Trade Center which was under construction at the time.

Shooting the bull with Vietnam buddies. I covered the war for over 10 years, from 1963 until its end in 1975.

Filming the Vietnam war. When I wasn't getting any footage the camera was unbearably heavy, but once I was filming it became miraculously light.

On the Great Wall of China.

Deska Lane is only one block long with a sidewalk running the length of the lane from where you could view the action— women dressed in flimsy nightgowns, sitting in doorways of little houses with a dim pink light coming from a single light bulb. The narrow path was crowded with groups of men in an endless line. Occasionally a man stepped out of the line and went to the door to get a closer look at what was available. If he liked her then he bargained the price. The women joked in English, Malay and a myriad of Chinese dialects with potential customers. At the end of the lane, at house number 36, I thought I would go over and talk to one of the 'girls.'

'You English?' she asked.

'No. American.'

'Oh, that very good. You know Davy Jones from USS Norris, DD859?'

'No, I don't believe I've made his acquaintance.'

'Davy's a swell guy. He see me every time he come Singapore and he always bring me a present.' She picked up a snapshot of a young sailor. 'This his picture.'

'Oh, he looks to be a handsome guy.'

'Okay, but don't waste my time. You want a little pussy? Twenty-five dollars for a short time. Fifty for a long time.'

'What is a short time?'

'Just until you come. A long time, one hour. Davy always take long time. He likes talk and smoke ganja.'

'What's that?'

'Hashish. In the States they call 'joint."

She became impatient. 'So come on, you want girl?'

I took a perfunctory glance at number 36, whose age I guessed to be about 45. She was plump and sloppy looking. Her hair was done up in paper curlers and she was missing a couple of teeth in the front. She watched me closely, waiting for an answer as to what price range I preferred. I wanted to extricate myself as neatly as I could so I figured that if I gave her a few dollars it would more than compensate her for her time.

I looked at my watch. 'Gee, I didn't realize it was so late. I have to get back home now. Why don't I just give you $5 to pay for your time. I'm sorry.'

'Give me $15.'

I took a $10 bill out of my pocket and gave it to her.

'I'm sorry but I really have to go.'

'Yeah. Just get the hell out of here,' she said angrily.

So that was Deska Lane. Besides a collection of women to whom life had not been kind, I figured it was probably infested with cockroaches and rats. It was a sad place.

I walked to a street close by and was waiting on the corner for a taxi when a very attractive young girl approached me.

'Anything I can do for you?' she asked.

'I was just looking for a taxi.'

'You won't find one in this neighborhood.'

She had a very pretty face and wore a short mini skirt that showed off her shapely legs.

'Well, how do I get out of here then?' I said.

'Buy me an ice cream, and we'll see what we can figure out.'

'Okay, it's a deal.'

We sat on the stoop of an apartment house typical of the district, licking chocolate ice cream cones.

'You've been to Deska Lane, haven't you? Are you looking for a date?'

I didn't answer directly. 'How old do you think the women

on Deska Lane are?'

'I don't know. Maybe some are fifty years old and some even older.'

'Do you live near here?'

'No, but I can use my friend's room.' She indicated a place across the street.

'How much do I have to pay?'

'It's all up to you. Whatever you can afford.' She watched my face for a long second.

'You bought me an ice cream and seem like a nice guy, so I don't want to fool you.' She looked at me seriously. 'Things are not always what they seem to be at first glance.'

'What do you mean 'things are not always what they seem to be?''

I began to suspect that this sweet little girl was not a sweet little girl at all.

'Do I look like a boy?'

'Frankly no, but in Singapore I heard there are boys that masquerade as girls.'

'Do you like boys?' he asked.

'Well as boys, yes, but I don't think I could go to bed with one. Does that hurt your feelings?'

'Of course not. Sometimes I get a straight guy who is curious. Sometimes I get a guy who is so drunk that he doesn't care what I am. Ever been to Bugis Street?'

'No. What's that?'

'It's a night spot. It has open air restaurants and is the most popular meeting place in Singapore for boys like me. You can get beer and noodles there and watch the action, and pick up a boy if that is what you like. But it doesn't get rolling until after midnight. Would you like to go?'

'Maybe another time. I have to be up early in the morning for work.'

'What do you do?'

'I'm a photographer and I'm sorry I don't have a camera with me. I would really like to take your picture.'

'Oh really? You know I have been a photographer's model.'

Suddenly an idea struck me.

'Do you have any friends on Bugis Street? I could hire you as models for my fashion photographs.'

'What a wonderful idea. What kind of clothes would we wear?'

'Well, you'll be posing with my models, so you can wear any dress you have that you feel would be attractive and sexy.'

'I can find a few girls to pose. What would it pay?'

'Fifty dollars each for about an hour of your time. And we'd shoot right there on Bugis Street.'

'Oh, that's marvelous.'

'I must really go home now, but what do you say about meeting us tomorrow in Bugis Street at midnight with your friends? Four of you is all I can afford.'

'It's a date. Make sure you show up,' he said, shaking a cautionary finger at me.

'Don't worry, we'll be there,' I said, we exchanged names and went our separate ways.

The next morning at 7 a.m. I got a call from Susan Tan of the Singapore office of Mandarin Textiles. She said that Lindy had cabled her that we were coming and that she should give me any assistance she could. She was in the lobby.

I got out of bed, showered, put on a pair of slacks and a sport shirt and went down to the lobby to meet Susan Tan, who was 28 years old and a looker. She was very casually dressed with a tank top, a miniskirt that showed off a pair of very shapely legs and comfortable jogging shoes. Chinese women are usually very concerned about letting their skin burn, and go to great lengths to stay out of the sun, but not Susan. She sported a very handsome tan.

She told me she was manager of Lindy's Singapore office and worked with a guy that was a sort of gofer and chauffeur. She visited customers in Singapore and Malaya and could speak fluent Hokkien, Mandarin, Cantonese, Malay and of course English.

'What about shooting at a kampong today?' she said. 'It's a typical Malay village with houses on stilts and teams of bullocks pulling old style carts and such things. It's very colorful.'

'Sounds great. I'll wake up the girls.'

We boarded the spacious and air-conditioned company van and headed out into the Malayan countryside to Kampong Boyan, a small tapioca-producing village on the outskirts of the city. The distinctive kampong houses Susan had mentioned were built of teak with roofs of thatched palm leaves and elevated on stilts for ventilation and to prevent flooding during the monsoon season. The farmers kept their livestock and carts in the space under the house.

According to protocol, Susan introduced us to the village head and over a cup of tea she asked permission to photograph in the kampong. This took about a half hour and was spoken in Bahasa Malay. After the negotiations we just sat there twiddling our thumbs for almost another hour while we waited for Susan to finish the meeting.

The village head had agreed to us starting work immediately, but for modesty's sake he suggested the models changed clothes inside the house.

While the girls changed, I studied the village head's parrot. He had a green body and red head with black lines across his face. The bird wasn't in a cage, but perched on a wooden bar and had a chain on its leg. I tried to pet him and before I knew what was happening he rose up, fluttered his wings wildly, let out ear-shattering screams and tried to take a piece out of my arm with his sharp beak. One of the young sons of the house laughed and said something in Malay to Susan.

'Very funny. If he wasn't chained, that creature could have pecked out my eyes.'

'In the first place it is a 'she' not a 'he' and the boy says that the bird always attacks strange men, but is very gentle with women.'

Mei Ling came out wearing an orange silk dress that had a multihued flower print. It contrasted nicely with the dark wood of the porch walls and with the flamboyant green of the parrot's feathers.

'I want to get some shots with you and that parrot.'

'Not with me you don't. One thing I know is that parrots are very fierce.'

'This one is calm, especially with women. Believe me. Come on over and pet her.'

Mei Ling approached cautiously, petted the bird and finally agreed to the shot. Susan took off the leg chain and Mei Ling carried the parrot on her finger.

Cora came out more formally attired in a white dress with a shiny black leather belt drawn tightly at the waist. Her hair was rolled up into a bun and she held a white kitten in her hands and stood dreamily looking out from the veranda past waves of flame-colored flowers. In the background, bullock carts moved lazily over the dirt streets.

After finishing at the farm we went to a nearby rubber plantation. Apparently the rubber tappers only work early in the morning when the latex flows freely. We did manage to get one young Tamil girl, about 15 years old with a gold ring attached to her nostril, to strip a bit of bark off one of the trees and get a little sap running. She had very black skin and big beautiful brown eyes and was clothed in a torn, dirty dress that scarcely hid her naked breasts.

I got shots of the models posing alone and in pairs alongside the tapper who did her work with a long, curved stripping knife, and then wide angles showing the models in their brightly colored frocks with the dark forest of rubber trees in the background.

Except for my almost being eaten alive by that wicked bird we had a pretty fair shoot at Kampong Boyan.

'Now, I think we should go back to Raffles. We can relax a few hours, have a leisurely dinner and then I have a special treat planned. At midnight we're going to shoot in Bugis Street. I hired a bunch of gorgeous gals to assist us.'

'What do you mean 'gals.' On Bugis Street you could only mean boy-girls?' Susan said, correcting me.

'What?' said the three models in unison.

'Last night when I was poking around the seamy side of town I ran into one of those sort of guys and I made a deal for him to work with us and get three more 'girl-boys' to use as models.'

'So who did you met?' Mei Ling asked.

'His name is Baba.'

'Is she, or he, cute?'

'I don't know. I just met him on the street, mistook him for a girl, and over ice cream we reached a deal to shoot in Bugis Street. That's all that happened, sorry Mei.'

'You bought him ice cream? Isn't that cozy?'

'I've lived here all my life and I've never come in contact with those sort of guys. Singaporeans know they exist, but

Bugis Street is more an attraction for tourists and the British forces,' Susan said.

It was exactly midnight when we arrived at Bugis Street, and when Baba came to greet us the girls checked him out like he was a creature from outer space. 'He's adorable,' Mei Ling said. 'How could you resist?'

'I have a table over here,' Baba said, taking Mei Ling's arm.

We were led through a labyrinth of gawking tourists to a large table located next to a kitchen with a sign that read, 'Mee Hoon & Curried Lamb.' At the table were the 'girls' that Baba promised us, and they were dressed in their Sunday best for the occasion.

There was a tall number named Cherry. The sultry type, he wore a satin dress with a tiger motif and had extra long fingernails, painted black. Then there was a pretty Malay named Karina who wore a yellow floor-sweeping sarong with a long slit at the side that showed more than a bit of leg. The gown was bare at the shoulders and revealed the beginnings of a generous pair of breasts and he carried a dainty silk purse. Baba wore a black miniskirt with a gold stripe on the side and a gold belt around the midsection with a short, ivory silk blouse that was tied to show off a bare midriff at the bottom and a soupcon of breast at the top.

On the opposite side of the table was a 40-something who Baba introduced as Mrs. Puteh. Mrs. Puteh was obviously the boss of the outfit as they all spoke to him respectfully and he seemed to be keeping an eye on them. He wore a simple cotton frock with a flower pattern and his wavy hair was dyed slightly red and combed neatly. He had plucked eyebrows, a touch of face powder, light lipstick and was a little on the stout side. Baba whispered that if I didn't feel Mrs. Puteh was right for the pictures he was prepared to step down in place of someone younger.

'Oh don't do that. He's fine, perfect,' I said.

Baba's girls were serious workers, but great fun and well worth the $50 we paid them. We photographed hilarious scenes all around Bugis Street and had the full cooperation of a Guard's regiment who held our bogus females on their laps, feeding them noodles while our real girls modeled their garments all around them. The conviviality of Bugis Street put our models in the mood and their posing was inspired and the antics of the 'she-males' was side splitting. When we had finished we ordered some *mee hoon* and curried lamb and bottles of Tiger beer.

'I was wondering about your plans for your future,' I asked Baba. 'What will you do when you're older?'

'Well, I would like to make enough money for an operation and cut my … thing off and have it replaced so I could become a real woman. I want to go to Denmark and have it done by a real surgeon. I know several girls who have had the operation. They have sex and everything and are living like ladies. One friend of mine got married to a British sailor and she lives in England and is very happy and they are trying to have a baby.'

Was he kidding? Mrs. Puteh had her ear bent in our direction, and I asked her, 'What do you think of Baba having the operation?'

'I think it's crazy. I have everything I want without that stupid operation. I have many lovers and couldn't be happier. Besides it's a pipe dream, Baba will never have enough money to leave Singapore.'

Karina put in a few words, 'I agree with Baba and there are ways of getting money.'

Cherry said, 'Why become a real woman? It's no secret that nine out of 10 women wish they were men. As we are both, we have the best of two worlds.'

'How do you figure that?' Mei Ling asked.

'We are already men and we can be women anytime we want by dressing like a woman. I get an erotic sensation from silk under things and a designer dress. I definitely identify with that side of my personality,' Cherry said.

'Have you ever had sex with a woman?' Mei Ling asked.

'Yes, once,' he whispered and looked at Mrs. Puteh to make sure she didn't hear.

'I picked her up. Or she picked me up, right here in Bugis Street.'

'Oh that's interesting. Tell me about it.'

'There were several of us around the table with a big party of German tourists. We were all drinking beer and feeling good. This woman, Erica, was with her husband and was sitting next to me and she kept asking me personal questions. Could she touch my breasts and how big was my private part? She even put her hand under my skirt.'

'Oh it's not very big,' she told me.

'It gets bigger when I get hot.'

'Can a woman get you hot?' she asked me.

'Why not? Give me $25 and $10 for the hotel and watch me react. What do you say?'

She looked warily at her husband. 'I'll do it,' she said.

'He was so drunk he didn't realize she was picking his pocket for the money. We stole away from the group and got a room in that little hotel across the road and she made love to me.'

'Did she like it?'

'Oh, very much. She was really excited and kept giving me big wet kisses. She wouldn't let me take off my dress. Only the panties. I think she was a little kinky.'

Mei Ling was surprised. 'Did you get an erection?'

'Why not? The experience was very interesting, but I'd much rather have had her husband.'

'What do you think Mei? Do you want to try?' I asked.

'Okay, but I want Baba.'

'Sorry, no women for me,' Baba said apologetically. 'I think you are very attractive, but I never had a woman and I am not about to start tonight. I'm sure that Cherry would oblige you.'

Mei Ling reflected. 'No, no. I guess if you're not interested I'll forgo the experience.'

21

ZHOU ENLAI

The Auricon sound camera was designed to use 100-foot-long rolls of film that ran two-and-a-half minutes. This was really too short for newsreels but some forgotten genius figured out that if he could cut away the 100-foot-long magazine and replace it with a 400-foot-long version then the camera could record for longer. So he found a hacksaw, got to work on the Auricon and overnight that became the industry standard. It worked well almost all the time but on one crucial assignment it abandoned me. That catastrophic screw up involved one of the foremost political figures of our time.

Alan Stein was a wealthy businessman from Van Nuys, California who had connections at KTLA, the biggest and most prestigious TV station in Los Angeles and in his free time he covered news stories in Asia for them. He had some routine business which had made him rich, but which he kept secret because he wanted to project the image of an intrepid news correspondent.

I first met him when he hired me as cameraman for a story about a U.S. Army DC-3 that crashed just moments after takeoff on its way back to Taiwan. To get to the crash site we climbed up the very steep Mt. Butler in a rain storm, slogging through thick mud and slime.

When we arrived, paramedics were already covering the bodies and preparing to take them down the mountain. Parts of the aircraft had exploded and were spread over a wide area of the hillside. Police guarded the site, shivering from the wet and the cold. It was a distressing scene.

We were greeted with typical warmth by chief inspector Shelley of the Hong Kong police. 'What the hell are you doing here Farkas?'

'Mr. Stein here is the correspondent from KTLA and...'

'Who told you that you could come up here?'

'We just assumed...'

'Don't assume, just turn around and go back down.'

'We just want to get a few shots and then we'll go.'

'Am I speaking English or Hottentot? Don't take any shots and go down the mountain, now,' he said.

'Look inspector,' Alan spoke up, 'I have a satellite reserved for tonight and KTLA is standing by for the story. We only need about ten minutes to do the filming and we have authorization from Government Information Services to cover it.'

'Not this story you don't. If you don't want your press cards confiscated you will get off this mountain, pronto. You know I can arrest you.'

'On what charge?' I asked.

'Disobeying my orders. Now get off the mountain.' He was incensed.

'Is there something that makes this different from other plane crashes?' Alan asked.

'No questions, just go.'

We were frustrated but couldn't disobey a direct order from the chief inspector, surrounded by subordinates, so we had to leave the mountain.

'He looked serious,' Alan said. 'Why do you suppose he is so pigheaded about our staying here?'

'I don't know. Maybe something is on the plane they don't want us to see. Aw Christ, after all the trouble we had getting up, we have to go back down in all that mud and muck and what's worse we don't have a thing to show for it. I am sorry about your satellite.'

'Oh, that was bullshit about the satellite. I was just giving it the old college try.'

He called me up the next afternoon with another assignment. He sounded excited and asked to meet me at the FCC immediately. He arrived in a cab carrying a valise.

'Can you travel?' he said.

'Of course.'

'Then tonight we head for Bandung in Indonesia to interview Zhou Enlai.'

'What?' I replied in amazement. 'That's marvelous. How the hell did you arrange that?'

'It was all fixed up by the KTLA stringer at the Bandung conference. Our plane departs at 6:30 p.m. Can we make it?'

'We've got to make it.'

After rushing to get visas we checked our bags at the Pan Am ticket counter and while waiting for the departure we went to the restaurant for a sandwich. We were chatting and oblivious to the time when I noticed a Pan Am plane taxiing to the runway.

'Could that be our flight?'

'Oh my god,' was all Alan could say.

We rushed to the Pan Am check-in desk and there on the monitor was Flight 22 listed as 'DEPARTED.'

'How can this be?' Alan said, pleading after the fact. 'We were having a coffee and the plane left without warning.'

'You should have checked the monitor,' the agent said unsympathetically.

'They don't have a monitor in the restaurant.'

'They are all over the airport. You should have checked.'

'What are we going to do?'

The agent apprised us of our options.

'Garuda has a flight leaving at 7:30 a.m. tomorrow morning and I could get you on that. It reaches Jakarta by early afternoon and you can get a flight for Bandung at 3:15 p.m. Are you interested?'

'Definitely. By the way, what happened to our bags?'

'They are on our flight. I'll send a telex and let them know you will be arriving on the Garuda flight and that your bags left without you.'

I don't know why, but working with Alan seemed to be ill-fated. On our first story we had climbed Mt. Butler in a rain-storm, slogging through mud and got nothing. Now this time round, our interview with one of the world's great leaders was in jeopardy. Our appointment with Zhou Enlai was at 11 a.m. the next morning so Alan phoned his stringer in Jakarta and tried to put it off until late afternoon.

We arrived at Bandung airport the next morning and were met by the stringer, a bespectacled girl named Nelly. She recognized us immediately, smiled and waved two thumbs up as a sign of success.

'We meet Mr. Zhou at the press facility at 5 p.m. We must get your press passes and a release for the equipment. It must be checked out before you can take it into the conference hall. Then we should go and set up quickly as there isn't much time.'

Thanks to Nelly, the people at the press office were already waiting for us and they accommodated us with all due haste. Then at the entrance to the conference hall we had to endure a crew of inspectors going through every piece of equipment we had. They checked out the film cans, unscrewed the headphones and made us hook up the sound amplifier to the camera so they could see that it was not a dummy, concealing a bomb. They were very thorough and it was tiresome for us, but I guess it had to be done.

Once in the press room Nelly set up a comfortable chair for our distinguished subject. I positioned the camera and the lights and she put on a pair of headphones and arranged the mikes. Everything was prepared and then in less than 10 minutes Mr. Zhou arrived accompanied by a man from the Chinese Embassy's information office. He shook hands with us all and we were ready to begin.

Less than 30 seconds into the interview I heard a noise from inside the camera and had to stop the shooting. I switched the camera off, and then on. It made that terrible noise again and then stopped. Alan turned to me in dismay.

'What's wrong?'

'I'll have to open the camera. It'll be just one second.' Alan looked worried.

'I'm sorry sir,' he told Mr. Zhou. 'Just a problem with the camera. It'll just be a minute.'

I opened the camera and found that the film had jammed

in the gate. I tried looping it through again and it jammed again. I thought it might be the magazine so I changed it and tried again. Same problem.

'If you can bear with me a moment, sir, I think the magazine motor needs adjusting.'

I sat on the floor and took the magazine off, got out my tools and started fiddling with screws on the motor. I didn't actually know what I was doing and when I tried it again it still didn't work. Mr. Zhou Enlai, prime minister of the People's Republic of China, sat there and smiled. And truly, I must have looked comical sitting on the floor, surrounded by tools, attempting to fix the camera.

Alan came over, trying to look cool.

'What can we do?' he whispered nervously.

'I don't know. If Mr. Zhou has the time I can perhaps find another camera,' I said out loud.

Mr. Zhou nodded in a friendly way and told me to get another camera. Sweating, I asked Nelly to join me and we left Alan trying to engage the Chinese leader in small talk.

Nelly, of course didn't know where to get another camera, but she said there was a photo studio just down the block and we could ask them. Failing that we would just have to go back and tell them the interview was off.

Nelly got into an extended conversation with the man in the photo shop. I had given up all hope.

'He has one,' she said.

'What? Where? Can I see it? What kind is it?'

'I don't know. We'll see.'

The man came out of the backroom with a large wooden box marked Auricon. I was elated. It was a huge camera with 1,200 foot magazines and worked off the main electricity source instead of batteries. I'd heard about them but I had never seen one before. I asked Nelly if we could hire this guy to help us work the camera. She said that he didn't have a press pass, beside it was his father's camera and he didn't know how to operate it. We made a deal and bought two 1,200-foot rolls of film from him and then hurried back to the conference hall.

We couldn't convince the inspectors that they should give this camera a hasty inspection so they took about 15 minutes to inspect every part. I was sure that Mr. Zhou had already deserted us. It was 45 minutes since we left him there to shoot the bull with Alan. As we opened the door we saw Alan laughing at a joke that Mr. Zhou had made. They were getting along fine.

I instructed Alan and Nelly to set up the monster tripod while I loaded the magazines. I figured out the loading system very fast and we hooked up the microphones to the amplifier. We tested it. Everything seemed to be working alright. We started again.

We were lucky this time. We had just kept a world leader sitting around for almost an hour. He was more than understanding but it might just as well have gone the other way. So I figure you can never completely rely on mechanical devices like the Auricon camera. As perfect as they might seem, something can always go wrong. What can you do? Learn to pray.

22

MARY

I find the combination of saltwater, itchy sand and beating sun extremely unpleasant, so I seldom go swimming at the beach. Sometimes though, when a friend browbeats me into it, I reluctantly agree to accompany him.

My pal Dicky Woo worked in the control tower at Kai Tak airport and his one claim to fame was eloping with Dorothy Shaw, the daughter of Run Run, the film magnate who was considered the L.B. Mayer of Chinese films. When Run Run found out about the marriage he offered Dicky $100,000 to annul the nuptials and just go away, which Dicky happily agreed to do.

One Sunday he got me to accompany him to one of the grubbiest beaches in existence — Repulse Bay. Aptly named, as far as I was concerned. The sand hid all kinds of garbage, so you had to be very careful where you stepped and you were always wary of the nature of what was crawling around or floating in the water. Nonetheless another friend Guy Searls, the one who had helped set me on my course as a news cameraman, rented a hut for the season on that beach where he entertained mainly Asian airline stewardesses. About 30 years old and a perennial bachelor, the girls fondly called him 'Uncle Guy' because of his mother hen attitude of looking after them.

Guy had built up one of the most comprehensive files of mainland China bigwigs in existence, giving the facts and figures of even the most obscure Communist officials in the most obscure locations. Americans weren't allowed into China at the time and 'China watching' was widely practiced, so Guy's file was a handy facility for China reporters. When he wasn't broadcasting for CBS radio or working on his files, he could be found under an extra wide umbrella in front of his hut with about five or six lovelies around him. He was lolling about on the beach one day when an urgent cable from his boss arrived at the CBS Hong Kong office.

'Proceed all haste Musoori India for story Tenzin Gyatso 14th Dalai Lama spiritual leader Tibetan Buddhism ruler forced flee over Himalayas when Chinese Communists occupied his country stop Dalai Lama believed living reincarnation of Buddha greatly revered by his people stop Cannot stress too much historic implications and importance this event stop We holding open radio lines your transmission rush rush rush Honkers has details air tickets advance money but you must proceed with all haste repeat all haste'

Unfortunately, Guy didn't see the cable as he was incommunicado at his hut on the beach reposing in the sun. It was too late to go when he finally saw it and the head office in New York followed it with a second cable, saying simply, *'You're fired. Repeat you're fired.'*

I must say Guy took it all stoically and simply went back to updating his files and enjoying the time with his 'nieces.'

The sun was unusually hot on the day I joined Dicky Woo at the beach, and against my better judgment, I took a dip in the ocean just to cool off. The water was disgustingly warm and didn't offer much respite from the sun so after a few minutes I returned to Guy's hut. He wasn't there: it seemed that all the girls and Dicky had gone swimming. The only person left on the porch was an attractive girl in a very chaste, one-piece bathing costume. She looked at me doubtfully.

'This hut belongs to Guy Searls,' she told me, figuring I was an interloper.

'I know. I'm his guest.'

'Oh, I'm sorry. I'm Mary Jo Kay.'

'I'm Marvin Farkas. Are you one of Guy's stewardess friends?'

'Well I'm more of an interpreter,' she said. 'I work for Hong Kong Airways.'

'You're an interpreter?'

'Sort of. I was transferred from BOAC for my languages. I speak Korean, Japanese, a couple of dialects of Chinese, English, Portuguese and a little French.'

'Very impressive,' I told her. 'You're not Chinese are you?'

'No. I'm Korean but I was born and brought up in China, in Shanghai.'

'Oh, Shanghai, I'd like to hear about that.'

When I was settled comfortably under a beach umbrella

she told me about her life in China.

The Japanese had seized Shanghai in 1937 and they occupied the city until the end of World War II. During the occupation, Mary studied at a Japanese school but there wasn't any serious interruption to her education when the Japanese went down in defeat. Mother Kay conveniently converted the whole family to Catholicism and Mary was enrolled in the Loretto convent school. After that life went on as before until the Communists came to power in 1949.

In the wake of the Communist takeover the Kay family lost everything and for the first time they knew real poverty. The 10 Kay children took their meals in two shifts, each time eating a little rice with vegetables and very occasionally fish or bits of meat. Mother Kay washed the family clothes and made six meals a day and that is all she had time to do. Father Kay operated a hardware store in front of their house but business wasn't good.

One day a couple of plainclothes police showed up at the Loretto school trying to uncover evidence proving that the 'Legion Of Mary,' a Catholic youth group, was a band of counterrevolutionaries. They took the teachers and students one by one to police headquarters and grilled them. Finally they were made to sign a 'confession' saying the Legion was a subversive organization that carried out treasonable acts against the motherland. Most figured they had no choice and signed the iniquitous piece of paper, but Mary resisted. After returning to the police station every day for two weeks but stubbornly refusing to sign, her mother told her it was hopeless to resist and she must give in. Shortly after, the government closed down all religious schools in China. Mary's mother tried to get visas to Korea for the family, but the Chinese authorities refused her request saying the Kays had no papers showing that they were actually Koreans.

Mary's schoolmate, a Portuguese named Virginia Da Costa had a wealthy father who wanted to leave Shanghai, but first he had to figure a way to get his money out. He hit on the idea of buying diamond rings and sending them to relatives to hold for him in Hong Kong. He gave rings to each of his daughters and to a few of his Shanghai relations and with her mother's permission he gave two rings to Mary. By bribing officials, he got her an exit visa out of China and a permit to enter Portuguese Macau by way of Hong Kong.

The Da Costa family was waiting for her at the Kowloon railway station when she arrived and the following day she headed for Macau where she was enrolled at the Santa Rosa Lima convent school. She subsequently returned to Hong Kong to work and just happened to be at Guy Searls' beach hut on that Sunday afternoon when I met her.

After listening to this much of Mary's tale I told her that I'd like to see her again and learn more about her life after Shanghai.

'Okay, but I'm flying tomorrow and the next day and the next day and the day after that. Let's see,' she said, calculating days of the week. 'I'll be busy until next Saturday.'

'Okay, so what about Saturday night?'

My friend Dicky Woo warned me that Mary Jo was a prude. He said he knew several guys that had gone out with her, but there was 'nothing doing.'

'There was this one guy, Frankie Wong,' Dicky told me, 'His family owns a jade mine in Burma and he is the sole heir to a pile of money. He went as far as getting engaged to Mary and gave her a small jade pendant, but got nothing in return.'

'What was he expecting?'

'He was going to marry her. He could expect her to show some, well, affection for him.'

'You say he was going to marry her?'

'That's off now. His family was against it. They thought he should have a wife who comes from a good family. You know, one with lots of money.'

'I'm not that fussy. She's very pretty.'

'Yeah, well Hong Kong is full of nice-looking girls. I'm just warning you that's all. I wouldn't want you to waste your time.'

For our first date Mary and I went to a Shanghai restaurant and she told me more stories, this time about her experiences as a stewardess. I noticed the infamous jade pendant on a chain around her neck so I asked her about it.

'I broke up with the guy who gave it to me and he wants it back. His family owns a whole jade mine in Burma, but he wants this little trinket back.'

'What a cheapskate,' I said.

'Well there is more to it than that, but you're right, he is a cheap guy.'

I didn't see her again until the following Sunday when we drove to Sheung Shui and had lunch at the Jockey Club with an Australian friend of Mary's from Shanghai, a man named Bob Daniels, a race horse trainer, and his Chinese wife Pansy. They lived in a small house on the club premises where Pansy's brother was also staying with them, a very obese Chinese gentleman who Mary kept referring to as 'Fatso.' 'It's so wonderful to see you Fatso.' And 'we must get together soon again Fatso.'

I was taken aback, and when we left I asked Mary if it wasn't rude to use a derogatory name when talking to him. She instructed me that the Chinese often call people by nicknames that allude to some physical feature like *fei lo* (Fatso), or *hak tsai* (Blacky) for a dark-skinned person, or *dai lap mat* (Big Mole). These names would sound offensive to Westerners, but to Chinese they were just a fact of life and they didn't take offense.

I enjoyed Mary's company, but we hadn't been dating long when I got an assignment to cover the independence ceremonies in Malaysia and had to leave town immediately. I left a message at her place telling where I was going and that I wanted to see her as soon as I got back.

23

MERDEKA

I was dispatched to Malaysia to cover Merdeka, the start of Malaya's independence. Hong Kong UP Bureau Chief Bud Merrick had gotten authorization to give me a US$3,000 advance for the trip. I drew down some of my contra from Cathay for airfare, took my Auricon sound camera, a Bell and Howell Filmo, got a supply of film from Kodak and set off.

Mohammed Sayed Alwi, the UP bureau chief in Kuala Lumpur or 'KL', met me at the airport. First thing I did was to get mixed up over the pronunciation of his name and he laughed.

'Call me Sali.'

Sali turned out to be a terrific arranger. He was good natured, humorous and a remarkable newsman who knew the in and outs of KL politics, and got us material we couldn't have got without him. The room he booked at the Railroad Hotel just across from train station was large and comfortable and cost me 33 ringgits at the increased Independence Day rate, which came to about US$11.

We discussed our coverage of the story over lunch at the posh Royal Selangor Club, a social club founded by the British in 1884. When we were into our *nasi goreng* a Singaporean

Chinese friend of Sali's stopped by our table. Sali introduced us. Her name was Hamida Bin Abdullah and she owned a factory in Malaya.

'Rosa makes beautiful pewterware at her factory over in Klang,' Sali said.

'I thought your name was Hamida?' I asked, not sure I'd heard right.

'That's right. It's a name I've adopted for when the British leave,' Rosa said. 'After they are gone it will be extremely difficult for me to operate here, if I'm not a Muslim.

'Is that true?' I asked. 'I thought that in the new Malaya all races will live together in peace and harmony.'

'Don't you believe it. The new government will try to break the stranglehold Chinese have on the economy by imposing forced partnerships with Muslims who will take at least sixty percent of each business. That's the reason I've adopted a Muslim name, to protect my factory.'

'So, what is your real name?'

She looked around cautiously to see if anyone could overhear and then said with a whisper, 'Rosabella Ho. Look, if you are going to cover Merdeka keep your eyes and ears open and you will see a lot of things that'll probably shock you.'

She looked at me with a meaningful expression for some seconds, didn't say anything further and left. It seems that change always sends businesspeople into a panic, but I figured I'd bear Rosa's warning in mind. As a newcomer, I didn't really know the political scene or what to expect from the new government.

'Rosa knows what she's talking about,' Sali said. 'She inherited the factory from her father who got it from his father, so her family's history of doing business in Malaya goes way back.'

'Very interesting. I'll keep my eyes open. Now, let's figure out how we plan to cover this story.'

'First, we should do some vox pop interviews with people on the street,' Sali said. 'I don't think you'll have any language problems as most people in KL speak English.'

We set up in front of the Secretariat building where we got government workers to stand before the camera and answer questions. Sali was my soundman and he worked the amplifier and carried a hand mike with some skill.

'For almost ninety years we have been servants and slaves in our own country,' said one chap. 'The British colonialists controlled our government, our businesses, our agriculture and now, thank Allah, we will finally be rid of them and reap the rewards for ourselves.'

'Will the Chinese be free to operate their businesses as before?' I asked, with Rosa's portentous warning ringing in my ears.

'Of course. We have nothing against the Chinese. As a matter of fact, things will be more open and everyone will be entitled to his share of the prosperity.'

We spoke to a couple of other people, but got more or less the same government line.

'Maybe I made a mistake, advising you to do interviews in front of the government offices,' Sali said. 'Let's go down to the business district and get some opinions from ordinary folk not connected with the government.'

We got out of our car in downtown KL in front of an old British relic, Robinson's Department Store. When our camera and microphone were spotted we were swamped by curious onlookers, and we began to capture some interesting opinions on film. I stopped a middle-aged English woman who was just leaving the store and asked her what she thought about the handover.

'It's a sell out. I'm fed up with the British government, allowing itself to be sold down the river by a bunch of Malays. We've put a lot into this country. We fought their bloody battles with the Communists, developed their rubber business, built tin dredges and supplied a market for their tin. Most of the industries in this country were built up by the British and what do we get out of it? We just walk out of the damn place leaving everything behind. It's a rotten deal and I am ashamed of the British government for allowing it to happen.'

We shoved our mike into the crowd and spoke to a young Malay man.

'The British have run Malaya since 1873. Sure, they built up the industries, but for whose benefit? The English supplied us with jobs, but they paid starvation wages. For years they milked us dry, and sent all the money back to England. But in two days time they will be gone forever, and I say good riddance.'

An elderly Malay man took a more moderate view. 'I will be sorry to see the British leave. They created work and we didn't do too badly. Naturally they took their share, but after all they had to get some profit for their trouble. I think that leaving here all at once is not a good thing. They should have been phased out, a few at a time.' His interview produced jeers from the crowd.

A young fellow seized Sali's hand with the microphone.

'The bloody Englishmen took everything and we got nothing back. Goodbye to the damned English.' He made a rude gesture with his middle finger and the crowd laughed.

It looked like the spectators were getting a bit obstreperous, and when they tried to grab the mike away from Sali I thought it was time to leave.

We did some filming at the railway station. Completed in 1910, the station was adorned with cupolas, minarets and scalloped eaves and looked like an enchanted palace right out of the pages of the Arabian Nights. As I watched the train come in, I fancied I saw a character step out one of the pages of the book and onto the platform, but on closer examination I discovered it was my old pal, Fred Marshall, affectionately known as The Schmeer Fink.

Fred, a sometimes producer of documentaries, traveled about with his cameraman Bobby shooting anything that occurred to him. He was a little light on brains, but had plenty of money and could afford to film, almost interminably. Bobby was a personable Burmese guy who, when he wasn't working for Fred, played piano in a Bangkok night club. He wasn't a great cameraman but that didn't seem to bother Fred who, as hard as he tried, could never seem to sell any of his films.

'We just came up from Bangkok,' Fred said in greeting.

'Here to film the independence celebrations?'

'The what?' he said, sounding surprised to hear about the Merdeka. He actually was in KL by accident.

'When does that happen?'

'It happens tomorrow night. The British will be leaving Malaya forever. It's a very historic event.'

'Yeah, we can do a whole documentary on it,' said Fred as he moved his hand over his head in a great arc to show the extraordinary work being fabricated in his mind. 'What do you say Bobby?'

'Sounds good to me, Fred.' Everything sounded good to Bobby.

'What hotel are you staying at?' Fred asked.

'The Railroad Hotel.'

'Okay. We'll stay there, too. What do you say Bobby?'

'Sounds okay Fred.'

'The town is sewn up tight as a drum,' I said. 'The manager told me they hadn't any rooms left.'

Fred couldn't hear what I told him, or decided not to pay any attention. He had inherited a considerable fortune from his father who on his deathbed decided it would be safer for his unpredictable son to live on a monthly income administered by a bank. So Fred got enough money to keep filming, pay his expenses, treat his friends to dinner and even to support a minor wife or two in Bangkok. He was a bit dippy, but he was a nice guy. Six foot two and weighing about 280 pounds, his hands were like two great slabs of beef. When he didn't shave he looked like a giant hit man, but he was actually as gentle as a lamb—except if he thought you'd crossed him, then watch out.

We filmed at the Jame Mosque, a superb building located at the confluence of two muddy rivers. A century ago it was at that exact spot that Kuala Lumpur was founded as a trading post by Chinese tin miners.

In Chinatown we found old shops in pastel buildings dating back to the turn of the century. The owners still engaged in characteristic Chinese trades. Rattan baskets were filled with 'thousand year old eggs,' dried and salted fish and a myriad selection of fruits and vegetables, some of which I had never seen before. Traditional medicine shops carried an array of strange seeds and pieces of bark and roots that were dispensed and weighed on old-fashioned Chinese scales. The air snapped with the aromas of Asian cooking. It was an extraordinary scene, but at this location we met some resistance to our filming. It all started when Sali pointed our microphone at one of the shopkeepers and tried to get him to say a few words.

'Hey, what you doing?' the storekeeper shouted angrily. 'Come on get out.'

'We just want to find out how you feel about the new state of Malaya?'

'I don't know nothing. Get out of here.'

The suggestion that we wanted them to appear on camera set off one shopkeeper after another and we found ourselves in the center of a bitter confrontation. They started swinging straw brooms and bamboo rods and I could see nothing for it but to withdraw to a safe place until I could think up another line of attack.

'This is a great place to shoot,' I told Sali. 'I'd hate to leave without getting something.'

'What about another street? There is plenty of this same kind of scene all over Chinatown.'

'Okay, but this time don't show the microphone until I get some local color shots. We can start the interviews with people on the street and leave the shopkeepers for later.'

I got some footage of people buying from hawkers and then we walked into a traditional Chinese medicine shop and without asking permission, got a full range of wide angle and close-up shots. Nobody seemed to notice my camera, so without stopping I motioned Sali to point the mike at one of the clerks. I asked him the usual question.

'I think Malays running government, good idea. They know Asian mentality. But not British, they always been outsider.'

'What about your daily life with the Malays?'

'We don't mingle, except for customer. They have their way of life and we have ours. I don't think anything different when they take over.'

We put the question to a Chinese woman on the street buying some water chestnuts.

'I looking forward to new government,' she said.

'Don't you fear that the Muslim custom of showing disrespect for the rights of women will affect you?'

She seemed insulted. 'I am Muslim and have always been treated with great respect by my husband. The opinions of other men don't matter to me.'

The interview ended abruptly, as the woman picked up her water chestnuts and walked away in a huff.

Back at the Railroad Hotel we discovered that Fred Marshall had gotten a room in spite of the manager's claim that 'there are absolutely no more rooms available.' Fred truly had a way of getting things done.

That night we had dinner in Petaling Jaya, a suburb of KL where open-air food stalls serve a variety of Asian dishes. We had Hainan chicken and rice with a side order of red chili and fresh ginger, and a crispy *kampong* fish baked in tamarind sauce. The food was great, but Fred's table manners were appalling. The front of his expensive silk shirt was soon speckled with large spots of chicken fat and yellow goo from the saffron rice, and I had to tell him a couple of times to wipe the grease off his chin. He ignored me and continued eating and talking about a feature he had recently produced.

The time finally arrived for Malaya to come of age. The newly built Merdeka Stadium was the venue for the main ceremonies and dignitaries and government officials crowded the platform. It was a few minutes to midnight and the flag pole was still flying the Union Jack. The sultan, the Yang di-Pertuan Agong along with soon-to-be Prime Minister Tengku Abdul Rahman, son of the sultan of Kedah state, shared the central places on the platform with the outgoing British governor.

Behind them was a large Malayan military band with a bagpipe contingent in kilts, the military wearing crisp khaki trousers, form-fitting tunics, dark green sarongs and smartly styled *peci*. Taking up the rear was a girls' choir attired in egg-yellow sarongs. In the press enclosure newsreel cameramen and photographers engaged in some last minute pushing and shoving as they jockeyed for position.

All was ready for the big moment. The clocks showed just two minutes to midnight. The British flag was lowered for the last time while the band played 'God Save The Queen.' Then the entire city was blacked out for a full minute and an eerie silence ensued. As the clocks struck midnight the lights went on all over the city and the new state was born. The Malayan flag was raised for the first time. The new national anthem was sung by the girl's choir amid the din of fireworks and the wild cheers of 'Merdeka, Merdeka' by the crowd of spectators numbering in the thousands.

I took a shot of a tableau of the four ethnic groups that would make up the new country, each holding onto one corner of the flag. A Malay, a Chinese, an Indian and a Caucasian. Equals, they could see great things in the future under the leadership of Tengku Abdul Rahman. We couldn't talk to the prime minister himself as the crowds were too great for us to move freely and besides, he was guarded by a company of armed soldiers. But a man from the information office came to the press enclosure and handed out invitations to a select group of foreign newsmen, saying we were invited to talk informally with the Tengku tomorrow morning at 10 a.m. at the Istana Negara.

Tengku Abdul Rahman was 54 years old at the time Malaya attained sovereignty. The gathering at the Istana included 20 members of the foreign press, invited with the express intention of introducing the Tengku to the world. We were served a Malayan breakfast and tea on the lawn. When the Tengku came out he mixed freely with the guests and answered most of the questions posed by the newsmen. He wore a yellow shirt and silk trousers over which was a sarong in typical Malayan style and the ever-present *peci* on his head. As he walked around the garden I saw him rearranging his sarong. I was fascinated and asked him if he didn't mind fixing it again for the camera. He laughed.

'Okay,' he said opening the sarong. 'Now if everyone will pay attention I am only going to do this once.'

He showed how he folded it at the side and the special way he tucked it in. When he was finished with the simple operation he lifted his hands in triumph and smiled and the crowd cheered.

He gathered the news people around him for an informal press conference and told us that of primary importance now was eradicating the Communist insurgency that had plagued Malaya since 1948. The battle was being won and he predicted an early end to hostilities. He did not plan any radical economic or social changes for the country. The rubber and tin industries were ripe for new capital and offered good returns. The existing free market economy was to be maintained.

He especially wanted to promote development in the poorer rural areas which were largely Malay. He had plans to build schools and clinics and extend basic transport and communication infrastructures across the nation. Coping with religious extremism and student and peasant agitations required some work, but his chief concern now was getting the business of running the government into motion.

'I must concentrate on educating our children and assistance for the poor,' he said. 'There is a lot to be done, and so if there are no more questions I will get to it and bid you all a good morning.'

We had witnessed a moment of history. The first day cover was a specially printed envelope decorated with a picture of the new Malayan flag and stamps that commemorated the transition from British to Malayan rule. I mailed one to Mary on that day, August 31, 1957, so that it would bear the Kuala Lumpur postmark on the exact day of the handover. Some people thought that it would become a very valuable historic memento.

24

ADVENTURE ON HAPPINESS STREET

The BBC was planning a documentary on Hong Kong for their 'Panorama' show and asked me to film it for them. A producer was sent out, accompanied by a freelance writer named James Morris. James had come right from covering Edmund Hillary's Mount Everest expedition for the London Times. (He later became famous as a female novelist named Jan Morris.) He was a personable guy who sent postcards to his kids with flowery descriptions of junks that 'glide round the fragrant harbor with silken sails that tremble in the breeze like the wings of butterflies.'

The producer wanted to portray the colony as a tiny bit of England nestled against the formidable breast of Communist China and James told the story of *taipans*, the businessmen that came from England's most affluent families and ran the great British business houses. For staff the taipans recruited young, well-educated Englishmen, taught them the business, paid them a pittance and put them into positions of responsibility and trust. The Chinese, on the other hand, held mostly menial posts without much chance for advancement.

The taipans lived in restricted enclaves in a world of caste-sensitive social institutions. Golf clubs kept a tight rein on membership and at cocktail parties the only yellow faces you would see were the ones serving drinks. Taipans were a fascinating adjunct to the story, but they were not exclusive to Hong Kong and were found in many parts of the world where colonial governments held power.

A company doing business in Hong Kong felt it unnecessary to include Chinese in confidential matters, with the exception of the compradors, the local intermediaries who were a necessity in untangling the complex web of Chinese business procedures.

Hong Kong's leading comprador was Robert Hotung, a Eurasian of questionable parentage who handled complicated transactions for the Hongkong and Shanghai Banking Corporation and, along the way, amassed a huge fortune. He became important enough — and rich enough — to have a 'Sir' inserted before his name and be remembered in the Queen's Birthday Honors. But even with his wealth and accomplishments, he still never received his longed-for dream of being accepted into the upper crust of British hierarchy.

We had to forgo an interview with Sir Robert as he was away in London getting hormone injections. He was well into his nineties and even at his advanced age he was known as a notorious womanizer. We were permitted to film his home, his several wives, his many children and servants and his simple office in a modest old building where he still used an abacus to do his mathematical equations.

The producer also wanted interviews with refugees that had been forced to leave China after the Communist takeover, so I arranged interviews with Mr. Lee and Mr. Chow, waiters at the FCC who had been with the club in Chongqing and Shanghai and spoke passable English. I also suggested my friend Mary Jo Kay for an interview.

Lee and Chow told of their adventures as they had walked

for weeks through the Chinese countryside pretending to be farmers. When they finally reached the border between China and Hong Kong at the Sham Chun River they didn't have any identification papers so they swam across at an unguarded point and wandered around Hong Kong before finding the FCC. The staff there concealed them until they were accepted into the colony in a general amnesty.

Mary told about her life in Shanghai, her family and how she rode the train from Shanghai and crossed over the Lowu Bridge carrying diamond rings for her friend's father. I recommended Mary mainly to impress her, but with her eagerness to talk she turned out to be an excellent subject for the interview.

I took Mary on assignments with me supposedly as an interpreter, but actually just to keep her around. We made a documentary for CARE on Cheung Chau, a small island inhabited mainly by fishermen. I put Mary in the film, acting the part of a social worker.

During our time on Cheung Chau we met Gus Borgeest, a Quaker who had founded a resettlement area for mainland Chinese refugees and rehabilitation center for opium addicts in Hong Kong on nearby 'Sunshine Island.' Gus helped people get back on their feet by giving them the tools and training to start a small farm on the island.

For his good work Gus received the Magsaysay award with a grant of US$10,000. Then, all of a sudden the government wanted to get into the act, and much to Gus's chagrin, decided Sunshine Island should be administered by a committee. As a result of wrangling over money and various stupid mistakes the committee destroyed the essence of Sunshine Island and in less than a year the project was closed down. Gus gave me his interpretation of a committee with no little amount of disgust. 'A camel is a horse designed by a committee.'

When our shooting wrapped, Gus invited Mary and me to watch a traditional Chinese wedding between a girl of 12 and a boy of 13. They went through the customary Chinese wedding routines and then their parents provided a feast of roast pork, fried pork, boiled pork and pork cooked in a hundred different ways. The bride lived on the junk of her young husband's family, doing all the usual household chores until she was 16 years old and they could begin their conjugal life.

I picked Mary up at the airport in a motorized sampan when she returned from trips and would bring her directly to my apartment on Tung Lo Wan Road, which was right at the water's edge. Very romantic and she loved it, but as my friend Dicky Woo had warned me, even though she practically lived with me, a few kisses were the extent of our love life.

'I have always thought of my airline job as temporary, until I find something that pays better or get married,' she said.

'Oh, do you plan to get married?'

'Well, when the right man comes along.'

I wasn't really interested in having a wife at this stage but just for conversation I decided to find out the kind of man she wanted.

'I really don't know. Anyway, I don't think about getting married right now, my life is fine without it.'

'I understand. I feel that way myself,' I lied.

So I left it at that. Bringing her home with me sort of singled her out as my girlfriend, even though our relationship was chaste. She told me bluntly that if I wanted to keep her

I had to be satisfied with things as they stood. She was very clear about that.

In the meantime there were various projects to keep me busy. I was asked by a Hollywood producer to find a double for Barbara Stanwyck to shoot scenes in Macau for an episode of The Barbara Stanwyck Theater called 'Adventure on Happiness Street. The task was an easy one. Fran Dominis, the wife of Life photographer John Dominis, was a dead ringer for Barbara Stanwyck.

Leonel Borralho, a jovial Macanese fellow and a colleague of mine from the *Tiger Standard*, acted as our liaison. He had been in trouble with the Macau police on several occasions for criticizing the Portuguese government in his stories. He was banished to Coloane Island where they sent political undesirables for sentences of anywhere from seven to 15 days. It was not a hardship situation as he stayed with a relative on Coloane, but it was a nuisance because it interrupted his daily routine of covering stories, sitting in his favorite coffee shop and shooting the bull with friends. In spite of the consequences, he continued to write what he saw as the truth.

Leonel said that according to protocol we had to visit the chief of police and show him the script and tell him what we were planning to shoot. As Macau was a small place we would not go unnoticed for long, so it was wisest to report to the authorities.

The peninsula of Macau was what the Portuguese termed 'an overseas territory' and they insisted it was not a colony. Over

400 years old, it was the oldest foreign settlement in China. It had lovely green hills and covered an area of only six square miles and at the time, the total population was about 350,000 with an interesting mixture of Portuguese and Chinese they call 'Macanese.' Charming houses in pastel tones and cobblestoned streets gave the impression of a village in Portugal. A barrier gate guarded by black soldiers from Mozambique formed the border with mainland China. At one time Macau was the main port for China's foreign trade but that declined after Hong Kong came onto the scene and the territory was reduced to a center for smuggling and gambling.

The gambling casinos played the strictly Asian games of '*dai siu*' where you bet on the sum of three dice and '*fan tan*,' a game played by separating a large pile of white buttons three at a time with a long chopstick and betting on what would be left over. The beautiful scenery, its aura of mystery, and its traditional style of gambling were what prompted the Barbara Stanwyck show to set an episode there.

Captain Joaquin Merced of the Macau police was a tall, thin man with a meticulously trimmed mustache and sparse hair parted in the middle and pomaded to his scalp. He was the perfect stereotype of a provincial Portuguese police officer. He spoke good English and he gave our script a cursory inspection. He then stared at us silently and tapped his fingernails on the desk. After a moment he spoke.

'For obvious reasons we want to keep Macau's reputation untarnished. The first objection I have is to the title, 'Adventure On Happiness Street.' The Rua de Felicidade was known for many years throughout the world as a red light district, so I think you understand that we do not wish to have attention drawn to its seamy side.'

'How are people in the U.S. to know that Happiness Street was a red light district?' I asked. 'You are speaking about a very long time in the past.' I thought, but didn't say, 'Most Americans have never even heard of Macau.'

'How are they going to know? How did your scriptwriter know? It was not by chance that he came on the name.' Captain Merced puffed slowly on his cigarette, and looked patiently at our little group.

'He just picked the most colorful name off a map,' I said, trying to explain. 'He wanted to give an interesting atmosphere to the story and he certainly didn't know it was a former red light district. If you read the script you will see that it is not what the story is about.'

Leonel signaled me to be quiet and let him do the talking.

'Captain Merced, Mr. Farkas is the director for the Barbara Stanwyck series and if he sees that the title must be changed, then it will be changed. Is that correct Mr. Farkas?'

'Well if that is what the Macau government decides, then I will go along with it.'

'How about we change the name to Avenida Rebeiro?' Leonel said, suggesting the name of Macau's main avenue.

'That will do wery well. But I hope you are serious about making the change?' the captain said.

To prove the point I took out my pen, crossed out the title from the front page of the script and wrote in 'Adventure on Avenida Rebeiro.'

'Now, what other objections do you have?' Leonel asked.

'Only the gambling scenes. You cannot film inside the casinos.'

'We know that and those sequences are not very important. In any case the interior scenes will be done in Hollywood. We just thought they would add a little bit of local color, but if you have objections?'

'I don't want to be difficult about this, but cameras are not allowed inside the casinos and I would appreciate it if you could limit the gambling scenes in the finished production.'

'Of course,' said Leonel. 'Now if you will sir, please give us a letter that will permit us to film in the streets, and we will trouble you no further.'

Captain Joaquin Merced of the Macau police didn't make any stringent objections to our shooting, but I guess he had to show who was in charge so thanks to our fixer we gave him that impression. At Leonel's suggestion we went ahead and filmed on the Rua de Felicidade and we could see no evidence that a red light district had ever existed there.

We had to get wide angle shots of Fran Dominis from a distance wearing a trench coat in her role as a double for Barbara Stanwyck. Actually, Fran looked so much like Barbara that Miss Stanwyck herself commented on the remarkable likeness.

Before going back to Hong Kong we had dinner at the Pousada de Macao, a lovely little inn right on the water's edge run by a Macanese named America Angelo. He served as chef and made us a superb African chicken. We had an exquisite view of the Pearl River estuary and as the daylight faded we could see drying fishing nets suspended from bamboo poles while sampans bounced languidly on the muddy waters.

So after a long day of shooting we boarded the 'S.S. *Fatshan*' expecting a restful three-and-a-half hour trip back to Hong Kong. But on board I ran into something that topped any TV script for originality.

I got into conversation with a man with a thick Russian accent who said his name was O'Brien. He told me that about six months ago he had left Hong Kong on the Fatshan for a day outing but Macau immigration discovered he didn't have a visa and refused him entry, and he was forced to return to Hong Kong. Back in Hong Kong the immigration authorities found he didn't have a valid Hong Kong visa, and they refused to let him off the boat. He was then shipped back to

Macau where he was again refused entry and sent back to Hong Kong who in turn refused to let him land. Since then he had been going back and forth, from Hong Kong to Macau and from Macau to Hong Kong. He had been trapped on the *S.S. Fatshan* for almost six months making the round-trips daily and paying his fare by working in the ship's boiler room.

O'Brien was a stateless person, coming he said from the industrial city of Shenyang in north China. Not having a passport he had somehow got a 'one way, one time' permit to travel to Hong Kong as a refugee, but after he tried to use it to go to Macau the immigration people wouldn't let him land again in Hong Kong. He was left totally without papers and was fated to travel back and forth on the *S.S. Fatshan* with no solution to his problem, and no apparent chance of reprieve.

25

MARRIAGE

It's a serious business, proposing marriage. But worst of all, the delightful freedom of bachelor existence would be gone forever. On the other hand, Mary was a good catch. I was 31 years old and I figured I wasn't likely to meet another girl with all her qualities. Most important, I was in love with her and it seemed she loved me too, so I decided to give it a shot.

I was inviting her to join the Farkas family and that would be the central theme of my proposal, so I decided to arm myself with photos of my family and friends. I made reservations at Gaddi's at the Peninsula Hotel. The grand dinner cost me HK$60 and towards the end of the evening I pulled out the pictures.

She looked at them with great interest but had a puzzled expression on her face.

'You're going to make me explain my behavior tonight?'

She looked me in the eye and asked me straightforwardly, 'Are you saying you want to marry me?'

'That was my plan. Why? Is it such a foolish idea?'

'I just wanted to know if that was the reason for this special treatment.'

'I guess it comes as a surprise to you?'

'Not really.'

'So, do you want to marry me or not?' I asked bluntly, not really as I had planned to pop the question.

She looked at me, tears forming in her eyes. 'I do, I do. I was waiting for you to ask for a long time,' she said. 'I was afraid that you might not.'

So it was settled. It was that easy and I really didn't have to worry so much.

'How about getting married in September? Summer is over and fall is just around the corner, so it's a good time to start a new life.'

'That sounds perfect,' she said.

Life is rarely perfect, however. The first one to throw a dampener on our plans was an old friend of Mary's, Father Mulcahey from her school in Shanghai. He invited us to lunch, we thought to congratulate us, but as the meal progressed his real objective emerged. 'What faith do you follow, Marvin?'

'My religion is Jewish.'

'Your religion? We Catholics consider there is only one religion. We frown on Catholic girls marrying outside the faith, but if you agree to marry in the church we can get around that.'

'What, as a Jew? How can I marry in a Catholic church?'

'You could be married in a part of the church called the

sacristy and we would consider that as marrying in the church.'

'Well, okay, if that's what Mary wants?'

'You can be sure she does.'

How could he be so certain what was in Mary's mind?

'Now about the children? Mary Jo would expect that they have a Catholic upbringing.'

'Mary hasn't told me anything about that. Anyway we aren't even married yet. When my children are old enough to understand, I will explain to them about the choices they can make.'

'Oh, no, no, no, you don't understand. It is absolutely mandatory that your children be brought up as Catholics and receive a Catholic education, and you must sign a paper to that effect before you get married.'

'Excuse me. I'm not a Catholic and I don't feel any compunction to sign my children's life away before they are even born. As I said, when they are at an age where they can understand all this, I will ask them and abide by their decision. Look, if they want to be priests or nuns that's okay with me, but it must be their own choice.'

'You are being very disagreeable Marvin. Remember, this is what Mary Jo wants and must have in order to keep her faith. We have simple rules, but they must all be followed. This is not bargain day. Two out of three is not good enough.'

'Then if we don't follow all the laws of the church, she will be excommunicated?'

'I can see that you have no intention of talking sense right now. Call me Mary Jo, and we can discuss it sensibly when you have made Marvin see reason.'

He left in a huff and forgot to pay the bill.

'What a biased man that is,' I said, looking at Mary. 'I hope I haven't hurt you?'

'No.' She took my arm and squeezed it. 'I was proud of you.'

Shortly before the wedding Mary got a letter from Father Mulcahey saying he was surprised to receive an invitation to the wedding party rather than the wedding itself. He mentioned that reliable people at the American Consulate had told him shocking tales about me and that she mustn't get married until he had time to check out those stories. And he wasn't the only one to give us grief.

Did you ever make a deal with a supposed friend who swears he has your best interests at heart, and then sticks it to you? Nick Kendall caught me at a very susceptible moment: my wedding day. I always considered him one of my better pals, but he pulled this little gambit on me in a most despicable way.

'You're going to need a car for after the ceremony, for your honeymoon,' he said.

'I know.'.

'Why not take mine?'

'Gee, that's very generous of you Nick.'

'What are friends for?' he said and then paused for a second. 'What do you say you give me three hundred bucks to defray costs?'

I was dumbfounded. What costs was he talking about?

'Come on Nick, you know I don't have any money.'

'Well then how about giving me that oil painting of the purple lady?'

So that was what he was after. I loved that painting which I had framed and hung in my living room to be admired by all my art lover friends. He surely couldn't want me to give it away just to use his car for a day or two?

He continued ruthlessly, 'You don't have $300, so give me the painting and you can use the car.'

'You mean you want the painting? To keep?'

'Of course, what do you think, I want to have it temporarily just to admire?'

'You drive a hard bargain.'

He wanted me to surrender a painting I had grown very fond of just to use his dented old '42 Buick — a car that guzzled gas, had bald tires and windshield wipers that didn't work. He'd got the old heap as a present from his Korean lady friend Mary Layfield who was married to a sea captain conveniently out of town most of the time. She bought Nick clothes and gave him money as well. He was my idea of a gigolo.

The 'purple lady' was a large oil painting I had picked up in Indonesia, the work of Queen Soenasis, the former monarch of West Irian. She was living in exile in Jakarta with her husband, the Rajah, at the home of Jane Wawarunta, a wealthy art patron. The queen was a very large and jovial lady and the painting in question depicted a nude woman of splendid proportions, purple in color surrounded by small vignettes of familiar Jakarta scenes. I fell in love with the picture the first time I saw it and she agreed to sell it to me for US$10. For me it had inherent value because after all, the artist was the queen of West Irian, the disputed territory in Indonesia.

At the time I acquired the painting I was with Bill Stevenson and we were interviewing the queen for our CBC story. She told us a remarkable tale about the royal family. It seems they always had a queen in West Irian and never a king.

'Why was that?' asked Bill.

'They were cannibals. When a boy was born in the royal family he was killed and eaten.

'So there was never a king in West Irian? Only a queen because when a king was born he was killed and eaten before he ever became king? So your people were cannibals?' Bill said, incredulously recapping her explanation.

'That's right,' said the old queen.

'Are your people still cannibals today?' he asked.

'Oh no, that was before the war,' she answered with a smile.

As we walked toward the marriage registry Nick reminded me again of his 'magnanimous' offer.

'So do we have a deal?'

'Come on Nick,' I said, pleading. 'Give me a break. I really love that painting.'

'Do you want the car or not?'

Being temporarily without funds leaves you at the mercy of every swindler who comes your way. We were only going to the Jockey Club in Sheung Shui to spend our honeymoon, but I had no way of getting there except with Nick's broken-down old bezou. I was so broke on my wedding day that my best man, Didi Ismail, had to pay the HK$11 for the marriage license.

I had ordered 12 cases of champagne for the wedding party on consignment from liquor wholesaler Gande, Price & Co. That is, what we drank we would pay for and we would get credit for all the bottles we returned unopened. No cash would change hands for quite a few months. It was a deal that could only be done if you were a foreigner. Mary told our domestic help, Ah Miu, that as soon as we left the party for our honeymoon she was to spirit away the unopened bottles. A cruel plot, but we were broke and we really couldn't afford all that champagne.

So we left on our honeymoon with a smoke-spewing old car and Nick took possession of my 'purple lady' — but I was happy with my beautiful bride.

26

CONMEN AND CHANCERS

After getting married Mary left her stewardess job but naturally drifted into other airline work. She set up shop as manager of the small KLM Airlines ticket office on the corner of Des Voeux Road Central and Ice House Street. The salary wasn't much but the perks were great: every year she got two free tickets to anywhere in the world.

In my life I constantly search for interesting people, and at one time I had figured the only truly extraordinary characters were in New York, but that wasn't true. Being on a busy corner, Mary's office attracted visitors. Some came in to ask directions, others to flirt and more just to pass the time. One day a certified wolf named Greg Archer dropped by, looking like an ordinary tourist with his Nikon camera and leather bag full of lenses. He said he'd noticed Mary as he passed her window and 'just had to introduce himself and take her picture.'

'What do you say to taking a little time off your job and going around town with me so I could get a few shots of you?'

'Are you serious? I have a job, I can't just leave,' Mary said, smiling. 'Are you a professional photographer?'

'No, I'm not. I'm a lawyer and I'm doing research for one of my clients, the committee for the Miss Universe contest. Do you have beauty contests here?'

'I don't think so. I've never heard of any.'

'I would really like to show my clients the great possibilities of Hong Kong for a Miss Universe contest. For instance, I could take pictures of you in different locations, perhaps one or two shots in a bikini on the beach.'

'Oh, I don't think I am suitable. There are plenty of girls in Hong Kong who would be delighted to have their picture taken by a talented photographer. I'm married and I don't think my husband would approve of my gallivanting around town with a stranger.'

'We wouldn't have to tell your husband.'

'Oh, I couldn't do that.'

He wished her an abrupt goodbye and left, but she passed on his story of the Miss Universe contest to my friend Gale McCarty.

'If he ever comes back introduce him to me. I have a few ideas on holding a beauty contest,' Gale said.

About a week later he passed by again and came in to say hello.

'I mentioned your Miss Universe connection to a friend and he said was interested in meeting you. Would you be free later today?'

'I have a meeting this afternoon with my bankers to transfer some funds,' he said importantly. 'I'm afraid today is out of the question but what about tomorrow?'

Mary phoned Gale and made an appointment to meet Greg for lunch at Jimmy's Kitchen. Gale was nervous about who was going to pay.

'Don't worry, this guy is loaded,' Mary said. 'I'm sure he intends to pay.'

The next day at 1 p.m. Gale showed up at Jimmy's Kitchen. He got a table and was about to give up after an hour when Greg finally arrived.

'I'm sorry to be late Gale, I was held up at my lawyer's office. It is Gale isn't it?'

'Yes. I was beginning to think you might have forgotten me.'

'I had a very busy schedule this morning with my lawyers. But let's order first. Oh yes, order anything you please, the meal is on me.'

Gale relaxed and ordered corned beef and cabbage, a house specialty, while Greg had a double T-bone steak with french fried potatoes and they each had a beer.

'Hong Kong is a perfect place to hold a beauty contest,' Gale said. 'We have a stadium and plenty of beautiful girls, but people here have never really thought about beauty contests. A Miss Universe competition might be too big to finance right off the bat. What do you think of starting with a Miss Hong Kong contest and next year when people understand the concept we can graduate to Miss Universe? I believe there are plenty of firms that could be talked into sponsoring.'

Greg mulled over the idea.

'Miss Hong Kong sounds good. We could probably organize it in a short while, but would you be willing to devote all your time to it?'

'I certainly would,' Gale said, feeling that he had stepped into a good deal.

Greg paid the bill with a credit card and they went to Gale's apartment to talk. It was a one-bedroom flat in an old building so the ceilings were high and the rooms were light and airy, though not large.

'This is fine,' Greg said, looking all around. 'We could make this our office. You have a telephone and typewriter, that would be enough to start off with. I like to keep things simple.'

Gale was taken aback. 'I hadn't intended to use my home as an office,' he said and then faltered. 'But if you think it fits the bill?'

'It seems comfortable and you're centrally located, and don't worry, I'll cover all your expenses. So now that we have an office let's get moving. We should have cards and applications for the contest printed and I'll plan a 'contest magazine' where we can place ads for the sponsoring companies and write brief stories about the contestants. That will make a little more income for us.'

Gale didn't see anything wrong with Greg's plan until he said, as an afterthought. 'I think that in order to work more efficiently, I should move in here with you.'

Gale was stunned. It seemed out of character for a successful lawyer like Greg Archer.

'But I have only one bedroom.'

'Oh, that's okay. I can camp out on the living room floor. It is only an expedient to get the work done without wasting time. You understand, don't you?'

Greg was going to stay in the living room, would be paying some of his expenses and they had an interesting business deal, so why not? Greg told Gale that to get things moving they must register the contest with the government.

'I'm going to go back to my hotel to check out and bring my stuff over here. In the meantime you go down and register the company, and include publishing a magazine.' And then as if it was an afterthought he said, 'Oh yes, and I'll need a key to your apartment.'

Gale paid a visit to the relevant government office and paid a fee of HK$1,000 to register a company which he called Greg/ Gale Contests, Limited. Meanwhile, back at the 'office' Greg had brought his clothes over in a set of very attractive matching suitcases. He was hard at work typing a letter to the newspapers to arrange a press conference when Gale came back.

'Oh, George, I mean Gale, that's right. It is Gale isn't it?'

'My god he's moved in and he doesn't even remember my name,' Gale thought to himself.

'Listen Gale, take this letter down to a printer's shop and get 30 copies made and then buy some envelopes and stamps to mail them. Keep track of the expenses, so I can pay you back.'

'I've already spent $1,000 registering the company.'

'As I say, keep a tab on what I owe you. Now get moving on copying the letters and while you are out see if you can get the names of all the newspapers in town.'

All these tasks finished, Gale returned to the apartment and found Greg hanging up his clothes on lamps and window frames and hammering nails into the wall. Before Gale had a chance to protest Greg told him he had called the Gloucester Hotel and talked them into providing a function room for their press conference, and now he wanted Gale to call the Pepsi Cola bottlers and get them to donate a freezer of Pepsis.

Gale was more than a little miffed.

'Look before we go any further, tell me why you're knocking nails into my walls?'

'I wouldn't have to do it if I had sufficient place to hang my clothes.'

Well Gale had several reasons to be angry, but Greg sloughed them off as not being relevant. He complained about the poor accommodations and acted like a martyr suffering these privations for the good of the project.

The only refreshments for the reporters were the Pepsi Colas which Greg/Gale Contests Limited got for free in return for promising to hang a Pepsi banner at their beauty show. Greg was great at handing out the bull and gave an excellent press conference. All of the papers considered the first Miss Hong Kong contest in the history of the colony an interesting news event and gave Greg/Gale Contests Limited good write-ups. When the stories came out they were besieged by girls anxious to compete. Gale was told to approach dress shops to get dresses and swimsuits for the contest which would be returned after the show.

Greg had an affair with one of the applicants, Miss Avril Lee. Gale thought this was in really bad taste as it left them open to criticism from the other girls if Avril 'just happened to win.' Greg had her sleeping over most nights in Gale's living room and they were making quite a bit of noise. Greg's welcome was definitely wearing thin.

Then everything began to go sour. The preparations took too long and the South China Stadium, which was the venue for the contest, pulled out. If the show was not going to come off, the shops wanted their dresses back, and the sponsors dropped out one by one. Gale went and spoke to the parties concerned, but they had the idea that Greg was a flake and they all seemed to know he was sleeping with a contestant and they wanted no part of him. Greg and Gale were forced to call the show off.

Some of the girls, especially Avril Lee, conveniently disappeared and refused to return the dresses. Greg/Gale Contests, Limited was facing several lawsuits.

Then one day Gale came home to find Greg shining his shoes with one of Gale's face cloths.

'What are you doing?' asked an irate Gale.

'What do you think I'm doing, stupid, I'm shining my shoes.'

'That's my face towel.'

'So what? I'm sick and tired of hearing you bellyache. I've had enough of you and this lousy apartment. Look at how you live! I should have known better then starting anything with a loser like you, you stupid bastard.'

'Get out of my apartment,' Gale screamed. 'But before you go, you owe me $4,680.'

'That's rich. Do you think I would give you anything? You ruined my Miss Hong Kong show. You're incompetent and lazy and I am glad to be rid of you.'

So Greg left, notwithstanding the fact he owed Gale quite a bit of money and that he had very cleverly got Gale to sign the business registration, take out the magazine license, and make all the deals with the dress shops and sponsors.

A couple of weeks later, following a complaint from the manager, the police were called to the Fourseas Hotel, a grotty little dive located in a remote corner of Kowloon. One Greg Archer had tried to pay his bill of HK$94 with a credit card that was no longer valid. Greg claimed it was all a mistake, he didn't know that the card had expired. He was arrested and held for trial. His bail was $500 which he didn't have but he had the balls to tell them he had a very dear friend named Gale McCarty who would surely help him out. Gale, poor fool, paid the bail and was told he was responsible for Greg until the trial.

Gale gave Greg $300 for a hotel and to buy himself meals but he discovered Greg was using the money to date bar girls. They had words and Greg walked out once again, but this time he disappeared for good. When the police discovered he had stowed away on a ship to Vancouver, they just washed their hands of him. But they questioned several people about

Gale McCarty and couldn't believe that he had taken all that crap from Archer, and yet helped him out when he was in trouble.

When Greg arrived in Vancouver he was arrested by the Royal Canadian Mounted Police and from his cell, wrote a letter to the *China Mail* saying one day he would really hold a Miss Universe contest and repay all his debts to the people who had trusted him. American Express hoped that he wouldn't forget the money he owed them for meals, Nikon cameras, lenses, a matching luggage set and a half a dozen expensive suits and monogrammed silk shirts either.

The sun must have been shining on Gale the day he went around to straighten out all that was owed by Greg/Gale Contests, Limited. He was fearful the affair would cost him thousands, but it turned out that many of the sponsors felt sorry for him and he only ended up paying a total of HK$300 – a small enough amount to pay to be rid of a cheap crook like Greg Archer.

Another colorful character was Harry Pelziger. I first ran into him in Taiwan while I was covering the Dachen Islands evacuation story. Harry was the U.S. Air Force public information officer for Taiwan, and was trying to convince the journalists to do a story on the Free China Air Force which had recently acquired F-86 jet fighters from the U.S. I was looking for an excuse to hang out in Taiwan, so I told him I was interested and went with him to the air base in Taichung. I filmed the brand new maintenance facility and the pilots training in their first jet aircraft. Harry really laid on a show for us, and I figured it made a fairly interesting story.

The nights were just as much fun as the days. Harry was a bon vivant and he invited me and my assistant Gale McCarty to a wonderful Chinese dinner at a restaurant called The Drunken Moon. Beside the unusual dish of live prawns, each of us had a beautiful girl by our side to assist us with eating. You literally kept your hands in your pockets and the girl did all the work and delicately served you each mouthful. My girl was rather disappointed when I took only one small sip of the Kau Liang wine, a 90-proof liquor which could lay you under the table in nothing flat. Harry and Gale had no such qualms about the wine and finished most of the bottle. After dinner you were free to take the girls back to your hotel, after making suitable monetary arrangements, to finish off what had been a most enjoyable evening at the dinner table.

The next morning Harry woke us early to partake of a special Taichung breakfast. We had snake meat congee and *yau ja gwai* (a fried wheat flour snack) which didn't taste bad at all and was apparently a specialty for fall weather.

We started back on what was ordinarily a 45-minute flight to Taipei in clear weather, but the black clouds came in fast and our 20-year-old rebuilt turbo prop C-45 was buffeted and battered and banged around until at one point I felt that we would never get off that plane alive. I looked over at Harry for reassurance but got none from that quarter. On the last part of the journey, although the rough weather hadn't abated, I had a strange feeling of tranquility. I had learned from doctors that when a patient knows that death is approaching something takes over his psyche, dulling his feelings somewhat as if he were drugged, and he becomes very peaceful. I believe that was my state of mind when after two hours we landed in Taipei in a driving rain.

I didn't see Harry until a year later in Hong Kong. He told me he had left the Air Force and was now in the film business in California. He was in Hong Kong searching for locations for a film called 'Pepper And Salt' about the adventures of two beautiful lady detectives, one black and the other blonde. His friends in Hong Kong had planned a party for him, but on that same afternoon he came to me looking extremely worried.

'Look I've got to go to Taipei. There is some misunderstanding about a deal I had and I must go and straighten it out. I'm afraid I'll have to miss the party,' he said.

'Is there anything I can do?'

'No, no. I have to take care of this myself. Thanks a lot. I'll be in touch.'

With those brief remarks he left, not giving me a clue as to the nature of his troubles, but the *South China Morning Post* ran the story the next day.

'Harry Pelziger a former First Lieutenant in the U.S. Air Force was arrested on his return to Taipei for trafficking in heroin. It is alleged that with an accomplice he conspired to send a package of heroin through the Army Post Office using his officer's ID. He is being questioned about a vast smuggling ring operating in Taiwan that ships drugs through the APO.'

At his trial Harry got 15 years and his whistle-blowing accomplice got a lesser sentence of 12 years. I found it hard to believe, but Harry confessed the whole thing and now at the age of 38 would spend the next 15 years of his life in jail.

Harry got a job in the prison leather shop sewing mail bags. He was the only foreigner in the prison and he was beaten severely by the other inmates on several occasions while the prison officials looked the other way. His devoted Chinese wife came to the prison every day with their children and stood outside in the street where Harry could see them through the bars of his cell window.

His accomplice in the smuggling operation was released for some unknown reason after serving less than a year and Harry's term was reduced to 12 years. Harry went ballistic but nobody took any notice. He wrote me that he was contemplating suicide, he couldn't do another 12 years in prison. Then strangely, he was paroled. They came to his cell one day with civilian clothes his wife had brought and told him he was free to go.

He continued to live in Taipei with his wife who staked him to a half interest in an automobile rental agency at one of the big hotels. He was partners with a young Australian and they did well. It seemed like his luck was finally changing, and he was settling down to the good life.

Then foolish temptation raised its ugly head and a brainless scheme for making a great deal of money came Harry's way. A Chinese guy he met in prison had told him about a wealthy aunt that had just died. In her will she had asked to be buried with her favorite gold necklaces and bracelets along with 50 gold bars to provide an income in the afterworld. The Chinese guy said his plan was to dig up the grave and get hold of the gold bars and the jewelry. The theft would not be discovered for seven years when it was the Buddhist custom to open the grave and remove the bones for cleaning. He figured Harry, with his checkered past, would be a good partner.

It was too good a proposition to resist and Harry approached his Australian partner for help. At first he wouldn't listen, thinking that Harry had flipped his wig. But Harry's explanation of how easy it was going to be to just dig up the grave and pick up all that gold was too much to resist and he finally agreed to take part in the plot.

They waited until a few days after the funeral, and then

on a moon-bright night they headed for the graveyard armed with pickaxes and shovels. The night before they cased the location and found everything in order except that this particular graveyard was also the local fishermen's favorite spot to dig worms. The Chinese partner told them that fishermen were superstitious and deathly afraid of ghosts. He proposed that he and the Australian would do the digging, while Harry dressed up in a sheet with holes for the eyes and if he saw fishermen he would walk slowly down the hill, mumbling is his most sinister voice, 'Woo, woo, woo.'

While his partners did the digging, Harry roamed the perimeter of the hill in his ghost costume. For about two and a half hours, he saw nothing suspicious. Then suddenly, he caught the low murmur of voices and in the dark he saw a group of fishermen coming towards him. He immediately started his eerie chant.

'Woo, woo, woo,' he said, but the fishermen continued to approach.

He chanted louder, 'woo, woo, woo,' but still they came.

'Woo, woo, woo,' he finally shouted. When he could make them out clearly, he saw they carried guns. Harry was really scared. He ripped off his ghost costume and ran back as fast as he could to alert his two companions at the grave site.

'Robbers,' he cried frantically. 'Robbers, with guns!'

His partners were just prying the lid off of the coffin when Harry came running up. They threw down their shovels and were preparing to run when they were surrounded by eight men with guns, cocked and ready to fire. They turned out to be detectives that were onto their plot.

The sorry group didn't realize it, but an undercover man had been tailing the dead aunt's nephew for a number of days. For the second time in his Taipei career Harry found himself in handcuffs, being led away to jail.

A short time afterward when I was in Taipei I tried to find Harry and his lawyer told me the story of his madcap exploit. He said that the group was out on bail and awaiting trial, but he didn't want to give me Harry's address. He said it was better if Harry had no contact with anybody but his family at the time.

I got a letter a short time later from Harry. He was in Los Angeles. He related to me how he had escaped from Taiwan with his wife and children, sneaking onto a plane with no bags and landing in California with only the clothes on their backs. The truth of the matter, as told to me later by his lawyer, was that the Taiwanese government had let him 'escape' just to be rid of him. He really was a thorn in their side.

The last word from Harry Hope (his new name) was that he was living in a sprawling house in the San Fernando Valley with his devoted wife and two children almost directly under the big Hollywood sign and producing 'D' movies. Where he got the money for his lifestyle I'll never know. What I do know is Harry had a fondness for acquiring riches by fair means or foul. Maybe the clue lies with his ever-loyal wife: last I heard she was sporting a very valuable gold and jade bracelet and necklace that she had apparently brought with her from Taipei.

27

A GAGGLE OF FILM STARS

In my work there has never been a shortage of film stars. One of my more notable encounters was when I had an assignment from Movietone News to cover Clark Gable when he came to Hong Kong to film scenes for a real pot-boiler called 'Soldier of Fortune.' My instructions were to stay close to Gable and get footage of him whenever I could, and I got to know him and his director Edward Dmytrck quite well.

One evening between drinks Dmytrck asked me if I could arrange a date for Gable. It found it ironic that I was being called upon to fix up the great 'macho man of the silver screen,' and it brought to mind something that had happened years before.

At 19 years old I had decided to pack a few things and hitchhike around the U.S. in a search for adventure after my discharge from the navy. Hitchhiking wasn't considered dangerous in those days, and I seemed to pick up rides without much trouble. One afternoon in Ohio I got caught in a downpour and couldn't get a ride to save my life. I stood there on the side of the road with the rain coursing off me until the driver of a gravel truck finally took pity on me.

'I'm only goin' to Cadiz about thirty miles down the road,' he said.

That was fine, any port in the storm. Night was approaching and I figured I could find a small hotel in town, get some dinner and pass the night sheltered from the rain.

Cadiz was a really small town with not much going for it except, as I found out, that it was the hometown of Clark Gable. I got a room at a boarding house for $1.50 and then found the Home Restaurant on Main Street where I got a delicious three-course dinner for 35 cents. The restaurant was empty, but I found a great buddy in the short order cook who managed the place. There were several pictures on the wall of Gable as a young man.

'Did you ever meet Clark Gable?'

'Sure did. He came in almost every day with a gang of guys from the high school that he hung out with. A regular guy; didn't look like a movie star. I knew his mother, too.'

'Did he have a girlfriend?'

'Just one of the town girls. Not exactly pretty. A little on the fat side and she wore glasses but she was very smart in school and he liked that. He told me once that she was a little hefty for his taste, but there isn't much to chose from in Cadiz, so he hung out with her pretty regular.'

'Do you know why he left Cadiz and went to Hollywood?'

'No. Most of the guys leave town after high school. There ain't too much doing here, and it figured that he would go someplace else to find work. After his mother died he never came back.'

At that time I never dreamed that I would meet the 'great Gable' in person and knowing a bit about his past life in a small Ohio town didn't lessen his star quality in my eyes. In the weeks that I knew him I had dinner with him twice and drinks on several occasions but always I looked on him as what he was, a charismatic movie star. I was delighted by Dmytrck's confidential request to find a girl for Gable.

'He especially likes small, sexy women, very cute and with a bit of intelligence.' Dmytrck said.

I fixed him up with a reporter from one of the Chinese newspapers named Mimi Lau. She fit all the criteria and could discuss politics moderately well in English.

'Tell me, Mr. Clark,' she apparently said to him, speaking of the war in Korea, 'What your opinion of the 38 paralyze?'

Another time, Orson Welles arrived in Hong Kong to star in a film called 'Ferry to Hong Kong.' The entire film, exteriors and interiors were shot in Hong Kong on sets constructed on a stage built on a barren parcel of land between Aberdeen and Deep Water Bay. They built a replica of the motor vessel *Fat Shan* that looked exactly like the real thing. The story was based on a real person, though the plot was contrived and the hero was appallingly portrayed by Curt Jurgens. As the captain of the *Fat Shan*, Welles played his unbelievably preposterous role, doing what seemed like a takeoff of Charles Laughton in 'Mutiny on the Bounty.' At that stage of his career Orson was on a downward spiral and was obviously hurting for money.

One day, I got a phone call from a Frenchmen who told me he was a partner of Orson Welles and they were making a picture. He said it was a surrealist type of film and Orson would tell me all about it when I met him for the first day of shooting. They agreed to pay US$250 a day. Would I do the filming? Work with the director of 'Citizen Kane?', The finest film ever made? I would have done it without pay, but I didn't say so.

I was there at the appointed time and what a shock when I saw my idol. I hadn't realized Orson now weighed over 300 pounds. I was looking for the young Charles Foster Kane— svelte, dapper and handsome. I recalled reading somewhere that he said, 'The only thing I haven't beaten in life is glut-tony,' and looking at him I could believe it.

Although my mental image had been dashed, I still planned on getting some lessons in filmmaking from a man who had introduced some of the art's most innovative modi-fications. Orson told me that we were going to shoot mainly with a telephoto lens, handheld. That was already unusual. He made a rule that when we shot with a wide angle lens I must use the tripod tilted to the extreme, and we went all over the colony shooting in this bizarre fashion.

During two weeks of frustrating work I got no lessons from Orson, just instructions to shoot this and that in a most peculiar fashion. Although he was friendly, when we dined together he didn't want to discuss anything about the films he had made. He was absentminded and always seemed to be thinking about something that disturbed him, perhaps his enormous girth.

The Frenchman called on me and asked if I knew a lab where we could get the film developed. He gave me more than enough money with instructions not to make a print until I heard from him. Then, when the negative was devel-oped he asked me to leave it at a particular storage company. I did as directed and about a year later I was passing the storage company and stopped by to ask about the film. They said that a Frenchman had come about a month before and taken it all away, leaving no forwarding address. I never

heard from the Frenchman or Orson again and I never saw
a foot of the film we shot, so I don't know how it turned out.
But I can imagine.

28

SATYAJIT RAY

Mary was pregnant. Her tummy was swelling as the great day approached when we would become parents for the first time. Our landlord offered us a two-bedroom flat for HK$600 with a fireplace that, of course, we never used. But it was a good conversation piece when guests asked, 'Is that a fireplace?'

I was excited about becoming a father, but at this time when I wanted to stay close to home Cathay Pacific gave me an assignment that would take me around Asia for a few weeks, taking shots for posters and calendars. As usual, their ad agency Fortune International was in a hurry to have them finished, but I decided to stall so I could be close to Mary and went over to deliver my ultimatum. As I entered the office I overheard Earl Button the art director giving orders to his assistant.

'This project is a month old and we don't have one picture yet. Don't ask Marvin, tell him if he wants to do this job to get his ass over to Calcutta immediately and get me some pictures. Then when he gets back from there send him to the Philippines and then to Borneo, Cambodia and Japan. Keep him moving. We are way behind with this job.'

As I walked into Earl's office the first thing I did was mention that I was going to be a father.

'Isn't that great. Congratulations. Best of luck to the little mother,' Earl said and then went right into explaining the project.

'You are free to pick your own subjects but I want you to extract the essence of the place you're photographing. In Calcutta, your model's dress, her makeup and everything about her should say India. Find out what makes the place tick and then make it photographically exciting. You know how. Remember that the posters are being made to sell a location and will be four feet long and two feet wide so everything will hang out. They must be great. Any questions?'

All my resolve to stall the job was gone but Mary took it all with stoic good grace. She even suggested I look up her old Calcutta buddy, Peter Parr at the Tea Commission and buy her some Indian raw cotton. Mary said it was an unusual-looking material with a coarse finish and would make a nice skirt. Early the next morning I packed my set of 4x5 Linhof and my Rolleiflex and I was off to India.

As I was traveling on Cathay Pacific business, I managed to worm my way into first class where I had a nice chat with a stewardess who knew loads about Calcutta and told me where I could buy Mary's raw cotton. She also suggested shooting at the racetrack and historic Fort William, and she mentioned a statue of Queen Victoria commemorating her rule over India.

Seven and half hours after leaving Hong Kong we landed at Dum Dum airport. Calcutta is perhaps the most Indian city in India and one of the world's most crowded and colorful places. The center of commerce, finance and manufacturing for eastern India, it's a photographer's dream. People dressed in turbans and *dhotis*, peasants driving ox carts, barefoot coolies with huge loads suspended from bamboo poles, and cows walking serenely in the streets. These sights mixed with the sound of horns from taxis, cars, buses and bicycles all jockeying for positions on the overcrowded roads. During the day the city had a population of over eight million but when night came two million disappeared over the Howrah Bridge.

I checked into the Great Eastern Hotel, recommended by the stewardess, Shanta Mansukani, as supposedly the best hotel in town. The lobby looked a little seedy and while I was waiting in the check-in line I saw a large rat running across the floor. Feeling somewhat horrified, I brought it to the attention of the desk clerk.

He didn't even look up from what he was doing. 'What do you want me to do about it?'

'Nothing,' I said facetiously. 'I just thought I'd mention it.'

An Englishman in the check-in line said laconically, 'Welcome to India!'

I had made an arrangement with Dirk Brink at Deaks, the Hong Kong money changer. He simply gave me the telephone number of their man in Calcutta who would advance me as many rupees as I needed. Then when I got back to Hong Kong I could square my account with Deaks. That way I would not have to carry around U.S. dollars and change them on the street, which Dirk told me was a dangerous business.

I phoned the contact, Mr. Chandru Gupta. He had received

a message that I was coming and when I started to tell him about the amount of rupees I would need, he immediately hushed me.

'Please,' he said agitatedly, 'I will come to your hotel right away.'

'I am Gupta, I will be your guide,' he announced loudly on entering my room.

'What? I don't need a guide.'

Once the door was closed he explained. 'I'm not really a guide. I am the shroff for Deak and Company. I have your money.'

His very black hair was greasily pomaded to his scalp. He dressed in loose-fitting white trousers and a light pink shirt and he smelled of cheap *eau de cologne*. His glasses had thin black frames and his palm, when he shook my hand was wet and uncomfortable, as if he were holding a dead fish. He had a very fawning manner.

'You must be careful what you say. The police are every-where,' he said.

'Is what we are doing illegal?'

'Oh yes, very.' He got right down to business.

'I have brought you seventy thousand rupees, US$10,000.'

'Wait a minute. That's too much. I asked Mr. Brink for about US$3,000 in rupees that's all.'

'I've brought all these rupees. I can't take them back.'

'Well I could never use so many.'

'What am I supposed to do with them?'

'That's not my look out. I need only twenty thousand rupees.'

'Well can't you take the whole amount?' he said in a more conciliatory manner. 'You can return what you don't use to me, before you leave.'

'I don't want to get stuck with this huge amount because I

can't find you when I leave. Mr. Brink told me that I could lose a lot of U.S. dollars changing rupees in Hong Kong. I'm sorry, I can't afford to take the chance.'

Mr. Gupta took out a handkerchief and wiped off his glasses. He glared at me and reluctantly took 20,000 rupees from the pile.

'This is highly irregular. We don't deal in such small sums.' He turned to leave. 'Please don't call me again.'

With that he departed looking very annoyed. I discovered later that he was a freelance agent used by Deaks exclusively for this sort of currency transaction. I was glad to get rid of him but he left the aroma of that horrid, sweet-smelling perfume in my room.

Notwithstanding the rat in the lobby, the dirty water in the sink and the unctuous Mr. Gupta, I slept splendidly in my room at the Great Eastern and the next morning I checked in at the Cathay Pacific office.

Ramchand Bannerchee, the manager, was a very agreeable type. In his early 30s and a recent import from New Delhi, he had the look of a well-educated man and took an immediate interest in my project. He took me for tea and snacks in a restaurant just around the corner, and then he made a phone call and an Anglo-Indian girl joined us.

'I feel it isn't really right to talk in front of the other girls. We had word that you were coming so I took the opportunity of choosing Devi here to model for you. What do you think?'

'She's beautiful. I think she'd be perfect.'

'Don't feel that you have to say that,' Devi said modestly. 'We have other girls in our office that you could select. Maybe you'd like more time to think about it? I'm not even a hundred percent Indian.' She was refreshingly modest for such a beautiful girl.

'No, I'm serious. You'd be fine. You look a hundred percent Indian to me. What do you think Mr. Bannerchee?'

'She's perfect, except for her hairdo. Do you have budget for a hairdresser? We'd have to get one who is skilled at making Bengali hairdos. Very complicated, it takes an expert.'

'I'm sure we have budget for that.'

'That's fine. I'll have the hairdresser come to my office this afternoon.'

Later, as we lounged over tea, I asked Mr. Bannerchee about a fellow he'd said hello to on the way in. 'He was wearing an enormous rhinestone ring. Did you notice it? It looked sort of ridiculous.'

'That is Bal Chandrika,' Mr. Bannerchee said. 'He owns the biggest jute mill in this part of India. He is tremendously wealthy and that ring is definitely not rhinestone. In the heat of Calcutta most people dress in slacks and sport shirts and Mr. Chandrika dresses that way, too. He wears that huge diamond just to let people know that he is not an ordinary man. Otherwise, how are they to know to know how wealthy and powerful he is?'

'If it's a real diamond then he would be in danger of having it stolen.'

'Not much chance of that. Those two burly men sitting with him are his bodyguards and they go everywhere with him.'

At 2:30 p.m. two young Chinese hairdressers, apparently famous for making Bengali hairdos came to the Cathay office. They spoke lively broken English and Cantonese overlaid with an Indian accent. I could hardly understand what they said, but one of them was an artist of sorts and drew several types of Bengali hairdos on paper. I picked one and the hairdressers said it would take several hours to create so we arranged for Devi to go to their shop at 8 a.m. the following day.

I had some free time to look up Mary's friend Peter Parr and with the help of the *'Practical Guide to the Streets of Calcutta'* I found the Tea Commission's address on Clive Row, a street named for Robert Clive one of the founders of British rule in India. The British were gone, but not forgotten as everywhere I went I came across some vestige of the former empire.

Peter Parr had been a captain in the Indian army (actually the British army in India) and after 15 years had India in his blood and found it difficult to leave and return to an England he hardly knew. Upon discharge from the army he had managed to obtain a position at the Tea Commission and decided to settle in India. He was a pleasant, youngish-looking chap with a full crop of black hair and a rather large mustache. When he spoke he looked directly at you and resembled a drill sergeant, with square shoulders and a straight back.

Peter's office on the third floor of an old white plaster building was not elaborately decorated but cozy with a comfortable sofa, overstuffed chairs, and a simple wooden desk that appeared to have seen better days. Pictures of tea plantations lined the wall.

Peter had just returned from the hill stations in Assam where he had been inspecting the Darjeeling tea crop. I gathered he was a sort of a troubleshooter. I liked him immediately and after talking for a little while, I discovered he was free to accompany me to the Cathay office where I had to take care of some last minute details. The moment he saw Devi he fell head over heels in love. I don't believe she was taken with him though, and she politely rebuffed his advances.

'What a superb woman,' he said as soon as we left the Cathay office. 'Listen old man, do you mind if I ask her out?'

'Go right ahead, but didn't you find her manner toward you rather cool?'

'Merely a facade. Indian women are shy with foreigners. You must break down their resistance. In all my years here I have gotten to know the Indian woman's mentality quite well.'

'She's part English you know.'

'An Anglo Indian? So much the better.'

'I wish you the best of luck with her,' I said, adding 'old man.'

'What say we go to the Tolligunge Club for drinks and then after to the Calcutta Club for dinner?'

They say put three Englishmen together and you have a club. The Tolligunge Club was the watering hole for members of the Calcutta foreign community and surprisingly had no Indian members. Peter explained that the foreign community wanted a club of their own, and since liberation, foreign investors are kowtowed to around government circles, so on the subject of a purely foreign club, the Indians gave in without much of a fight. In any case Indians don't really feel relaxed around foreigners either, so they took over the remaining British clubs in Calcutta and restricted membership there to Indians.

Tolligunge was on the edge of town and had sprawling grounds that boasted a straight race course, the first I had ever seen. The club house was round and encircled by a veranda with slow-moving ceiling fans. It was an ideal place for enjoying your gin and bitters and watching the sun set on the British Empire.

'Where are you staying?' Peter asked.

'At the Great Eastern.'

'Ah yes, when I first came to Calcutta I stayed there for one night. I picked up this exquisite blonde in the lobby and registered her as my wife. We had a glorious night but when I was checking out in the morning, I discovered my bill was some astronomic figure. I told the man there must be a mistake, as I had only stayed one night. To which he replied, 'Yes, I know, but your wife checked in three months ago."

In India, people don't usually sit down to dinner until after 10 p.m. so it was well into the night when we left the Tolligunge. The Calcutta Club accepted only Indian members, but they allowed Europeans to have drinks at their bar and a meal in their dining room. It was a picturesque old building which the British members must have been hard pressed to give up. Inside, huge pillars surrounded a marble staircase and in a bit of irony, the walls were hung with pictures of the heroes that opposed British rule. At the top of the stairs, a little larger than the rest, was a photo of Gandhi leading one of his peaceful resistance marches.

As we sat talking Peter asked me very casually, 'Would it do you any good to meet Satyajit Ray?'

I was amazed that Peter should mention the master filmmaker.

'Do you know him?'

'Yes, quite well. If you want to meet him I could arrange for us to go over to his house after dinner.'

Satyajit Ray is a man I consider to be on a level with Orson Welles as one of the greatest filmmakers of our time. With little budget, using amateur actors and writing his own dialogue and background music, he directed beautiful and evocative portrayals of traditional Indian life.

I pictured him living in opulent splendor, like a minor maharajah, but his home in Calcutta was far from that. He lived in an unpretentious, two-story dwelling furnished with simplicity and practicality. The family had just finished dinner when we arrived and an aroma of curry permeated the house.

Satyajit Ray was quite tall, wore loose-fitting white trousers and an Indian tunic with a skirt that went down to his knees, and no shoes.

We were shown into the living room where we were served Indian tea and cookies.

'This is Marvin Farkas,' Peter said. 'He has a company in Hong Kong that makes documentary films and was very anxious to meet you.'

'Do you know Brian Brake and Nigel Cameron?' Ray said, mentioning the respected Hong Kong-based photographer-writer team. Brian Brake, the photographer, had done a lot of work for Life magazine.

'Yes, slightly.'

'If you see them please tell them hello. They are dear friends.'

'After seeing Pather Panchali I couldn't resist the opportunity to meet you. It was a beautifully told story and I was impressed with the way you gave real value to the lives of impoverished people.'

'In India, a majority of the people live in a kind of poverty that the western world finds hard to understand. What I try to show is that there is value in everyone's life and these poor folk live normal lives. I show their religion, close family ties, their loves, their laughs, and everyday ordeals of finding work and putting food on the table. They live unremarkable lives, but with the additional adversity that comes from poverty. It is a bit complicated, but those are the stories I tell, and if that is what you saw I am pleased. Naturally my films are aimed at Indian audiences who understand the subject.'

'Is it true that you cast actors that have no experience?'

'It's true. They are complete amateurs for the most part that come from the poor backgrounds they are portraying.'

'I loved the scene of the dying old man and the grandson who gets him 'holy water' from the Ganges River.'

'The old man knew that the water was not clean and would probably hasten his death, but his faith transcended his fear of dying,' Ray said. 'Before he passed on he wanted to carry out this ritual of the true Hindu believer and drink holy water from the sacred river.

The actors give outstanding performances because they know the meaning of the scenes. Professional actors can play scenes once they are explained to them, but with my cast no explanation is necessary because each scene is an extension of their lives. That is the difference, and the reason for the realistic performances.'

'I have an idea for a film that shows a different side of life in India and is a complete departure from what you have done before. Would you be interested in making a film that takes place in an upper middle class setting? It concerns a young married couple and their problems when they come into a huge inheritance.'

'So far I have done films only about poor people.'

'Wouldn't you enjoy the challenge of a complete departure from your other films? After all there is more to India than the Ghats of Benares.'

'Let's say I was interested in taking on your project, would you be prepared to do the film on my terms?' he asked combatively. 'I approve the script, adapt it, write the music, direct the film, and I do not have to discuss with anyone about how

I spend the budget. The producers are not permitted on my set during shooting, and the only time I see them is when I show them the final cut, about which they have no say. Does that sound fair?'

'It doesn't sound fair, but it sounds like what I thought you would say. I must confess that my idea for a film is just something that I thought of on my way over here. The prospect of meeting you got my creative juices flowing. I don't have a feature project right now.'

'It doesn't really matter because my time is taken up with projects for the next three years.'

My chat with Satyajit Ray was much too short. There was much more I wanted to say to him, and of all the people I met in India, there was no one I wanted to talk to more than this brilliant filmmaker. In that modest home, on the outskirts of Calcutta, I began to learn to appreciate the real art of making movies.

29

THE BRIDGE AT LOWU

Ah, the best-laid plans of mice and men. I arrived back in
Hong Kong ready to start planning my first trip to the
U.S. with Mary when I was suddenly swamped with news
work which I couldn't, in all conscience, turn down. I had
to make almost daily trips to the closed border area of Hong
Kong and what has become an historic site — the Bridge at
Lowu.

On the border I ran into Father Poletti picking up five nuns
who had been thrown out of China, for their 'counterrevolutionary activities.' They came from Inner Mongolia where
they had been under house arrest for over a year. Father
Poletti told me that the powers that be in Rome had lost all
touch with them.

The elder nun was the spokesperson and conducted an
impromptu press conference. A big-boned, Irish woman
about 50 years old, she came from County Tyrone and told
the assembled group about their ordeal in a rich Irish brogue.

The nuns had worked in Taiyuan, Shanxi province and
when the Communists got into power, local officials warned
them of difficulties conducting religious services. They
didn't feel particularly threatened at first, but gradually the

harassment became intolerable and when they were threatened with arrest they thought it best to flee.

On a dark night they took the church van and headed into neighboring Mongolia where there was a Catholic church in Hohhot. The church had been abandoned, the building was looted and lay in shambles.

'How long were you able to keep going?' I asked.

'Not long. The Communists got hold of us and we were accused of holding illegal church services and preaching lies about Jesus and we were closed down. They said we told seditious stories to gullible people and gave Bible classes to children. They also accused us of giving people medical treatment for which we were not qualified, and going to people's homes to commit what was considered the greatest offense of all, proselytizing our religion. They said we deliberately defied the Chinese authorities and played on the weakness and lack of education of the poor souls of Inner Mongolia and they demanded we make a confession. It didn't seem to matter that it was coerced, as long as there was a confession.'

The nuns spent a year locked up in their house. The yellow wind blew from the Gobi Desert and covered the floors with an inch of sand. They spent most days cleaning, only to be hit again and again. Then came snowstorms and they didn't have enough firewood to keep warm and nothing but candles for light. They ate mostly boiled mutton and washed it down with milk from pregnant horses. A sweet old lady brought them sorghum every once in awhile, and another woman brought tea leaves, but not often.

When it seemed things couldn't get worse, devoted parishioners who had thus risked everything to support the church suddenly turned on the nuns. Even children who had attended Bible classes told deliberate lies about their activities.

'One night, after praying for God to forgive us, we confessed the whole lot,' the elder nun said. 'That confession was our key to freedom because within a week we were read a decree, expelling us forever from the People's Republic of China. We were hustled aboard a train and after a week's travel we crossed this border.'

'Where are you headed now?' a reporter asked.

'First to Rome to tell their story to the church hierarchy and then for re-assignment somewhere else,' Father Poletti said, answering for them.

He gathered the nuns together and was preparing to leave the bridge when a police officer called to him.

'Can I see you a second Father?'

'What's the matter?'

'It seems that the Chinese sent over a stretcher with a European man that is very ill. I believe he has terminal cancer and doesn't have long. Can you give him his last rites before you leave?'

'Is he Catholic?' Father Poletti asked.

'I can't tell, he is barely conscious.'

Father Poletti took off his knapsack, pulled out his stole and while the five nuns stood solemnly by, their hands folded in prayer, Father Poletti knelt over the man and administered his last rites. Then he stood beside the nuns and watched silently as the man was carried from the bridge to spend what precious little time he had in the free world.

Rich and successful Chinese, too, felt the force of Communist vengeance. If they weren't expelled they were sent to the countryside for 're-education,' meaning to plant rice and dig ditches.

Shanghai was a particular target for the new government. With its strong foreign influence, the city had experienced a period of phenomenal commercial and industrial growth, far more so than the rest of China. The Communists claimed that the success was capitalistic and at odds with their ideology. Always jealous of Shanghai's accomplishments, the leaders moved to knock it down a peg or two. They took capital earmarked for infrastructure projects away from Shanghai to use in other parts of China. When foreigners and Chinese entrepreneurs were thrown out, Shanghai shrunk back into nothing more than a third class, hopelessly overcrowded and poor city.

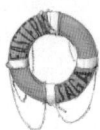

One hapless group coming over the Lowu Bridge was comprised of left-leaning Fulbright scholars from America who had received grants to study in China. They were received cordially at first, but after a short while were unceremoniously dumped by the Chinese who decided they had little to offer their revolution. We interviewed some of the scholars as they came back across the bridge. They were very fond of the Chinese people, they said, and couldn't understand what had happened.

But the most extraordinary bunch of misfits to come over the bridge was the 'turncoats.' They had fought in the Korean War and defected to the Communist Chinese side after being captured. Some married and set up home in China, but a small group of them decided to return to the U.S. and we met them on the bridge.

'They give us filthy, unheated houses to live in. We worked in the fields with peasants from before the sun came up until it was dark. The food was uneatable. We got better treatment in the prison camp.'

'Well, you subscribed to the Communist ideology didn't you?' I asked.

'What are you tryin' to say; that we're freakin' Communists?' one member of the group said angrily. 'We're loyal Americans. We love America.'

'Then why did you choose to live in a Communist state and be a traitor to your own country?'

'We weren't traitors. We were tricked by the Commies. When we found out what was up we wanted to go home.'

'Do you know that the United States government takes your defection very seriously? You will have to stand trial, and maybe even go to jail?'

'We'll take whatever punishment is comin'. They couldn't hang us for making a little mistake, could they?' he said seriously.

I shrugged my shoulders. 'We'll see.'

I heard scores of tales about fugitives from China who crossed the border over the Lowu Bridge. Businessmen and women, priests and nuns, scholars and teachers, schoolchildren and countless others. It may have just been a tiny bridge but in the crossing, shattered hopes and dreams started to knit together again.

30

HE SPEAKS ONLY TO GOD

In the 19th century, France began to colonize what they called French Indochina—Vietnam, Laos and Cambodia. They continued to rule with few interruptions until the 20th century when strong nationalist groups seeking to smash the yoke of European domination started a war aimed at driving the French out. In 1954 the French went down in humiliating defeat and Vietnam was partitioned into North and South. The North aligned itself with the Soviet Union and China, and the South was propped up by the United States. In an attempt to re-unify the nation and dump a corrupt government (and their American cronies), a faction supported by the North and calling themselves the Viet Cong started a guerrilla war. Civil wars supported by the Communist bloc also simultaneously broke out in Laos and Cambodia. The war raged in Southeast Asia for years until in one final push in 1975, North Vietnam over-ran the southern capital of Saigon and the Vietnam War was over. Political accord was established and Vietnam was again a unified nation.

The Vietnam War was my chance to take part in history being made. I like covering dynamic events and the people that make them happen. I don't like filming dead bodies, though I got more than my share in the 12 years I covered that war. In the case of Vietnam, it was the politics that I found fascinating.

Two guys who worked out of the UPI office had teamed up to write stories against the war and the people that controlled it. Their work had a big impact. Neil Sheehan was the UPI's Saigon bureau chief and David Halberstam was a *New York Times* correspondent who worked out of the UPI office.

Neil was a brash Irish kid, a slim, fair-haired brooding character who pulled no punches and went straight for the jugular with his stories. David was fresh out of university with button-down shirts, khaki trousers and buckskin shoes. He had a full head of thick black hair, wore spectacles and looked more like a young university lecturer than a war reporter. He wrote with purpose and forethought, resolving to bring down the perpetrators of the Vietnam debacle.

Like an old vaudeville act, Halberstam and Sheehan sat opposite each other across a shared desk typing away with the rapidity of two machine guns. They were like avenging angels and they took on the architects of war unremittingly. They would stop briefly to talk over a point and then go back to typing. They kept sources on tap that they selected carefully, to back up the facts of their articles. Neil often said that he didn't trust the word of anybody above the rank of sergeant.

One eminent victim of their scorching attacks was Madame Nhu, the politically active wife of Ngo Dinh Nhu, the brother of South Vietnam's president. Madame Nhu was a Catholic and she mercilessly baited the Buddhist majority, with a special focus on monks. Halberstam and Sheehan likened her to a venomous reptile that had to be eliminated and with their typewriters they went at it full force. Thanks to them, word of her wicked celebrity spread and she was in great demand with the press; she began charging US$500 for an interview. When asked about the Buddhist monks who burned themselves to death in a protest of the war, she notoriously said, 'Come, join me for a Buddhist barbecue. If they don't have matches I can supply them.'

Madame Nhu may have been mean spirited, but she wasn't stupid. She realized she was in great danger in Saigon and I suspected when we were called to the airport to cover a quick trip she was making to Paris to take her daughter to a posh finishing school it would be the last we would see of Madame Nhu. When I got back to the UPI office, I found Halberstam and Sheehan with wicked smirks on their faces. They rubbed their hands together and said something like, 'That takes care of that. Now let's get General Harkins' and set their typewriters blazing away at their latest victim.

Another recipient of the scorn of these two newsmen was Ngo Dinh Diem, the 62-year-old president of South Vietnam. In 1955 as prime minister, Diem overthrew the government of

Emperor Bao Dai, declared South Vietnam a republic and fraudulently named himself president with support from the U.S. who was increasingly worried about the Communists in the North. Diem then refused to hold the elections which had been agreed upon under the 1954 Geneva Accords to reunify the country. His justification was that the people in the North would not be able to vote freely, although Diem's government was itself accused of fraudulent election practices and wholesale corruption.

Agitation by the Catholic-led government was especially strong resulting in the arrests of thousands of Buddhists who made up the majority of citizens in the country. Diem accused the monks of being infiltrated by Communists, an assumption that was supported by a U.S. fact-finding team. Religious friction between the Buddhists and the government continued to grow and political protests in the form of self-immolation by the monks were frequent. The Viet Cong began an all-out war on the Vietnamese army and their American advisors, and then on November 1, 1963 Diem's regime came to an abrupt end.

Just before that date our UPI Television News camera crew was granted an interview with Diem. At the presidential palace we were searched thoroughly and our camera equipment was meticulously checked by the palace guard. We were warned by the guys at UPI to watch out for flying bullets as it was no secret that Diem might be assassinated at any moment.

Diem used the same phrase in all his interviews. 'You must give us a chance to exterminate the Communists. Please support our efforts. I can see the light at the end of the tunnel.'

Ah yes, the light at the end of the tunnel. I was so mesmerized by the thought of his being assassinated that I kept staring at him as I attached the microphone to his lapel. I imagined that I would see him lying there, in a pool of blood; he must have known they were out to get him.

Three days later there was a coup and a general called Big Minh took over the country. Ngo Dinh Diem and his brother Ngo Dinh Nhu were blindfolded, loaded into a police wagon and driven away by a loyal palace guard made up of the most carefully selected and elite soldiers in the South Vietnamese army. The captain in charge of the abduction asked for orders over the walkie-talkie.

'We are cruising around the city. What shall we do with them?'

A voice from the other end came, 'Shoot them.'

The squeamish captain couldn't believe what he heard. 'Oh, my God,' he said.

'Just shoot them and make sure you don't spill any of their blood in the van,' came the retort.

So I guess that's exactly what happened. We went to the cemetery that night with a crowd of newsmen, dodging enormous mosquitoes while we waited four hours for the bodies to arrive for burial. They never turned up. There were two freshly dug graves, side by side but the caretaker told us he didn't know who they were for. Diem and his brother were never seen again.

Did the persistent vilification of Diem by guys like Halberstam and Sheehan play any part in bringing about the coup and assassination? It's hard to say, but when I was at the airport the next day shipping the film of the empty graves, a ground stewardess from Air Vietnam proposed an alternative theory.

'Thank God for the Americans,' she said, clapping her hands with delight. 'They killed Diem and his awful brother Nhu.' She looked straight into my eyes. 'Thank you for liberating our country from these terrible people. Thank God for the Americans.'

One aspect of my coverage of the Vietnam War was that I occasionally got to interact with some very important people. They probably wouldn't remember me, but I had presidents, prime ministers, ambassadors and four-star generals before my camera.

However Henry Cabot Lodge, the American ambassador to South Vietnam, a graduate of Harvard College and an illustrious member of the New England aristocracy had little to say when I was doing a story on the American Boy Scout troop in Saigon. The bureau chief at UPI thought it might make a good off-beat story, and to my surprise who should be there handing out merit badges but Ambassador Lodge. A tall, handsome man in his early 60s, he was in shirt sleeves with his trousers held up by a pair of multi-colored suspenders.

The scout meeting was in the basement theater of the U.S. Operations Mission building, but it could have been any building in the States.

'If I'd known you were going to be here I would have brought a sound camera,' I said to him.

'Really?'

'Yes. You're an important man and you on camera would have given substance to the piece.'

'Why?'

'Because people want to hear what you have to say.'

'About the Boy Scouts?'

'About anything. If you can wait five minutes, I work at UPI just down the street, and I could get my sound camera.'

'No,' Mr. Lodge said emphatically.

'What about the war? Talking about the war? That would be interesting.'

'I doubt it.'

'You could talk on any subject and people would listen.'

'I don't like talking.'

'You mean you don't like talking in general, or you don't like talking to a camera?'

'Both.'

'But you're the American ambassador. You must have talked at some time in your life to reach such a significant position.'

'Influence,' he said.

'You could talk about that. How you got the job of ambassador. What the position means to you.'

He shrugged his shoulders and started to walk away.

I half shouted after him. 'What Vietnam means to you, how you feel about the American position in Vietnam, what you think the outcome will be!'

Mr. Lodge was almost out of the door of the theater when he turned and said, 'Forget it' and was gone.

He had brushed me off in about 10 single-syllable words. He had turned out to be a true, upper class, close-mouthed New Englander, which reminded me that old poem:

> *So this is good old Boston,*
> *The home of the bean and the cod.*
> *Where the Lowells speak only to the Cabots,*
> *And the Cabots speak only to God.*

Actually I don't know how valuable having an on-camera interview with Henry Cabot Lodge would have been. As ambassador he sat in his office all day and attended official functions. His perception of the American position in the Vietnamese war would have been very blinkered.

When I arrived back at the UPI office with my non-story, Richard Lindley, my reporter of the moment was waiting impatiently for me. I especially liked working with British correspondents like Richard. They were articulate and possibly more thorough than the Americans who relished being in the thick of things but then produced watered-down versions of the story accompanied by pictures of themselves in heroic situations. British reporters liked stories which had a beginning, middle and end, and they often worked on them long after their American counterparts had theirs in the can and were back on the veranda of the Continental Hotel sipping gin and tonics and reliving their close calls on the battlefield. The Americans got the story, but not in the detailed manner of the British.

'Where were you?' Richard asked.

'Well I have this story of Henry Cabot Lodge presiding over a Boy Scout meeting that I really ought to ship,' I said sarcastically.

'We are supposed to go to Pleiku with President Thieu. He's giving Maxwell Taylor a tour of Montagnard camps. We have to pick up a helicopter at Tan Son Nhut, so get your sound gear and let's get out of here. We might have missed the story already.'

I grabbed my sound camera and a couple of rolls of film,

and in less time than it takes to tell we were in a beat up blue and white Peugot taxi headed for Tan Son Nhut airport at the breakneck speed of 28 miles per hour.

Richard was baffled. 'Why do you do these ridiculous stories about Boy Scouts that interest nobody? We have an important story to shoot. Maxwell Taylor is the chairman of the Joint Chiefs of Staff and he came direct from Washington and is being shown around the Montagnard encampments by none other than the president of South Vietnam. We might be able to get an interview with him, and find out how the war is going, right from the top.'

'Sorry, Richard.' The only bit of snobbery about him in my eyes was that he insisted on being called Richard, never Dick.

We were going in a party of about 20 helicopters to Pleiku, a mountainous region several hundred miles to the northwest of Saigon. The Montagnard were an indigenous mountain people from Vietnam's Central Highlands. They were known as fierce fighters, and President Nguyen Van Thieu was leading an expedition to show General Taylor and the press how the people of Vietnam from all walks of life were rallying to the government's side in their battle against Communism.

The Montagnards lived in thatched roof shacks in small fortified hamlets, surrounded by barbed wire ditches armed with sharp excrement-smeared wooden stakes. Around the perimeter tin cans containing a few pebbles hung on the barbed wire. They served to sound the alarm should intruders try to get into the encampment.

Some of their fighters were older than you might expect soldiers to be, and some were merely 12- and 13-year-old boys and girls. Most carried M1903 rifles, relics of World War I. All were dressed in rags, and a few smoked pipes which contained a strong narcotic. American Special Forces were advising them on modern guerrilla warfare and the use of the weapons.

'How do you like this duty, soldier?' General Taylor asked one of the U.S. Army contingent.

'Great, sir. These are the nicest people in the world, but when you get them riled, look out. They are fierce fighters.'

'What about the children I see here? Are they as young as they look?'

'Well, about thirteen or fourteen years old. Girls fight alongside the boys. They have a young leader who is only fifteen and he leads not only the kids, but the older men as well.'

'Could I meet him?' the general asked.

'Yes sir,' said the American advisor and called to one of the boys to get their leader.

A skinny young boy laden with two hand grenades, a .45 pistol on a cloth belt wrapped around his waist, and an M16 with a bandolier of bullets around his neck, appeared. He was a handsome boy with brown skin and big white teeth. He smiled shyly when he was introduced to General Taylor.

'Has he been in any battles yet?'

'A couple of nights ago they went outside the fence and picked off about thirty Cong that were attacking. They lost six of their own men in the skirmish. Would you like to see the graves?'

The general raised his hand. 'No, that's okay. What about the food? Do you eat their food or just subsist on K-rations?'

'About half and half,' answered the soldier. 'They have some strange concoctions and don't eat meat, but what they eat is surprisingly tasty. Except for the insects. I've gotta stop at pan-fried water beetles. We have our own water and occasionally take a sip of their wine. It's really strong, like 90 proof. We give them supplies of K-rations but they prefer their own food.'

At this point President Thieu came up to join our group. 'Would you like to look at the living quarters?' he asked General Taylor.

Their huts were built of logs with openings left for windows. Huge leaves served as curtains and the entry door was army issue tarpaulin. The nights were cold here and everyone used blankets. The Montagnards slept on thin mats on the floor of the huts while the American advisors slept on regular army cots.

We had a brief interview with President Thieu about the Montagnards. Richard asked some direct questions.

'Do you feel that these mountain people are sophisticated enough to understand what Communism means?'

'They are loyal to our government and many have lost their lives fighting the Communists.'

'I asked if they realize that the enemy they are fighting is Communist?'

'Of course they realize the political significance of the enemy, and they are prepared to fight them and protect their homes and their way of life.'

'Are you trying to say that the Viet Cong want to wipe out the Montagnards and take this … clearing in the forest? What could they want with this remote and almost uninhabited part of the country?'

'It is part of their drive to take over the entire land and indoctrinate all the people with their ideology.'

'Are the Montagnards being paid?'

'Just a pittance.'

'Wouldn't they do the 'right thing' just for the money?'

'Of course not. They need little in the way of worldly goods. They are a primitive people and the small amount of money we give them is not an incentive to fight our enemy. Rather they are motivated to fight the Communists to preserve their way of life.'

We cornered General Taylor. 'What do you think of President Thieu's account of why the Montagnards are fighting the Viet Cong?'

'I don't know all the facts but there is reason in what he says.'

'I can't understand why he brought you all the way out here to meet a primitive tribe. Do you think this is important to your report when you get back to Washington? And why so many helicopters?'

'Well, I requested to see what the American Special Forces are doing in-country and the large number of helicopter gun-ships are for security.'

'What is the next thing on the agenda?'

'I am going to meet all the field commanders this afternoon and discuss how to get this action over with in the quickest possible way. Any more questions?'

'Just this: are we winning or losing?'

'Of course we are winning, but I will get a clearer picture when I speak to the field commanders.'

31

RISING UP OF THE PUNJAB

It was one of those sunny, lazy days in Phnom Penh,
Cambodia and I was dining al-fresco at the Café De La
Poste on succulent artichokes in vinaigrette sauce with ITN
correspondent Mike Nicholson and my soundman Frank
Price. War action in Cambodia was languishing and we
couldn't find any stories to shoot, so we were just waiting
for headquarters to send Mike home to London and me and
Frank back to Hong Kong.

After lunch we strolled back along the quiet streets to the
UPI office to check the wire. At that time UP and ITN coop-
erated on newsreels. At the office we found a message from
London instructing us to proceed to Pakistan with all possible
haste. The Indus River, which normally irrigated the farms of
the Indus Valley, was overflowing through the northern sec-
tions of the country. The floodwaters were making their way
steadily south and were expected to reach Karachi in a few
days, and if that happened more than half the country would
be flooded. We rushed back to the Hotel Le Phnom and in
less than an hour were packed, checked out and headed to the
airport to catch a Pakistan International plane to Karachi.

On arrival we met the UPI bureau chief Ronnie Pena, a

recent import from Hong Kong. Ronnie suggested we head-quarter ourselves at the northern edge of the flooded region in Lahore, the capital of Punjab Province. We took a flight to Lahore that afternoon and checked into the Intercontinental Hotel. While Mike did the rounds of government offices to check out the story, Frank and I checked out the town.

Frank was an American, but he looked like a local with his huge beard and even the doorman at the Intercontinental mistook him for a fellow Pakistani. He was a big fellow, a shade over six feet tall with a gigantic frame and huge hands. He had spent two years in Goa with the Peace Corps and could speak Hindi quite well, and even a smattering of Urdu, the local Punjabi language.

We wandered the Diamond Market, the entertainment area of the city. On the way we met a disheveled character who offered to be our guide to the delights to be found there. He spoke in whispers like a street huckster keeping a lookout for the police. He conversed with Frank in Urdu and said he was going to take us to see the seamy side of Lahore where we could meet exciting, 'loose' women.

We followed him to a house just off the main drag and after climbing a rickety staircase, we entered an apartment with one large room. Inside, men sat around with an array of musical instruments. A mini organ, worked by pumping with the foot, a few tom-toms and strange-looking pipes, and one guy had a saxophone.

There were also two rather attractive, barefoot girls

wearing the *salwar kameez*, a sari-like dress with loose-fitting trousers drawn in tightly at the ankles and little bells. They wore brightly colored scarves over their heads and each one had a gold ring through her nose and thick, black mascara round the eyes. Frank had a little discussion with our guide about the price to get the show going, and when we came up with the cash the orchestra started to play and the two girls to dance.

They undulated their bodies, stamped their bare feet, rang the little bells and swung their heads to the beat of the tom-toms. The dance became more erotic with their ample breasts rising and falling, but just when things were getting interesting the music stopped and the girls disappeared with amazing speed.

We were about to follow them out when the door swung open, and a blind beggar dressed in a loin cloth was led in by an apparently deranged man with a week's stubble on his face.

'Oh, this ought to be interesting,' Frank said. 'He's what they call a *babu* or a *sadu*. A teacher. He can tell our fortunes.'

'Oh bullshit. I'm not interested in having my fortune told. Anyway they don't look like teachers, they look like beggars, and I don't want to be taken for any more money.'

The disabled man stationed himself in front of the door and wouldn't let us out without giving him some rupees. I was tiring of Lahore's Diamond Market but before we left the area we had a bowl of mutton curry soup with fresh lime juice from a steaming cauldron set up in the street. It might not have been sanitary but at least it was tasty. When I looked around for Frank I found him talking with a man wearing a filthy white shirt, grimy oversized trousers and a scruffy turban on his head. He was smoking a pipe with a piece of silver foil over the top of the bowl. The man shook hands with Frank, and then Frank took the pipe, put it into his mouth and started to puff. I was flabbergasted.

'What the hell are you doing, sharing a pipe? Are you crazy?'

Frank just smiled and pointed to the pipe.

'Ganja,' he said. 'Hashish.'

He marched ahead, puffing on the pipe as wreaths of sickly, sweet-smelling smoke circled his head.

The next day we got out of bed early and headed for the Lahore Flying Club where Mike rented a Piper Cub from which we could film the floods. Then, we were to fly to Bahawalpur to join a contingent of Pakistani Air Force helicopters that were dropping CARE food packages in the stricken areas.

I was seated alongside the pilot so I could shoot from the window. Mike was fairly comfortable in the back seat but Frank's heavy frame was scrunched down in a place where there was no seat, just a small empty space. He had the tripod, extra batteries and film on his lap.

On the way to Bahawalpur the pilot landed the plane on a strip of land alongside some railroad tracks where about a thousand people were stranded near the submerged city of Kanpur. The people, mostly farmers were encamped in the open. Women, some with babies at their breasts, were cooking japatis in earthenware pans in one part of the abandoned train station. There were flies everywhere—on the food, on faces, on lips, on noses.

Those people had been stranded for five days and had lost most of their belongings. Their only hope was a train that was rumored to be coming to take them away from the floods, which showed no sign of receding. The families had small supplies of vegetables and flour, but when that was gone they would go hungry. Their situation was hopeless. We couldn't reassure them, only sympathize with them and try to raise awareness about their plight. We would depart in our plane for a warm meal and a comfortable bed, but what had this forlorn group to look forward to? It seemed to make no sense. In the end we had to take off and leave the hapless farmers at the Kanpur train station, waiting for a train that might never come.

We arrived in Bahawalpur about 5 p.m. just as the Pakistani Air Force pilots were having tea in pukka British military style. They sat around a large table covered with a baize cloth set up on the grass in front of their helicopters. The tea was poured from a highly polished silver tea service by two army mechanics who doubled as servants. The pilots were munching on specially baked nutritional cookies that had just happened to fall out of a CARE package.

'Why don't you chaps sit down and join us for a cup of tea?' inquired Captain Ismail with a very proper British accent. He was delighted to meet Mike.

'I say, did you ever happen to meet my old schoolmate Dickie Sharaz in London? He's one of you television chappies.'

'Oh no, I haven't had the pleasure,' Mike said.

'I assume you are here to cover the floods?'

'You assume correctly. Will you be flying tonight?'

'It is pointless to fly at night as it is almost impossible to find locations without light from the ground, and people are constantly moving to keep ahead of the floodwaters.'

The pilots seemed very friendly and I saw a chance to put a word in.

'I wonder if it would be possible for us to go along on one

of your flights? I would love to get close-up shots of the faces of the flood victims as you hand out relief packages. Their expressions would tell the whole story. Then I could get on the ground and show your helicopter coming in, from the point of view of the victims.'

'Sounds very interesting, but it might be difficult. Ordinarily there would be no problem, but we have to make room for General Kahn, the chief of relief operations, and his staff. He really doesn't get along well with reporters. There has been some criticism about 500 cases of CARE packages that went missing and the local press is holding the general responsible. I'm afraid what you ask is difficult at this time. If you could wait a day until he leaves?'

'I'm afraid that will not be possible. We have deadlines,' Mike said.

'I know, more's the shame,' Captain Ismail said amicably.

This was a real setback. We had come all this way and were counting on going along with the helicopters, and now it seemed it wasn't going to happen. While we were agonizing over the situation one of the officers told us that transport had arrived to take us to a guest house where they had made arrangements for us to have a bed and a meal. We crammed into the front seat of a Land Rover and Frank shook his head in dismay.

'You blew it,' he whispered.

'What do you mean?' Mike asked anxiously.

'Marvin blew the whole deal. Saying he wanted to take pictures of the starving masses and show the looks on their faces.'

He turned to look at me. 'You blew it man.'

Mike looked concerned. 'How do you know?'

'Look, I know these people. They are proud and they are not going to take you out so you can shoot pictures of their countrymen in wretched circumstances. If only Marvin could have shut up I am sure we could have gotten a ride with them. As it is, they had to make up the story about the general.'

'Aw, you don't know what you're talking about,' I said.

'I don't, eh? If we were accepted in their group they would have invited us to join them for dinner instead of preparing it separately for us. I know the traditions of these people. We have been ostracized and are going to have to eat alone and it's all your fault.'

Mike seemed to believe his story. 'Oh, Christ Marv, why couldn't you hold your tongue?'

'I'm sorry, Mike. I didn't realize.'

After a half hour riding over an extremely bumpy road we arrived at the guest house. In Pakistan accommodations in small towns were usually quite rough, and the government made guest houses available with clean rooms and a full staff of servants for visiting dignitaries so they could take showers, get meals and rest comfortably. The room they gave us was large enough for the four of us including the pilot of our plane. It had traditional beds with ropes stretched across the frame just under the thin mattress. They didn't look it, but we found them very comfortable.

When dinner was announced we went down to the dining room and to Frank's dismay, found the pilots waiting for us to join them. So he was wrong. His Peace Corps days had been spent in India, not Pakistan, and he'd probably passed his time under a haze of ganja smoke.

32

ALI BHUTTO

The next day another of Frank's theories was debunked. General Kahn cancelled at the last minute, leaving room for us to fly with the group. But only two seats were available and so Frank was left back at the base to reflect on his erroneous assumptions.

I got all the shots of the relief operations I needed. I was even dropped off so I could get pictures of the helicopter coming in and close-ups of the faces of the flood victims. The Pakistani Air Force couldn't have been more obliging.

Afterwards, we had a nice curry lunch with the pilots at their encampment, and then took off in our Piper Cub for Lahore with Frank stuck in his space at the back muttering to himself.

We didn't make it all the way back to Lahore. We were planning to fly over Multan to get pictures of the flood scene from the air on our way back, but due to an unexpected development we ended up landing. Not aware that we had received instructions from the tower I asked the pilot to circle over the flooded fields.

'No can do, Sahib, boss.'

'Why not?'

'The president's plane is landing and I have instructions to get out of the sky, pronto.'

Mikes face lit up. 'You mean Ali Bhutto?'

'That's the man.'

'I met him on a story in London. Maybe if I talk with him we can get an interview.'

'You know President Bhutto?' Our pilot was impressed.

'Okay, land the plane. I'll try to talk to him.'

With the plane on the ground we were instructed to get ourselves off the tarmac immediately. When the president is in the vicinity press passes mean nothing. We were expelled unceremoniously onto the street in front of the airport and into a crowd of about 50,000 screaming Pakistanis, pushing and shoving in an attempt to get a glimpse of Ali Bhutto. A large contingent of police armed with metal-tipped bamboo poles called '*lathi*' were viciously beating back the crowd. Some of the good citizens of Multan were knocked to the ground, but they seemed to accept this form of brutal restraint as a matter of course.

'Bhutto,' the spectators shouted excitedly, even before he came into sight. 'Bhutto, Bhutto.'

We were in the middle of the mob and it was all I could do to hold on to the camera to prevent it being knocked to the ground, and me with it.

Immediately after landing Bhutto came out of the airport and waved his arms to the crowd. He was surrounded by police who beat a path for him through the shrieking mass.

'Bhutto,' they waved their arms in greeting. 'Bhutto, Bhutto.' It seemed like uncontrolled adoration for their leader.

'You guys try to get out of this crowd and wait for me,' Mike said, already moving away. 'I will get to Bhutto some way.'

When the president had passed we were able to take refuge by the wall of a building, Frank shouting in Urdu to clear the way. We waited for half an hour, and had about giving up on ever seeing Mike again when we saw him making his way toward us.

'Okay,' he said. 'Come on. The president is going to take a helicopter trip to the flooded area and he kicked a couple of his aides off the plane to make room for us. I'm sorry Frank, there are only two places, you'll have to find some place to wait for us.'

The aircraft was an old Russian-built helicopter with huge rotors already turning when we arrived. We climbed aboard, and seconds later the aircraft lifted off, and we began our journey with the man that held the offices of president and prime minister of Pakistan, Ali Bhutto.

We didn't know it then but it was to be the last time we would see him. Soon afterwards he was accused of ordering the murder of an opponent and arrested by his successor, General Muhammad Zia Al-Haq. Later, in spite of massive protests on the part of leaders in the West, Ali Bhutto was hanged at the age of 51.

Bhutto seemed moody and unapproachable. He stayed in his seat and didn't talk to anyone.

I couldn't take any shots out of the small windows with my rather awkward sound camera, and anyway they looked as if they hadn't been cleaned since the plane was commissioned.

Mike and I sat there and wondered what was going to happen. Bhutto paid no attention to us. He just kept looking out the window, and shaking his head in disbelief at the devastation. Then he called one of the crew, and gave instructions to land on some high, dry ground.

'What do we do now?' I asked Mike.

'Search me,' he said and tried to catch the eye of Bhutto to remind him of our presence.

A crewman came over to speak with us. 'The president asks that you join him.'

We followed Bhutto as he made his way to a crowd of flood victims. There was no screaming mob here and I got the impression that some of the farmers didn't even know who he was. A couple of his aides handed out relief packages while Bhutto asked them how they were affected by the flood. And then he turned to us.

'You want an interview?'

'Yes, sir.'

I gave Mike the hand microphone, put the camera on my shoulder and started to shoot.

'Mr. President,' Mike started. 'How do you plan to attack these horrendous floods?'

'I'm afraid we must let nature take its course, but we have to get help to the people caught up in the disaster.'

'Does Pakistan have the resources to help three million flood victims?'

'Unfortunately, no. We need assistance. The United States, Britain, Japan and Germany have offered money and food and technical support.'

'What do you mean by technical support?'

'They are sending engineers to advise us on strengthening the barrages, or levees as you call them in the West. In the face of such devastation they must be reinforced. We hope the work will be done in time to stop the floodwaters before they reach Karachi, our largest city with over five million inhabitants.

'There hasn't been a lot of rain, so what do you think caused the floods?'

'Some people believe that India, as a means of revenge, opened the flood gates of the Punjab, the five rivers that flow into Pakistan.'

'We heard that, too. Do you believe it?'

'How am I to know? We have continuing disputes with India over Kashmir, and there is the recent war over the secession of East Pakistan in which India took a part, blatantly interfering with the sovereignty of our nation. Perhaps this is related to those troubles?' President Bhutto shrugged his shoulders. 'Who knows?'

'What do you think?'

'This is not the time for speculation. It is a time for action, or those unfortunates that are in the path of the floods will suffer further.'

'There are those that believe since you took on the dual role of president and prime minister your government has become repressive, that you have been trying to adopt the methods of Red China.'

'That is not true. I admire the Chinese for the way they have united their country after thousands of years of domination by foreign powers, war lords and corrupt regimes. I don't copy every aspect of government from China, but I feel we have a lot to learn from their success.'

President Bhutto looked angry. 'Switch off the camera please.

'I thought this was going to be an interview about the

floods. I do not want to go into a discussion of our politics at this time.'

Mike was a little embarrassed.

'I'm sorry, sir. It's only that with this rare opportunity for an interview with you I got a little carried away.'

He signaled me to start the camera again.

'More than fifty million people have been affected by the floods,' Bhutto said. 'People are dying, many will never see their homes again. A great deal of farmland has been ruined. Food is scarce. Much of our water is polluted. We need staple food supplies, tents to house our homeless. We need engineers, we need helicopters to move flood victims and we need medical supplies and qualified medical people. We need all these things and we need them in a hurry. Thank you.'

He shook both our hands and walked back to the helicopter.

We were dumbfounded.

'Was that the interview? Do you think ITN will run it?' I asked.

'Of course. After all he is Ali Bhutto, a most difficult man to get in front of a camera. We also got him speaking, one-on-one to victims of the floods, right in the disaster area, and got an interview in which he just about accused India of starting the floods. It's good stuff, and it's exclusive.'

Mike went to attend to some business while Frank and I loaded the equipment back into the plane. When he got back he informed us that he had fixed a ride for himself to Karachi on an Air Force C-130.

'Give me all the film with a dope sheet. I'll write a story on the way there, record it on my recorder, and then ship it on the first available aircraft to London. I'll return to Lahore tomorrow.'

The next day he failed to show in Lahore. We figured he might have missed the plane, or met a girl. On the third day of fruitless waiting, a stewardess from the Pakistan International Airlines approached me in the hotel lobby and passed me a message from Mike.

'When you get this I will be back in London. The assignment editor felt that we got the story we needed and has directed me to come home immediately. You are needed in Pakistan by CARE to shoot film of their package drop. The CARE representative in Lahore will explain. Frank can go back to Hong Kong. Thanks for everything. We got another winner, Mike.'

33

THE WILD MEN FROM BORNEO

As a child I remember seeing the *Wild Men From Borneo* at the circus. Dressed in loincloths and carrying spears, they were introduced by the sideshow barker as savages that came from far, far away where they lived in caves and lived on tiger meat and wild berries. When I was young the *Wild Men* were always one of the most memorable circus acts for me, but as I grew older I could see through the theatrics of the *ooga-booga* language and painted faces and they lost their wonder.

But then I actually came across the wild men from Borneo — in Borneo. They really do exist.

Sitting in my office, wondering where my next assignment would come from, I got an urgent call from the NBC bureau chief Ron Nesson. Their staff cameraman was away from Hong Kong on another assignment, so could I go along with him to cover Vice President Hubert Humphrey's fact-finding trip to Malaysia, Vietnam and Indonesia? I didn't have to think twice about it. Ron said we were to take a commercial airliner to Kuala Lumpur, where we would pick up *Air Force Two*.

They called it *Air Force Two* when the vice president was on board, but it was actually the same plane we knew as *Air*

Force One. The plane was a Boeing 707 equipped with special communication electronics, a bedroom and conference space for the vice president, and a forward compartment with first class-type seats, tables and electric typewriters for the press.

In Malaysia, Humphrey paid a visit to a rubber plantation and a tin-dredging operation. He met the Yang di-Pertuan Agong, Malaysia's figurehead leader elected for a five-year term from among the 12 sultans, the hereditary rulers of the Malay States.

In Vietnam he met President Nguyen Van Thieu and got an update on the status of the war. Then, dressed up in a bush outfit purchased specially for the occasion from Abercrombie and Fitch, the vice president pep talked the troops in the field, awarded medals for bravery, shook hands and signed autographs for the hometown boys from Minnesota.

Indonesia was the last stop on his whirlwind trip and the highlight was a speech he gave to the farmers of Semarang, promising them 'food for work.' The farmers cheered and waved little paper banners with his initials, HHH, taken from the wrapper of a locally made toilet paper. They started work digging an irrigation ditch which ran about a mile. But once Humphrey left the scene the work stopped and the farmers went back to what they were doing before they were interrupted.

Air Force Two dropped us off in Jakarta and started back to Washington. So much for a 'fact-finding' tour.

We topped off our piece about Humphrey with a story on rice production, and as we had come such a long way Ron thought it would be a good idea to give NBC a couple of other stories to earn our keep, so to speak.

We did a story on Sukarno's 'unfinished projects' and even got to talk with the great man at the mountaintop house with exquisite views he had built for his Japanese wife, Dewi. Since he was deposed, Sukarno had been living under virtual house arrest, but was permitted to move around with armed guards. Simply attired in black, loose-fitting pants, a white T-shirt and a *peci* perched on his head, he wasn't permitted to do an interview but we were allowed to talk with him and had some stimulating conversation and laughs about nothing in particular.

We thought we had come to the end of our trip in Indonesia but things didn't turn out that way. The following morning at breakfast I showed Ron a piece I had found in an English newspaper written by Jeff Williams, an old friend from AP. The story was about an indigenous group called Dayaks on the island of Kalimantan just north of Java. They were feared for their ancient headhunting practices, but now apparently the Dayaks were murdering Chinese settlers as retribution for the killing of one of their high chiefs.

Ron's journalistic instincts were aroused and after breakfast we rushed to army headquarters and spoke with General Hartono, the officer in charge of Kalimantan, a restricted military area. When we asked for permission to go there to do the Dayak story, the General laughed so hard that his quaking paunch almost snapped the buttons on his figure-hugging shirt.

'Yes, I have heard that fairy tale. What rubbish. Believe me, it is just the fantasy of a Christian missionary. If you want a real story we have one about Chinese Communists fighting our army in Kalimantan. They are remnants of units left in the jungle by Sukarno. The emergency has passed, but that ragtag army refuses to come out and they keep harassing our troops. Now that is a good story, and what's more, it is actually happening, not a figment of someone's imagination. I can supply transport, and ten armed bodyguards to protect you while you do the story.'

'Thanks a lot for the offer,' Ron said. 'It is very tempting, but we would really like to see for ourselves if Jeff's story has any substance.'

'In that case I cannot give you permission to enter Kalimantan.'

'I'll tell you what. You give us permission to go, and if we find Jeff Williams' article is, as you say, without substance, we will do a story to expose him.'

'I don't know,' the general said.

Ron did a lot of talking in the next half hour and the upshot was that the General agreed to let us go and search out the truth of Jeff's story while keeping his story as an option. Ron figured that a gaggle of headhunters cutting off Chinese heads, drinking their blood and eating their livers was a far better story than a standard war-type one.

At 5:30 the next morning we boarded a Garuda Airways DC-3 heading for Pontianak, the capital of West Kalimantan. The route took our aircraft through the mountains and was nerve wracking as those peaks rose about 200 hundred feet above our flight path. The air was extremely turbulent and I couldn't eat breakfast. The journey seemed to last much longer than the 90 minutes it actually took us to get there.

Upon arrival Ron contacted Captain Mohammed Malik, the army's public relations officer, who shook his head in disbelief when he learned what we were after.

'Jeff got that story from some holy roller, Christian cleric,'

Captain Malik said. 'He hasn't even been there.'

We argued our case, and he shook his head once again. 'If General Hartono gave you permission to do it, then go ahead, but I believe you are making a mistake. You should also be aware that when you enter that area you do it alone, you will have no bodyguards to assure your safety.'

'You say there is a possibility of danger in Dayak country?'

'I am saying that we do not have the men to patrol everywhere in Kalimantan Barat. The Dayaks are savages, so we cannot say for sure that the area is safe. As far as accommodation here, we have only the conference room, no beds just the bare floor. We can give you blankets to spread out, but that is all. It seems we have been overrun with newsmen and all the rooms in the guest house are taken.'

Obviously the price for not doing their story.

As luck would have it we ran into Jeff Williams in a coffee shop. He seemed to be deep in thought and was making notes on a follow up to his Dayak story.

'Well what the hell are you doing here?' he asked.

'As a matter of fact, we were looking for you,' said Ron. 'We want to check up on the story you wrote about the Wild Men from Borneo.'

'You are interested in that, eh? The army says that the story is all lies but I can tell you it I got it from an unimpeachable source and the facts are even more horrendous than my article. Sit down and have a *kopi* and I'll fill you in. Are you interested in going up to that area?'

'We didn't come all this distance to fake the story,' Ron said.

'I got the lowdown from an American clergyman named John Goodman, a Christian missionary who works with the Dayaks. He lives up there among them, but recently brought his wife and two children to Pontianak because he feared for their safety. I am interested in going up there, and seeing things firsthand. Maybe we can all go together.'

'Captain Malik says that there is risk for us if we go up there? Is that true?'

'Maybe, but I spoke to Reverend Goodman and he is willing to drive me there in his jeep. If he is willing to go, and he knows the Dayaks, I guess it's worth taking a chance. Come on, let's go over to his house and discuss it with him.'

Reverend Goodman's home in Pontianak was a little white-framed house surrounded by palm trees and a low picket fence. It had a sign over the front door reading, 'Outer Regions Mission.'

The reverend was about 40 years old and stood six feet two with an abundance of chestnut hair and poised carriage. He spoke earnestly about the problem with the Dayaks.

'Their attacks on the local Chinese is a heartbreaking mistake. The Dayaks confused the band of plundering Chinese Communists that really killed their leader with the farmers that live in the region.

'A group of about twenty settlers sought sanctuary in our church to escape the gangs, but a band of Dayaks forced their way in and slaughtered eleven of them with bolos and knives adorned with red streamers right in the church and in front of my family. The remaining settlers ran, but four more were caught outside and killed.'

'Oh my god,' Ron was horrified.

'What are the red streamers for?' I asked.

'They signify blood. Dayaks are people of the blood. An apt name, don't you think?'

'What did you do then?' Ron asked the reverend.

'After a few minutes, when they had all gone, we got down on our knees and prayed.'

'You prayed for the Dayaks?' Ron asked in disbelief.

'We are all God's children. We dug a pit and buried the

fifteen bodies outside the church, then left for Pontianak out of fear for our own lives. This was just one incident we witnessed, but I know many have been killed, perhaps more than three hundred. There are no soldiers or police in that area and we don't expect that the people who carried out this massacre will ever be brought to justice.'

Jeff looked seriously at Reverend Goodman.

'You offered to drive me up there to check out the scene myself. Is that offer still on?'

The reverend shook his head.

'Of course. When would you be ready to start?'

'We have a deadline to meet so we would have to go almost immediately.'

The clergyman looked as though he might have thought better of the promise he made the day before. He said weakly, 'Do your friends want to go too?'

'Yes, if we can all squeeze into your vehicle.'

'We have a large Mitsubishi Jeep, almost like a van. Actually the canvas roof is leaking a little so we would have to buy some plastic to stick over the hole. There is a place in town...'

The reverend's wife suddenly cut in. 'Wait a minute,' she said, obviously afraid, 'Are you mad? We just ran away from those crazy savages. How can you promise to take these men back there, into the mouth of hell?'

'I promised,' Reverend Goodman said. 'Besides I should go back to check that the church is alright.'

'I don't care if the church is alright,' his wife said. 'We are safe here and besides it's beginning to rain.' Her eyes rested on our little group. 'Look, dinner is ready. Let's discuss this sensibly over some hot food.'

We knew that the reverend was our only chance to get to Dayak country and over dinner we tried to convince his wife.

'Mrs. Goodman, I understand your anxiety about our

making this trip, but we are newsmen and the world is waiting for our story,' Jeff said kindly. 'Mr. Goodman has promised to take us, and he is our only link to this tragedy. We have been counting on his promise.'

'I know you are guided by the best principles and you must get your story, but it is now dark outside and raining. We can put you all up for the night and then in the morning we can assess the situation.'

'We don't have the luxury of time,' said Jeff. 'We must leave tonight.'

Reverend Goodman reminded her, 'I did promise dear. But if we see any sign of trouble we will come back, that is my word to you and the children.'

'You will not wait until morning?' his wife asked.

Jeff looked kindly at her and then put his hands on hers in a calming way.

'I wish we could.'

There was a dramatic silence for a few seconds. 'Now where can we get the plastic to plug up that hole in the roof of the jeep?'

We put a plastic tablecloth over the hole in the roof of the jeep, picked up soda biscuits and soft drinks and then set off for Dayak country. It was 8.30 p.m. when we started our journey into the unknown. All we knew about the place we were going to was that there were savage headhunters that drank human blood and ate the livers of their victims. Not a comfortable prospect to be facing on a cold, dark night as the rain came down in buckets.

34

THE JAWS OF HELL

We reached the Kapuas River on the edge of town and found the man who operated the ferry asleep with his feet on a desk. We shook him awake and explained we needed a ride across the river. He shook his head and said he had closed up shop for the night, but for triple the normal fee he could be persuaded to make one final crossing. After money had changed hands, Reverend Goodman drove the jeep aboard the unseaworthy ferry, the ferry man sounded his warning bell then maneuvered out into the river, and we made the seven-minute crossing.

On the other side we had to wake the proprietor of a petrol station who filled our tank with an old-fashioned hand pump. It was a laboriously slow process, and while he went about it I noticed a sign by the road. I couldn't make out the words and I asked Reverend Goodman about it.

'I'll translate it for you,' he replied with a tiny chuckle.

'You are located on an imaginary circle on the surface of the earth at latitude zero degrees. This circle divides the northern hemisphere and the southern hemisphere into equal distances.'

He summarized for me, 'You're standing on the equator.'

The rain didn't let up and we had to drive slowly over muddy pot holes. The Dutch colonizers obviously hadn't thought it necessary to build decent roads in this part of the country. It was very dark and we couldn't see anything from where we were sitting in the back of the jeep, so I entertained them with lines from Marx Brothers films, and when I ran out of those I took out my ukulele.

I kept up the show for almost three hours, until we reached a guard post straddling the road. It was the last army post in, shall I say, 'neutral territory.' The reverend spoke to the soldiers. They were surprised to see us and to hear of our mission, but our papers were in order so they let us into the closed area.

We had entered Dayak country and from here on we were totally on our own. It was well after midnight and our eyes were trained on the road ahead when from the darkness a dim red glow appeared in the sky. As we moved farther up the road, the light got brighter and after another mile we saw an entire village ablaze.

A line of barefoot men were exiting the village, each carrying a prize. A huge mirror inscribed in Chinese, a table, a chair, some clothes, pots and pans, family pictures, books and ledgers. Some carried daggers and bolo knives, and others held old-fashioned rifles with long, rusty barrels. The rifles had red streamers attached.

'You wanted to see Dayaks? Well there they are,' the reverend said.

'Good lord, they've burned down every house in the village, and most likely whole families were locked inside,' I said, aghast.

'What can we do?' Ron asked.

'Not a thing. We can't stop here. We've got to keep on going and try to act as if we didn't notice anything.'

We watched the fires with horror and it was hard to follow

Reverend Goodman's advice and act as though nothing had happened.

'I feel so helpless,' Ron said.

'I assure you we are taking our lives in our hands just by being here,' the reverend said.

We slowed down and kept up with the line of Dayaks leaving the village. A group of them recognized the reverend and spoke to him.

'They want a ride,' he said. 'I told them we have a full load.'

He drove the jeep at a snail's pace.

'Whatever you do, don't take your camera out,' he said to me. 'Can you see if they have their rifles aimed at us?'

'No.' I said. 'They just keep walking, as if they were in a trance.'

'Look at that guy carrying a chair on his head. Oh, he's from my neighborhood,' the reverend said, brightening a bit. 'I hope he's going to donate it to the church.'

His levity seemed out of place but nobody said anything. For what seemed like hours we crept slowly along the line of Dayaks.

'Look at the pace they're keeping.' Jeff said.

'And they can keep it up interminably,' Reverend Goodman said. 'They never seem to tire.'

Finally we got our car out in front of the line and picked up speed.

'How many people do you figure live in that village?' Ron asked the reverend.

'About fifty or so.'

'Do you think that any of the villagers got away?'

'Not very likely,' the reverend said. 'They move stealthily and the Chinese were probably not expecting them. There have been Chinese in these parts for hundreds of years, and up until recently they got along well with the Dayaks and even intermarried. When their great chief was murdered the Dayaks went berserk, and started killing every Chinese in sight. They see no difference between the Communists that murdered their chief and these innocent souls.'

Dawn was approaching. The rain had stopped and the early morning sun rose rapidly over the mountains. It came first as a combination of reds and yellows washing over the trees and leaves and finally settled as clear, bright daylight. The crisp blue sky was so magnificent it almost shut out the nightmare, but we knew the specter of those innocent people, dying in their homes would be with us forever.

All of a sudden Reverend Goodman stopped the car, and through the bushes we saw two dead bodies trapped in the tall grass in the stream. They were men dressed for farming who might have just come from the fields, except for one thing — there were cavities where the cervical vertebrae of their necks were exposed. They didn't have heads. By the look of it they had been lying there in the fast running stream for several days and the cool water had preserved their bodies and washed away the blood. The Dayaks had apparently resorted to the grisly practice of decapitating their enemies, a tradition they hadn't followed since the Japanese occupied the area during World War II.

We got out of the car and Ron did a 'stand-upper' into camera with the bodies in the background. I got shots from every conceivable angle of the bodies, as well as the general area of the idyllic setting.

Reverend Goodman looked agitated. 'Look, we'd better get out of here. If we're caught by the Dayaks anything could happen. Remember they are very primitive people and they might consider us their enemies, and you can see what happens to their enemies.'

'Shall we bury the bodies?' I asked.

'Oh no. We don't have time. We'd better leave right now.' The reverend looked around nervously. 'I guarantee you we will come across other such incidents on the road.'

A few miles further on we found a monstrous, stomach-turning scene at the side of the road — a bodiless skull swarming with maggots. The vermin jammed the mouth, eyes and nose cavities and had partly eaten away the hair and the skin of the face. Not far away was a bloated, headless body which was also creeping with maggots. I got out of the car, and recovering somewhat from the initial shock, started to film while internally debating the sense of recording such grossly repulsive scenes. I felt compelled to shoot them, but playing them on air was up to NBC and seemed unlikely.

'Please work fast. I'm very nervous,' the reverend said, looking around for signs of Dayaks.

'They live in this vicinity and you never know when we will be discovered.'

'All the bodies are cut open in the same place, on the abdomen,' Jeff said. 'Is there any reason for that?'

'Yes, that is where they cut out the liver. They have been following that ritual for many years.'

'Why the liver in particular?' Jeff asked.

'It has a religious significance. They eat the liver raw for transference of the soul of the person they have killed. Then they drink the blood, but only from the veins that run to the heart because they believe that will give them wisdom and strength.'

He was looking nervously in all directions. 'Let's discuss this later; I feel very uneasy.'

After exhausting the photographic possibilities at the location we got into the jeep and headed for the church. On the road we passed another headless body, but Reverend Goodman refused to stop.

The church was of the kind one finds in small towns in the U.S., only smaller and roughly hewn with a conical tower and cross perched on top. The church building housed a prayer hall and an apartment where the preacher and his family lived. Two faithful Dayak tribesmen guarded the premises. The church had a large kitchen where we ate a breakfast of bacon and eggs with toast and coffee prepared by one of the Dayaks. The family had brought pork products back from the States, although it had required a sizable bribe to get them through customs in this Muslim country. Nothing was impossible in Indonesia if you were willing to pay for it.

'You dug a grave to bury the bodies on the church grounds? Is that right?' Ron asked the reverend.

'Yes. I'll show it to you.'

He pointed out a large area where the earth had been speedily shoveled to make a rough pit. There was a simple cross made of two pieces of wood nailed together at one end.

'We'll have to film a few of the bodies to make the story credible. I'm sorry.' Ron said.

Ray and I set to work with shovels and quickly uncovered three of the bodies. You could make out the legs of other bodies protruding from under the dirt. It was really gruesome. We ended our film with a shot of Reverend Goodman saying a prayer at the makeshift grave, and then we shoveled back the dirt to cover the bodies.

'Okay, I think we've got enough here,' Ron said. 'Let's hit the road and see what else we can find. And to think the Indonesian Army said this story was a figment of Jeff's imagination.'

Thirty minutes of driving brought us to a still-smoldering village. Dayaks were walking around and a pair came over and unsmilingly took our hands, running their index finger across our palms. According to custom, they had filed down their four upper front teeth, carried huge bolo knives, went barefoot and wore red bandanas. I tried smiling at them but they only returned icy stares. We saw dead cows lying all around, but I thought better of looking for bodies of Chinese farmers. We were a million miles from civilization and sur-rounded by vicious savages and it occurred to us that we could be murdered on the spot and no one would ever know. Ron decided it was not a good place to do an into-camera report, and in fact it was best to get the hell out of there ... fast.

We didn't think it wise to push our luck so we kept our camera out of sight and left the burned-out village. A little further up the road we came across a farm house with three poles supporting a cooking bowl in front and a sign that read '*ruma Daya.*' Apparently the Chinese family had been run off and Dayaks had taken up residence. It looked quiet and I said to Ron that we could probably shoot some interesting film there.

'Okay but be careful,' he said.

I took a few shots of a neat little vegetable garden, and then peeped in the open door and saw a bare-breasted woman cooking food and three children playing on the floor.

'May we come in?'

She took no notice of me.

Without warning a dozen fierce-looking men dressed in loin clothes and carrying knifes with red streamers sprang from behind the trees and confronted me. I called to the rev-erend for assistance but as he stepped out of the car a couple of men took hold of his arms and dragged him to the front of the house. Two others forced Ron and Jeff out of the car and then at knife-point led me to join the group of prisoners. The leader, who was also brandishing a huge knife, spoke with a good deal of braggadocio. He ran his blade suggestively across the preacher's throat after finishing his tirade. Reverend Goodman translated what he said.

'I told him that you were news reporters doing a story about their struggle against the Chinese Communists. He said he thought I was lying. I told him I recognized some of his men as members of my church and they would tell him I was a Christian and didn't tell lies.'

'What did he mean running the knife across your throat?' Jeff asked.

The reverend looked concerned. 'He said that if he discovered I wasn't telling the truth he would cut off all our heads.'

'Do you think he meant it?'

'It's difficult to know what he meant. But if he wants to, what would stop him?'

Ron got an idea. 'How about interviewing him?'

'Are you kidding? I'm not going to ask him to do an interview.'

'An interview with a Dayak would make great film. Go ahead, ask him.'

The reverend hesitated, and against his better judgment started talking to the leader. I saw a smile play on the Dayak's face, then amazingly he agreed to the interview. I figured we had no time to waste so I hoisted the camera to my shoulder and instructed my soundman to point the shotgun mike at the leader who had never seen a microphone before and thought it was a weapon. He raised his knife defiantly, but the reverend quickly explained our equipment. The leader touched the microphone's foam cover, satisfying himself that it was harmless. Ron started the interview and the reverend translated.

'Tell us your name and age?'

'I am Atak. I am twenty years old and I come from Balik Arian, twenty kilometers from here.'

'When did you first start to wage war against the Chinese?'

'Ten days ago. We were told by a government man about the murder of our great chief Aziras and four of his Iban warriors. I gathered together the fiercest fighters in our village and we went out to seek revenge.'

'You were told of the murder of your chief by a man from the government who knew what actions you would take against the Chinese?' Ron couldn't believe that the Indonesian government went around inciting the Dayaks to commit murder. 'How were you able to distinguish the Communists that actually killed your chief from innocent Chinese farmers?'

'We kill all Chinese.'

'Have you personally killed anyone?'

As answer to the question Atak raised his hand with the knife and proclaimed in a loud voice, 'With this knife I have executed three hundred Chinese.'

His men raised their weapons and cheered.

'Do you cut off the heads of your victims?'

'We burn down their houses and when we find them in the fields or on the road, we kill them and cut off their heads.'

'But why?'

'To relieve the agony of the gods. They demand the heads of our enemies.'

'And do you eat the liver of your victims?'

'Yes, and we drink their blood to give us strength in battle and wisdom in our life.'

One of his men opened a little pouch, and took out what looked like a piece of black meat. He thrust it at Ron with a silly giggle on his face.

Atak laughed. 'He is offering you the taste of a Chinese

liver.'

In that moment, Atak seemed like an impudent child who made up stories to excite our imagination. Reverend Goodman drew our attention to the bluish pallor of his skin which he got from drinking blood. If they committed these appalling acts to appease their gods, the good clergyman had a long uphill pull to convert the Dayaks to Christianity.

At the end of the interview Atak led all his men in a rousing, '*Hiddup Daya, hiddup Daya.*'

Reverend Goodman then translated a shocking disclosure. 'He asks if you want to see the prisoners. He says they have captured nine Chinese girls.'

'I won't film them harming any girls,' I said.

'He says they are protecting them, and tomorrow they will bring them to the soldiers for safety.'

'Okay, let's take a look,' Ron said, answering for our group.

A couple of his troop went into the house and returned with nine frightened Chinese females. Two girls about 11 or 12 years old were holding each other and crying, and then there were four girls probably in their 20s, two older ones about 35 or 40 and one who was more than 60. Reverend Goodman asked them several questions but couldn't get them to say a single word. They just stood there, staring at us. It was a paradox. The Dayaks had murdered Chinese farmers indiscriminately, but treated these frightened women with respect and kindness.

We had seen enough of Dayak country and needed to return the reverend to his family and then go on to Jakarta to ship our film. As we drove out early the following day, after spending the night at the church, we passed Atak and his group leading their hostages at a blistering pace to the soldiers, as they promised.

On the way to the airport we stopped at a huge warehouse

in Pontianak which was a refuge for the Chinese farmers and their families. More than a hundred families were camped together on the concrete floor. A ship was apparently coming from China to rescue them, but they weren't interested in leaving. One old farmer said that they would wait and when it was safe they would return to their farms. They had suffered greatly at the hands of their captors, but they still wanted to return and live peacefully with them. We learned later that the Dayak uprising had left about 300 Chinese dead and 55,000 displaced.

In New York about two months later, I dropped by NBC News to borrow a copy of our Dayak story for a family screening. When I returned it to Mac Johnson, the assignment editor, I mentioned that I'd noticed it hadn't been edited and it seemed they hadn't used the story.

'That's right,' he said, explaining that if we had contacted him beforehand he wouldn't have okayed it. 'We were pissed off with Ron for wasting all that money on a non-story. He should have known better.'

'What do you mean a non-story? Dayak tribesmen murder several hundred Chinese farmers with the blessing of the Indonesian government and you consider that a non-story?'

'Who cares? Indonesians killing Chinese, Chinese killing Indonesians, what's the big deal? The average American is not interested in stories like that.'

'How could they not be interested?'

'If they were killing Americans or Americans were killing

them that would be a story.' As an afterthought Mac said, 'Your footage may find its way into a documentary one of these days but as far as NBC is concerned it was just a monumental waste of money. Ron really should have known better.'

I was disappointed that NBC hadn't used our story but perhaps there was some truth in what Mac said. If it didn't involve them, then Americans just didn't want to know about tribesmen living in some jungle somewhere who cut off the heads and drank the blood of innocent people. They were content seeing the *Wild Men From Borneo* at the circus.

35

NEW YORK AND BACK

Our daughter was born in New York and thus became an instant American citizen. We had gotten extraordinarily cheap tickets on Trans Global Airlines, an American carrier making its inaugural trip after which, I believe, it closed down. After what seemed like a never-ending series of stops in Taipei, Naha, Kobe, Wake Island, Anchorage, San Francisco, Denver and Chicago, we finally arrived at our destination. Actually, we had been lucky to get a flight at all because Mary was well into her seventh month. Most airlines wouldn't accept an advanced pregnancy on such a long trip, but I think that Trans-Global was prepared to bend the rules because it was strapped for cash.

Once we got to New York, Mary and I were wined and dined by friends wanting to meet my Asian wife on her first-ever visit to the United States. Mary played the part of a demure Asian woman to the hilt and wore a traditional Korean dress every time we went out. The socializing was great, but as we only had a limited time in New York, we had to focus on another key objective of our trip — applying for citizenship for Mary.

A certain obscure immigration law allows the spouse of

an American working overseas to get citizenship in a matter of few weeks instead of requiring three years of residency. It is one of the government's best-kept secrets, and you must be aware of its existence because they won't tell you about it. It's known as 'expeditious naturalization.' But to get that we would need help.

'We're going to the old Twentieth Century Fox studios to meet Burt Reinhardt,' I said to Mary. 'He's the guy who gives my assignments. I've never met him face to face before and I hope we can get a letter from him to use with immigration to get you one of those fast citizenships.'

Burt was a busy news executive who had started as a lowly office boy and worked his way up. He now gave assignments to UP cameramen all around the world and he invited us to look over his operations of which he was rightly proud. Of course, my favorite part of the tour was the library which at the time was the biggest news film archive in the world. He found the listing of films tagged with my name, and we got to see copies of stories I had shot, of police searching Chinese junks in Hong Kong, interviews in a marketplace in Malaya, deserted farms on the Dachen Islands and ox carts heading across the Howrah Bridge in Calcutta. The trouble with shooting news film is that cameramen seldom get to see the results of their work.

'If I can prove I'm legitimately employed overseas by a news company, I believe I can get Mary expeditious naturalization,' I said to Burt. 'I need a letter from you saying that I am a cameraman working for UP Movietone, stationed in Hong Kong, and that I'm in New York on home leave and will go back to resume my duties in due course. Do you think I can get a letter like that?'

'That regulation is a new one on me, but if a letter will help I can give you one … in honor of your first baby.'

Armed with the letter we went downtown to the immigration office and Mary filled out a multi-page application form. Then an assistant led us into an office where four men waited like a jury to hear her case. One of the men took her application form and read the letter from Burt Reinhardt, then passed it around to the others.

'You presently have a Korean passport, but you come from China?' he asked.

'Well my parents lived in Shanghai before the war, and I was born there. I am the oldest of ten children, all born in China. Actually I have never been to Korea.'

'Then how come you have a Korean passport?'

'It was the only one I could get in a hurry.'

'Where did you learn to speak such good English?'

'I studied at an American convent in Shanghai. I also speak two dialects of Chinese, Korean, fluent Japanese and a little Portuguese,' Mary said to him, none-too-shyly.

'Did you notice that man who was leaving as you came in?' one of the adjudicators asked. 'He's from Puerto Rico and has lived in New York for nine years, but he can't speak intelligible English. He's failed every language test we gave him. Uncle Sam doesn't want citizens who don't even go to the trouble of learning English after nine years.'

'Then I must take an English test?' Mary asked.

'Not you. It's obvious you speak English very well. Do you know anything about American history? Do you know, for instance, what the stars represent on the American flag?'

'Yes. Each one stands for a state. There are,' she paused,

'Fifty-one states? Alaska and Hawaii have just become states and, and …' Mary said, stumbling as she tried to remember the crash course I gave her on the subway. I wondered how she came up with 51 states.

The immigration officer corrected her. 'There are only fifty states.'

'Well, I thought it was the … Philippine Islands?'

'Oh no, not yet,' he said, laughing.

They asked her all about her life in China and Hong Kong, where we met and one or two more history questions about George Washington and Abraham Lincoln and the U.S. Constitution. They asked her the name of the current U.S. president.

'Eisenhower,' she said without hesitating.

'Well, that about does it. You passed your personality and history tests with flying colors, so we will recommend you for expeditious naturalization. Congratulations.'

'Is that all it takes?' she remarked.

'There are one or two other formalities for our bureau in Washington, but there shouldn't be any difficulties from here on.'

'There is one thing I must warn you about. It's against the law to swear in new citizens sixty days before an election, and one is coming up on November 4. If you can wait until after that, I don't think you'll have any trouble becoming an American.'

'No problem. We can wait,' I said happily.

When we got down to the street I noticed a frown on Mary's face.

'I was just wondering, what if the government finds out that letter from Mr. Reinhardt is a fake?'

'It's not a fake. I am their man in Asia, just the same as a full-time employee. The letter is on official company stationary and has the signature of the vice president in charge of production, so don't let it bother you.'

We left immigration headquarters elated and headed toward Canal Street, a street filled with chattering Asians speaking a multitude of strange dialects. One thing I found interesting was that most Chinese people in New York lived the same lifestyle they had in Asia. They lived close together, their children went to Chinese schools, they conducted their business in the traditional way and ate only Chinese food. Many didn't even speak a word of English. They had an existence that was far different from the 'average' American, so what was the big attraction of living in America?

'They can make money and live free here,' Mary explained. 'In China they can only say, "yes, yes". America is the place where they can put their foot down, and say "no". They want the freedom to choose, but they feel more comfortable bringing their traditional way of life with them.'

We stopped at a crowded Chinatown restaurant called Harmony Palace for a dim sum lunch. As we walked in one of the restaurant captains stared at us.

'Mr. and Mrs. Farkas? How are you? Do you remember me? I'm Steve Hung from Mei Sum Restaurant in Hong Kong.'

We often went to Mei Sum (or Maxim's) for afternoon tea with a circle of friends, and Steve was the maître d'.

'Steve. Of course. What the heck are you doing here?' I said, shaking his hand.

'This is my restaurant, well I am part owner. I came over about a year ago and started the restaurant with a partner. Come on, I'll find you a place.'

It was absolutely packed. He put us at a large round table that was already occupied, and we made our own corner to eat. Sharing is customary at Chinese restaurants when no tables are available.

A group of men were sitting at the opposite side of our table speaking Chinese. I noticed one of them looking hard at Mary and me, as though he knew us. He had a wispy beard and his hair was thick and black. I couldn't place him though.

'My god,' Mary said, whispering. 'It's Corky Kuo.'

'What? Are you sure?'

Corky Kuo was one of our group that gathered at Mei Sum in Hong Kong. He was short and I remembered him as having a clean-shaven face with slightly graying hair. He was originally from Shanghai and was the Chinese sales manager for KLM and Mary's boss. He had an annoying habit of grabbing the check every time we had tea. That was okay to start with, but eventually it got a little irritating. He excused it by saying it was a 'Chinese custom.'

Mary told me it was Corky's routine, after selling an air ticket, to exchange the Hong Kong dollars for English pounds by writing a check on his personal account at the Barclays Bank in London. This worked well for KLM, and after a while the manager, Jacob Van der Groot, let Corky make all the foreign exchange for the company.

Then Corky called in sick one Friday and Monday morning the manager found a telex on his desk from Corky's bank in London. His latest check, for 30,000 British pounds had bounced. Van der Groot was staggered. He called the bank and asked them to verify that they had not made an error. They told him that Corky had only a negligible amount in his account. He then phoned Corky at home, but got no answer. He went to his apartment and banged on the door. Still no answer and the building superintendent refused to open the door without a warrant from the police.

'Look you damn fool I have to get into Mr. Kuo's apartment. He may be lying there deathly ill. He may be dead.'

'No,' the landlord said. 'He's not dead. He went out Friday morning with a couple of bags, said he was going to China and would come back on Sunday.'

'Well he hasn't come back has he? I think a crime has been committed.'

Van der Groot was desperate but the superintendent was adamant, so he went to the police station and returned with a couple of constables, and when they finally got the door opened they found Corky's clothes gone and his bed made. He had flown the coop with KLM's 30,000 pounds.

In the course of their investigation the police discovered that Corky had also helped himself to his best friend's passport. The case was put in the hands of Interpol which traced him to Paris where he applied for a visa to the U.S. He left the passport at the American Embassy, but didn't return to pick it up. They then found out that he had mysteriously turned up in London and from there his trail got cold. To avoid further embarrassment, KLM surprisingly withdrew the charges and decided to live with their loss. Van der Groot was fired and returned to Holland where he lived in the hope of one day finding Corky Kuo and extracting retribution.

And that was the story as far as we knew it.

'I don't see the resemblance,' I said to Mary.

'I tell you it is Corky with a beard and minus the gray hair.'

'Is that Mary Jo?' he said, looking closely at us. 'And Marvin?'

'I thought it was you Corky.'

'The name is Chi Wai. Chan Chi Wai.'

'Oh I see,' Mary said. 'Well, I guess you don't see anybody from the old Mei Sum crowd in New York?'

'No, except for Steve Hung. I come here to have tea almost every day. Steve knows my situation but never mentions it.'

We chatted for a while. 'So, where do you live?'

'Somewhere in Chinatown.'

Mary asked if he knew that KLM had dropped the charges against him.

'Oh, yeah.'

'Then why the beard? What do you have to be afraid of?'

'First, there is the matter of immigration. Then the US$300,000 I owe the people who helped me to come here. With a weekly twenty percent interest rate it must be well over one million by now. I must be extremely careful, or I might wind up floating down the Hudson River in a cement jacket. Actually, I feel relatively safe here. Two out of every five Chinese you see on the street in Chinatown are here illegally.'

I don't know where he got his figures.

Corky then looked seriously at the two of us.

'Now you have my secret, and I would like to feel that is safe with you.'

He picked up our check and left.

On the day our first child was born we rushed Mary to the Doctors Hospital on Cathedral Parkway just on the edge of Harlem at 2 a.m.

'It's a girl,' the nurse said as she held back the blanket so I could see the evidence. It was a cute little baby girl with lots of black hair and big brown eyes.

Mary had gone into labor quite suddenly and after a four-hour wait, our very healthy 8lbs 3oz baby came bouncing out and we were a family of three — a fact that would take a little getting used to.

My father and mother, though they were separated, came to the hospital together and my father insisted on picking up the bill. He also paid Dr. Irene Shapiro for her work on our behalf.

So, that was all there was to it. After a day at the hospital we brought the baby home for the inevitable fawning and flattering by relatives and friends who came to get a look at the 'Chinese baby.' After an intensive search through her numerology book for guidance, my mother decided that her name could only be Marjorie. That was okay by us: Mary, Marvin and Marjorie.

There was only one piece of unfinished business to take care of before we left New York. We received a letter in the mail saying that Mary had been accepted as a citizen, and there would be a swearing-in ceremony at the Foley Square Court House on November 8. We took the baby with us and joined about a hundred people in the courtroom. The new citizens raised their right hands and repeating the judge's words, swore allegiance to the United States of America. The judge then told them they should not ever forget they had taken a solemn oath to defend the country against its enemies in word and deed. They should look at it as the most important day of their lives; a day for celebrating.

'Share this event with the rest of your family; go out to a restaurant, eat a good dinner, go to the theater. Do something to mark this day. You are now citizens of the greatest country in the world. You can be proud. Welcome to America.'

The judge waved both his arms in greeting, and left the courtroom.

We had a grand dinner at my mother's house, featuring matzoh ball soup and Hungarian-style stuffed cabbage. The house was full of relatives and we were presented with two orchestra seats to the Broadway hit 'The Flower Drum Song.' The judge was right that it was truly a day to remember.

After three very eventful months in New York, we got Mary Jo and Marjorie Kay American passports and, within a few days, we were on our way back to our home in Hong Kong. My father drove us to the airport.

'Take good care of your little family Marvin,' was all he managed to say as he choked back tears.

We had passed a pleasant period in the city of my birth, New York, surrounded by relatives and friends, and now we were headed back to Asia to continue our life and whatever lay ahead for us. Only we were returning with one more piece of precious baggage than we came with. The future looked good.

AFTERWORD

I could go on telling more stories of my adventures, but I believe you have enough to digest at this point. I covered the Vietnam War for 12 years and saw many horrendous manifestations of man's cruelty to man, but I'll leave that for others to tell.

What I've told you is some of my personal experiences from the time I left New York for Hong Kong in 1954 until the 1960s. I did a lot of traveling around the world and had a few adventures along the way — a lot more than I could fit in this book.

The tales are all true, except for some of the dialogue which, 50 years later, I cannot remember accurately. But I feel I've got the gist of the conversations and after so much time the exact words are of little consequence.